THE BLUE, THE GRAY, AND THE GREEN

unCIVIL WARS

SERIES EDITORS

Stephen Berry
University of Georgia

Amy Murrell Taylor
University of Kentucky

ADVISORY BOARD

Edward L. Ayers
University of Richmond
Catherine Clinton
University of Texas at San Antonio
J. Matthew Gallman
University of Florida
Elizabeth Leonard
Colby College

James Marten
Marquette University
Scott Nelson
College of William & Mary
Daniel E. Sutherland
University of Arkansas
Elizabeth Varon
University of Virginia

The Blue, the Gray, and the Green

Toward an Environmental History of the Civil War

EDITED BY BRIAN ALLEN DRAKE

The University of Georgia Press   *Athens and London*

A different version of chapter 2 previously appeared as "Dying in the Desert" by Megan Kate Nelson, *The Civil War Monitor*, vol. 2, no. 1 (Spring 2012): 48–53, 71–73.

Chapter 4 is adapted from *Nature's Civil War: Common Soldiers and the Environment in 1862 Virginia* by Kathryn Shively Meier. Copyright 2013 by the University of North Carolina Press. Used by permission of the publisher. www.uncpress.unc.edu.

Chapter 5 is adapted from *Arcadian America: The Death and Life of an Environmental Tradition*, by Aaron Sachs. Copyright 2013 by Yale University Press. Reprinted by permission of Yale University Press.

Chapter 8 is adapted from *A Golden Weed: Tobacco and Environment in the Piedmont South*, by Drew Swanson. Copyright 2014 by Yale University Press. Reprinted by permission of Yale University Press.

© 2015 by the University of Georgia Press
Athens, Georgia 30602
www.ugapress.org
All rights reserved
Set in Berthold Baskerville by Graphic Compostion, Inc.

Most University of Georgia Press titles are
available from popular e-book vendors.

Printed digitally

Library of Congress Control Number: 2014955518

ISBN 978-0-8203-4714-1 hardcover
ISBN 978-0-8203-4715-8 paperback
ISBN 978-0-8203-4775-2 e-book

British Library Cataloging-in-Publication Data available

CONTENTS

Acknowledgments   *vii*

INTRODUCTION. New Fields of Battle: Nature, Environmental History, and the Civil War   *1*
  Brian Allen Drake

ONE. Fateful Lightning: The Significance of Weather and Climate to Civil War History   *16*
  Kenneth W. Noe

TWO. "The Difficulties and Seductions of the Desert": Landscapes of War in 1861 New Mexico   *34*
  Megan Kate Nelson

THREE. Yancey County Goes to War: A Case Study of People and Nature on Home Front and Battlefield, 1861–1865   *52*
  Timothy Silver

FOUR. "The Man Who Has Nothing to Lose": Environmental Impacts on Civil War Straggling in 1862 Virginia   *67*
  Kathryn Shively Meier

FIVE. Stumps in the Wilderness   *96*
  Aaron Sachs

SIX. "The Strength of the Hills": Representations of Appalachian Wilderness as Civil War Refuge   *113*
  John C. Inscoe

SEVEN. Nature as Friction: Integrating Clausewitz into Environmental Histories of the Civil War   *144*
  Lisa M. Brady

EIGHT. War Is Hell, So Have a Chew: The Persistence of Agroenvironmental Ideas in the Civil War Piedmont   *163*
  Drew A. Swanson

NINE. Reconstructing the Soil: Emancipation and the Roots of Chemical-Dependent Agriculture in America   *191*
    Timothy Johnson

TEN. Walking, Running, and Marching into an Environmental History of the Civil War   *209*
    Mart A. Stewart

EPILOGUE. "Waving the Muddy Shirt"   *225*
    Paul S. Sutter

Contributors   *237*

Index   *241*

ACKNOWLEDGMENTS

"Credit where credit is due" is one of the better idioms, and the overwhelming share of any acclaim for *The Blue, The Gray, and the Green* belongs to its contributing authors. It has been a great pleasure to edit the work of such insightful scholars, and they have all been kind enough to forgive me for (or at least to ignore) any editorial fumbles on my part.

It was also a pleasure to be present at the creation; the book's chapters began life as papers for the third annual UnCivil Wars conference, held in Athens, Georgia, in October 2011. Thus, many thanks are due Sam Thomas and the T. R. R. Cobb House for hosting the conference sessions and keeping us fed and watered in between. Thanks, as well, to Vince and Barbara Dooley for opening their home to our motley crew for both the conference's keynote address – delivered with panache by Mark Smith – and its inaugural dinner. The Watson-Brown Foundation and the University of Georgia's Willson Center for Humanities and Arts earn a tip of the hat for their financial contributions. The authors and the editor alike are grateful for the intellectual insights of conference commenters James Giesen, David Moltke-Hansen, Kathy Newfont, and Albert Way, and of two anonymous readers for the University of Georgia Press. Particular thanks are due Paul Sutter for his thoughtful observations at our closing dinner and for his similarly thoughtful conclusion in this volume.

John Inscoe not only wrote a chapter for *The Blue, The Gray, and the Green* but also assisted me as an unofficial consultant and guide to the intricacies of editor-hood. Similarly, Mick Gusinde-Duffy has been a diligent and affable champion of the manuscript at the press. Finally, as conference co-organizer as well as a friend, Stephen W. Berry II deserves a snappy present-arms for the myriad ways in which he furthered this project.

THE BLUE, THE GRAY, AND THE GREEN

INTRODUCTION
New Fields of Battle
Nature, Environmental History, and the Civil War

BRIAN ALLEN DRAKE

Jack Temple Kirby was a staunch supporter of the union – the union, that is, between Civil War studies and environmental history. In 2001 Kirby, a historian at Miami University (and later the Bancroft Prize–winning author of *Mockingbird Song*, an environmental history of the American South) penned an online essay for the National Humanities Center in which he wondered why the two academic fields had never gotten together. Environmental history had, at that point, at least two decades of impressive growth behind it. Civil War historians, meanwhile, had spent those same twenty-plus years marching away from a narrow focus on battlefield events and sectional crises to explore the lives of individual soldiers, freed slaves, women, the home front, motivation, memory, and a host of other topics. Both fields were doing interesting and even provocative work but doing it separately. Why?[1]

It was not because there was nothing new to say about the Civil War. "My graduate school mentor [had] joked that the Civil War era was overcrowded," Kirby recalled, and that there was nothing left to write about but "'The Sex Life of Lincoln's Doctor's Dog.'" It was not actually true, of course, as his mentor well knew. "The African-American experience of the war was only then getting sympathetic attention," Kirby observed, "along with political issues both large and local. Women and the war awaited eager scholars and readers, later." Yet in 2001 the environment had somehow failed to make it onto the list. Kirby blamed geography. While the Civil War was an eastern topic, he said, environmental history was a child of western history, born and raised across the wide Mississippi, and simple physical separation went a long way in explaining why neither discipline was doing much reading in the other's books and articles. The rest of the essay offered suggestions for how a marriage between environmental history and Civil War studies might proceed and what it might look like.

The cornerstone of any good marriage is familiarity, and one can imagine both sides looking a bit warily at the partner that Kirby the matchmaker intended for them. Civil War history has always had something of a reputation for confirmed historiographical bachelorhood, and although its interests are far more diverse than they were twenty years ago, that diversification was long in coming. Social historians, meanwhile, have until relatively recently tended to avoid "mere" military history, devoting themselves to labor, class, race, gender, and the broader civilian "subaltern"; historian Maris Vinovskis famously called them out in 1989 for "losing the Civil War" in particular. Now, here was Kirby issuing another call for setting up house. Who, exactly, his readers might have asked, was this spouse-to-be?[2]

It's a good question, especially from the Civil War side, because environmental history is nothing if not an eclectic and sometimes even enigmatic field, and historians of the war would not have been the first to be confounded by it. The short answer would be that environmental history is the study of the interactions between humans and nature across time. Like the social history turn that influenced it greatly, environmental history seeks to give voice to actors whom our historical narratives have traditionally ignored. Unlike with social history, however, those long-ignored voices do not belong to humans alone. Geography, climate and weather, natural resources, flora, fauna, microbiology, and the like have also shaped human history, environmental historians argue, and people have in turn shaped them. History, in other words, unfolds within a larger web of dynamic ecological connections, and to ignore that is to miss a good chunk of the human experience.

It is also true that few, if any, human experiences in American history were as profound as the Civil War and its aftermath. The statistics delineating the war's human carnage are a kind of historical mantra, as are the moral and political debates about race, economics, and freedom that brought the two sides to blows in 1861 and dominated their reunion after 1865. The work of a phalanx of historians, some of them among the profession's best, has left few stones unturned in those particular historiographical patches. Indeed, there is perhaps no period in American history that has received more and better attention than the Civil War era. Why, then, should its scholars care about nature, when their labors have already been so fruitful? What could an environmental approach tell them about the Civil War experience? Why should they – or anyone else, for that matter – even consider Jack Temple Kirby's marriage proposal?

To begin, given the attention to detail in other areas, it is simply odd that so little thought has been given to nature's place in the Civil War story. This is unfortunate from a coverage perspective, but the drawbacks go beyond that. While it might not have the potential to transform Civil War studies in the way that social histories have, an environmental-history approach *can* tell us many things we didn't know before and can also allow us to reassess some things we *thought* we knew. As its contributions to other fields suggest, environmental history can locate and turn over new stones in the Civil War field as well as reposition some older ones. With that in mind, a short survey of environmental perspectives in non–Civil War military history will give shape to the "environmental gaps" in Civil War studies and help elucidate some of its potential contributions.

Environmental history's roots run deep and wide. Many schools of thought have shaped it: social history, the Annales school, the work of western historians like Walter Prescott Webb and James Malin, agricultural history, the history of science and technology, political economy, the geographical sciences, biology, and ecology, to name only the major contributors. As a distinct field, it emerged in the United States in the ecologically minded 1970s and grew slowly in the 1980s and early 1990s. Its most significant accomplishment at that time was to fundamentally change the historical narrative of early North American history by uncovering the vital role of "virgin soil" diseases in the decline of Native populations and their dispossession by Euro-Americans. From there the discipline matured and expanded, informing everything from the history of American agriculture, forestry, wilderness preservation, and other forms of land use to urban sanitation, race and gender relations, religion, and postwar politics. It also moved beyond the borders of the United States to take regional, transnational, and global perspectives. While its influence has never equaled that of social history, environmental history has nevertheless become an indispensable category of analysis alongside the social history trinity of race, class, and gender.[3]

It wasn't quite true, as Jack Temple Kirby claimed, that there had been no environmental perspectives on the Civil War before 2001. His betrothed couple had dated casually before then, as it were, even if early practitioners were not environmental historians per se and did not conceive of their work in environmental terms. Weather, for instance, has long been an obvious factor in Civil War histories, as anyone familiar with the Seven Days campaign, Burnside's Mud March, or Sam Watkins's travails in his memoir *Co. Aytch* could attest. Photographs of shattered trees, dead animals, and battlefield detritus have been similarly ubiquitous ("Military historians preoccupied with combat on specific landscapes *almost* do environmental history," Kirby noted in his essay, "and environmentally-minded readers may deduce from conventional texts ecological aspects of warfare"). More to the point, Ella Lonn's 1933 book *Salt as a Factor in the Confederacy* argued that a major obstacle to Southern victory was its lack of salt, which was necessary for everything from curing meat and butter to tanning hides. Here was an argument, grounded in ecological realities, that a modern environmental historian would have recognized immediately; the surrender at Appomattox was a consequence of Leibig's Law of the Minimum, so to speak. In the 1960s, historian Paul W. Gates plowed both Union and Confederate fields with *Agriculture and the Civil War*, touching on the effects of drought, frost, and flood on crop production. But overall, Kirby was spot-on; while other fields moved to incorporate an environmental viewpoint, military history in general, and Civil War history in particular, seemed to hold itself back in reserve. This probably had a lot to do with the sheer potential of social history; since so little scholarship had been produced concerning the experiences of women, African Americans, common soldiers, and so on, it stood to reason that scholars would focus their attentions there. Perhaps bringing nature into the mix seemed like too hazardous a mission for a field still working out the implications of the social history turn.[4]

After Kirby's essay, however, some slow progress came. In 2002 environmental historian Ted Steinberg dedicated nine pages to the Civil War in *Down to Earth*. Two years later, *Natural Enemy, Natural Ally: Toward an Environmental History of Warfare* featured one chapter on the Civil War amid studies of India, Japan, Finland, South Africa, and the Pacific islands. Mark Fiege's "Gettysburg and the Organic Nature of the American Civil War" argued that Lee's famous 1863 raid into Pennsylvania was more a foraging expedition than a strategic move, as overgrazing and scarce rations in Virginia drove him northward in search of food and fodder, and there he utilized the local geography to brilliant tactical effect. In 2005 Lisa Brady joined Steinberg and Fiege with her essay "The Wilderness of War," in which she interpreted the 1863 Vicksburg campaign, the

1864 Shenandoah Valley campaign, and Sherman's march through Georgia as Union attempts to sever the South from its "agroecological foundations," that is, its pastures and fields. For several years, however, these three pieces remained the only significant works of Civil War environmental history.⁵

Meanwhile, scholars of other wars were doing a much-more-thorough job of incorporating environmental history into their work, and in the process they uncovered some fascinating connections between nature and military experience. World War II was the prime example. Back in 1995 the journal *Environmental History* got things started with a short piece titled "The Impact of World War II on the Land." In 2001 Edmund Russell produced *War and Nature*, a groundbreaking study of the reciprocal links between chemical warfare research and postwar pesticides like DDT. *Natural Enemy, Natural Ally* featured several chapters on the war, and between 2003 and 2011 *Environmental History* published articles on topics ranging from urban agriculture in wartime Finland to the global ecological footprint of aluminum production to the environmental context of Japanese American internment. Books by Judith Bennett and Chris Pearson explored the ecological legacies of American troops in the South Pacific and the meaning and uses of forests in Vichy France. The Cold War also received its share of analyses, as Jacob Darwin Hamblin analyzed the environment and geopolitics, Andrew Jenks wrote on the enduring environmental contamination from weapons research, and Mark Fiege explored the environmental sensibilities of atomic scientists at Los Alamos. John McNeill and Corinna Unger's *Environmental Histories of the Cold War* included chapters from fifteen scholars on everything from dam building to weather control. Charles Closmann's *War and the Environment* included an essay by Lisa Brady on Sherman's march but otherwise had a strong World War II/Cold War orientation. David Briggs's award-winning *Quagmire*, on imperialism, hydrological engineering, and warfare in Vietnam's Mekong Delta, appeared in 2012. Civil War scholarship on the environment, it was clear, had a lot of catching up to do.⁶

It was in this context that Stephen Berry and I hatched the idea for *The Blue, the Gray, and the Green*. In 2007 I came to the University of Georgia's history department, fresh from graduate school at the University of Kansas, where I specialized in the history of the post-1945 American environmental movement. Berry—then an assistant professor, now the Greg and Amanda Gregory Chair in the Civil War Era—arrived that same year. He had recently become interested in environmental history, having long been impressed by its analytical creativity, and as we got to know each other our conversations about our respective fields piqued my own interest in the Civil War. I was also influenced by our colleague (and a contributor to this volume) John Inscoe, by the work of several graduate students, and simply by living in the South, where traces of the war are still in the air as well as on the land. After a number of freewheeling discussions about the state of our respective fields—often centering on why they never seemed to get together—it seemed obvious to Steve and me that Jack Temple Kirby had been right: environmental history and Civil War history were a great match. We also decided that we should capitalize on that fact. When Steve suggested that we co-organize a meeting on Civil War environmental history as a part of the UnCivil Wars conference series sponsored by our department, the T. R. R. Cobb House, and the Watson-Brown Foundation, I leapt at the idea. The result was the October 2011 conference "The Blue, the Gray, and the Green," the first academic history conference dedicated wholly to the topic. It was our good fortune to attract a slew of impressive scholars, no easy task given the dearth of "Civil War environmentalists." The essays in this volume—the fourth in the University of Georgia Press's UnCivil Wars series—emerged from conference presentations.[7]

What, then, do these essays tell us about the Civil War? Since environment history deals with two very broad subjects—humans and nature—it can be an unwieldy methodological lens, and in answering that question it is useful to first have a sense of the field's thematic topography. Many scholars have offered their favorite interpretive frameworks and metaphors. Arthur McEvoy, for example, has argued that environmental history focuses on the interlocking, coevolving links between ecology, production, and cognition—that is, "the relationship between people, their work, and the world they live in." Similarly, for Donald Worster the practice of environmental history involves three levels of analysis. The first emphasizes nature's impact on human history, stressing the nonhuman world's "agency" in human affairs. The second analyzes the ways humans think about, define, and regard "nature" in science, religion, art, and culture, both popular and high. The third focuses on the places where people, drawing on their respective cultural values, physically engage the natural world in order to obtain what they need and want from it—the realm of agriculture, resource extraction, commodification and the market, and their related technology and material culture. John McNeill's interpretive trinity is similar to Worster's but simpler, broken down into the "material," the "political," and the "cultural" aspects of the human-nature interface. Paul Sutter, however, has recently offered a framework that eschews the three-tier approach for something even simpler. "All environments are hybrid," he writes, intricate and ever-changing fusions of human and nonhuman actors and activities. Thus, the best environmental histories weave McEvoy, Worster, and McNeill's various categories together into a "complex causal taxonomy."[8]

The following essays offer a Civil War–oriented sampling of that taxonomy. Some emphasize the active role of nonhuman nature while others place more stress on human cognition and cultural values, but all of them deal with hybridity in some way. However, by no means are they, individually or collectively, the final word on either what Civil War environmental history is or ought to be. As one of the first self-consciously environmental forays into Civil War studies, *The Blue, the Gray and the Green* is not and cannot be definitive. It does not presume to advance a sweeping and conclusive answer to the question of what environmental history can contribute to our understanding of the war as a whole. Instead, it offers a diversity of subjects and approaches in the hopes of showing what sort of distinctive contributions environmental history *might* make. It is a methodological smorgasbord, so to speak, a platter of interpretive hors d'oeuvres that serves as both an inspiration and a model for more substantial meals to come.

The first several chapters in this book emphasize nonhuman nature, and in the process they remind us that not only did nature matter in the Civil War, it sometimes mattered a great deal. Kenneth Noe's opening piece reveals that while the elements clearly affected marches and battles in a general way, they also had significant and quantifiable effects in very specific places. Furthermore, Noe shows that climate could be as important as weather, even away from the battlefield; the famous southern bread riots, for example, might have owed as much to bad harvests born of regional drought, flood, and frost as they did to the Confederacy's inflationary economy or logistical failings. Next, Megan Kate Nelson invokes regional climate to rescue the reputation of a shamed Union officer in New Mexico in 1861. Major Isaac Lynde surrendered to pursuing Confederates after leading his troops into the high desert on an ill-fated march from Fort Fillmore to Fort Stanton. Critics accused him of gross incompetence and his troops of drunkenness, but Nelson argues that extreme dehydration and heat were more practical explanations for their failure; a keen understanding of environmental conditions, she suggests, goes a long way to rehabilitating Lynde's soiled reputation. It also fosters a broader appreciation of the unique ecological context of the war in the West.

Stephen Berry has written that the Civil War constituted a "massive stir of the biotic soup" a là Alfred Crosby's Columbian Exchange, and the next two essays emphasize the active role of nonhuman nature in the form of contagious disease. Like Kenneth Noe, Timothy Silver begins by noting that weather and food scarcity were closely linked; in the mountains of Yancey County, North Carolina, rain, drought, and frost combined with a dearth of male laborers to create severe shortages. Silver moves next, however, to the effects of camp life on Yancey County's Confederate soldiers. Having grown up in mountainous isolation, their epidemiological innocence rendered them vulnerable to density-dependent illnesses as they merged with recruits from around the South in crowded, unsanitary training camps and battlefields. A comparable situation faced their Yankee opponents in the swampy, muggy 1862 Peninsula Campaign; Silver speculates that epidemic diseases played an underappreciated role in George McClellan's ignominious retreat to Harrison's Landing. Even the horses and mules that transported the armies and the livestock that fed them suffered intense bouts of glanders, hog cholera, and cattle fever. It would be years before their numbers in the South would rebound, significantly hindering the region's postwar recovery.

Disease was so prevalent among troops in the Peninsula Campaign and elsewhere in Virginia in 1862, Kathryn Shively Meier argues in her essay, that it was a major factor – perhaps the major factor – in "straggling." Soldiers of both sides routinely left the ranks without permission in order to administer "self care," which they much preferred to treatment in hospitals. Eventually, stragglers – unlike deserters – returned to their units; although mainstream treatments of straggling and desertion usually lump them together, Meier argues that an explicitly environmental approach allows us to make useful distinctions between the two. Showing little interest in such nuance, commanders blamed straggling on laziness, cowardice, and lower-class character faults, and dealt with the situation harshly. The irony was that "self care" likely went a long way toward keeping troops healthy and, in the long run, boosted both the number and the readiness of men available to fight.[9]

The next two chapters take us into to the realm of perception, ideology, and value. Terms like "nature" and "wilderness" are among the most complicated in American history, and environmental historians have made a cottage industry out of deconstructing their conflicting cultural meanings and the impacts those meanings had on both people and the environment itself. It is worth asking, then, how the Civil War experience both reflected and influenced those impacts. Aaron Sachs uses language, literature, and landscape paintings to muse upon the ways in which the war complicated and darkened Americans' imaginings about the meaning of wilderness in particular and nature more generally. Images of stumps, both wooden and fleshly, linked the defilement of human bodies to the defilement of nature, muddying older views of environmental destruction as Progress. Wilderness, too, took on new meanings because of the war. Before 1861 it had been as much a landscape of solace as menace. But the war's vast destruction shook Americans so badly that they began to lose faith in its capacity to heal spiritual and psychic wounds. That anxiety, ironically, helped to inspire the conservation and wilderness preservation movements of the late nineteenth century – movements that environmental historians have seldom connected to the conflict.[10]

Next, John Inscoe draws on period and modern literature to explore images of the southern Appalachians as wartime refuge, redoubt, and place of moral high ground. His close reading of the 1864 novel *Cudjo's Cave* and several short stories, memoirs, and reminiscences published after the war reveals an emerging northern literary image of the Appalachian "wilderness" as an island of morally upright antislavery and unionist sentiment amid a sea of decadent lowland slave-drivers. There was some truth to that image, for the real southern Appalachians were full of people with grudges against or ambivalence toward the Confederacy and its planter aristocracy. Escaped Union prisoners, too, experienced the mountains and their residents as friends and allies, and lauded Appalachian geography in their memoirs. The refuge offered by the region dwindled as Confederate and home guard units moved against deserters and resisters in savage internecine conflicts made worse by the difficult terrain. Yet more than a century later, the "refuge" idea persisted; Inscoe finishes by placing Charles Frazier's 1997 novel *Cold Mountain* in the tradition of much of the nineteenth-century writing that established those themes.

The last four chapters focus more overtly on "hybridity." First, Lisa Brady offers her thoughts on how the military theorist Clausewitz's concept of "friction" – the unanticipated and unpredictable problems that emerge during the execution of even the best-laid tactics – had an underappreciated ecological facet in Civil War battles. Drawing on Fort Donelson, Iuka, and Perryville as examples, she uses the quirky atmospheric phenomenon known as "acoustic shadow" to suggest that "friction" was as much an environmental issue as it was a product of human mistakes and foibles, as Clausewitz mainly defined it. Brady goes further, however, by arguing that nature-as-friction offers a "linguistic and conceptual bridge" between military and environmental historians who, though they share an interest in nature's effects on the war, lack a common analytical framework with which to speak to one another about it.

In his narrative about "bright leaf" tobacco farming in piedmont Virginia and North Carolina, Drew Swanson reveals how the war reinforced the region's production even as the Union blockade and the Confederacy's need for men, food, and fodder pushed in the opposite direction. Bright leaf, which was in high demand even in the absence of northern and global markets, generated large profits for, and intense competition among, the region's producers. Thus, they had little incentive to replace tobacco with food crops, and Confederate directives to that effect generated spirited resistance. Also, bright leaf grew best in soils ill suited for crops, which further undercut arguments for increased food production. In the end, large profits, local understandings of "best use" agriculture, and the ecological characteristics of bright leaf itself combined to make tobacco production unassailable, even in the face of the Confederacy's pressing commissary needs. For all the environmental changes the war wrought elsewhere, piedmont tobacco country proved highly resistant to them.

Timothy Johnson brings an environmental approach to cotton production during Reconstruction and afterward. The exploitation of African American sharecroppers is well known, as are the degraded soil conditions where they lived and worked. Less known, however, is the role that fertilizers played in both. After Appomattox, planation elites found themselves still in possession of their lands but bereft of the cheap, controllable labor source they had used to cultivate it. They also found that much of that land was ecologically degraded. Planters like David Dickson proposed the use of imported guano as a way to not only improve soil output but also to avoid the headaches associated with independent-minded sharecroppers. Indeed, guano would help keep them in line; a little-known but key element of debt peonage was the guano note, wherein croppers borrowed money for fertilizers against a percentage of the crop, much as they did with tools, seeds, and the like. Thus, guano served as a distinctly environmental link between the old system of slavery and the new sharecropping one, while also foreshadowing the rise of fertilizer-dependent industrial agriculture in the twentieth century.

Mart Stewart, inspired by burgeoning environmental scholarship on walking, follows with a comprehensive and provocative argument for a literal "boots on the ground" approach to the Civil War environment. The war, he writes, was a down-to-earth experience, an intense engagement with nature as well as between humans. More precisely, that engagement often came on foot. Civilians, slaves, and combatants on both sides walked, ran, and marched through the landscape as they foraged and hunted, lit out for freedom, or made their way to and maneuvered on the battlefield. Here, Stewart argues, we may find a powerful unifying theme for environmental histories of the war. By giving those histories legs, so to speak, we can see more easily the ubiquitous links between humans and nature during the war itself and in the years after. He begins by analyzing Francis Peyre Porcher's *Resources of Southern Fields and Forests* (1863). A guidebook to foraging in the countryside, Porcher's book united the Thoreauvian tradition of ambulatory naturalism with Confederate patriotism, linking the war experience to American nature-writing traditions. Next, Stewart draws on the saga of Charles Ball to elucidate the role of ecological knowledge and topographical awareness in runaway slaves' efforts to free themselves. Stewart ends by drawing important links between the practice of marching and the modernist, industrial-era regimentation that would do so much to alter American environments after the war.

Finally, in a probing epilogue, Paul Sutter considers the promises and the perils of Civil War environmental history and, echoing Lisa Brady, how environmental historians might make their work more accessible and useful to traditional historians of the conflict. With a sympathetic but critical eye, he discusses the limitations as well as the strengths of the book, but more important, he suggests some routes for future exploration. "Waving the muddy shirt" – his sly metaphor for environmental historians' insistence that "nature matters" – will not be enough to win the interpretive battle, he argues. The best environmental histories will instead have to have a keen sense of hybridity, dialecticism, and long-term impact; in particular, they will have to be acutely aware that the human side of the nature–culture hybrid remains vitally important. Why does environmental history matter for understanding the Civil War? Sutter replies that, if done well, environmental approaches will do more than stick a few green sprigs into traditional narratives. They will let us "[rethink] the very *matter* of the war, its lived material realities, and their formative relation to that roiling ideological formation that we call nature."

Common to all chapters is how they hew to the agenda set out in the UnCivil Wars series' first book. The essays in *Weirding the War: Stories From the Civil War's Ragged Edges* took as their inspiration the idea that we can see the war with more clarity if, ironically, we embrace its "fractal" nature and explore "a single story, incident, or phenomena that leaves us with questions about the war we thought we knew." This involves, among other things, focusing on events and actors seldom appreciated by even the best of recent Civil War historiography. Nature was one of those "fractals"; essays by Amy Murrell Taylor and Joan Cashin brought an environmental perspective to the history of emancipation in Kentucky and wartime food shortages in the South, respectively. *The Blue, the Gray, and the Green* continues in that vein. On one level, it seems painfully obvious that nature mattered in the Civil War – recall those photographs of battlefield destruction and the stories of illness, starvation, and marching in the mud. But the following chapters reveal that nature mattered in ways we have not always appreciated or even considered. By both their breadth and their specificity, they show us that the environment weirds the war, as well. They also take up Jack Temple Kirby's suggestions concerning avenues of exploration. His essay urged historians to look at forests, farmland and agriculture, livestock, the urban landscape, disease, and environmental protection, including the ways in which the war affected them after 1865, both in and beyond the South. *The Blue, the Gray, and the Green* touches on nearly all of these topics, and then some.[11]

In the end, *The Blue, the Gray, and the Green* is not and will not be the final word on Civil War environmental history. It is only an opening statement in a historical conversation rich with possibility. Much work remains, and some of it has already begun; contributors Lisa Brady, Megan Kate Nelson, and Kathryn Shively Meier have recently published some of the first books in the field, joined by Jim Downs's *Sick from Freedom* and Andrew Bell's *Mosquito Soldiers*. But the road ahead is long – Jack Kirby followed up Maris Vinovski's call for a social history of the Civil War with a powerful one of his own, and in answering him there are miles to go before we can stand down. It is our hope that this book encourages a steady forward march.[12]

Notes

1. Jack Temple Kirby, "The American Civil War: An Environmental View," online essay for the National Humanities Center, July 2001, http://national humanitiescenter.org/tserve/nattrans/ntuseland/essays/amcwar.htm; Jack Temple

Kirby, *Mockingbird Song: Ecological Landscapes of the South* (Chapel Hill: University of North Carolina Press, 2008).

2. Maris A. Vinovskis, "Have Social Historians Lost the Civil War? Some Preliminary Demographic Speculations," *Journal of American History* 76 (June 1989): 34–58.

3. The literature of American environmental history is vast. For broad discussions of the field's major topics, ideas, written works, and primary sources, see Paul Sutter, "The World with Us: The State of American Environmental History," *Journal of American History* 100 (June 2013): 94–119; Mark Fiege, *The Republic of Nature: An Environmental History of the United States* (Seattle: University of Washington Press, 2012); Ted Steinberg, *Down to Earth: Nature's Role in American History*, 3rd ed. (New York: Oxford University Press, 2012); Carolyn Merchant, ed., *Major Problems in Environmental History*, 3rd ed. (Belmont, Calif.: Wadsworth, 2011); and John Opie, *Nature's Nation: An Environmental History of the United States* (Belmont, Calif.: Wadsworth, 1998). For broad non-U.S. works see Edmund Burke III and Kenneth Pomeranz, *The Environment and World History* (Berkeley: University of California Press, 2009); J. Donald Hughes, *An Environmental History of the World: Humankind's Changing Role in the History of Life* 2nd ed. (London: Routledge, 2009); I. G. Simmons, *Global Environmental History* (Chicago: University of Chicago Press, 2008); and John F. Richards, *The Unending Frontier: An Environmental History of the Early Modern World* (Berkeley: University of California Press, 2003). The leading proponent of "virgin soil" studies is Alfred W. Crosby; see *The Columbian Exchange: Biological and Cultural Consequences of 1492* (New York: Greenwood, 1972) and *Ecological Imperialism: The Biological Expansion of Europe, 900–1900* (New York: Cambridge University Press, 1986).

4. Sam R. Watkins, *Co. Aytch: A Confederate Memoir of the Civil War* (New York: Simon and Schuster, 2003); Ella Lonn, *Salt as a Factor in The Confederacy* (New York: Walter Neale, 1933); Paul Wallace Gates, *Agriculture and the Civil War* (New York: Alfred A. Knopf, 1965).

5. Steinberg, *Down to Earth*, 89–98; Richard Tucker and Edmund Russell, eds., *Nature Enemy, Natural Ally: Toward an Environmental History of War* (Corvallis: Oregon State University Press, 2004), 93–109; Lisa M. Brady, "The Wilderness of War: Nature and Strategy in the American Civil War," *Environmental History* 10: 421–47.

6. Ferenc M. Szasz, "The Impact of World War II on the Land: Gruinard Island, Scotland, and Trinity Site, New Mexico as Case Studies," *Environmental History Review* 19 (Winter 1995): 15–30; Edmund Russell, *War and Nature: Fighting Humans and Insects with Chemicals from World War I to Silent Spring* (Cambridge: Cambridge University Press, 2001); William M. Tsutsui, "Landscapes in the Dark Valley: Toward an Environmental History of Wartime Japan," *Environmental History* 8 (April 2003): 294–311; Rauno Lahtinen and Timo Vuorisalo, "'It's War and Everyone Can Do as They Please!': An Environmental History of a Finnish City in Wartime," *Environmental History* 9 (October 2004): 679–700; Chris Pearson, "'The Age of Wood': Fuel and Fighting in French Forests, 1940–1944," *Environmental History* 11 (October 2006): 775–803; Connie Y. Chiang, "Imprisoned Nature: Toward an Environmental History of the World War II Japanese

American Incarceration," *Environmental History* 15, no. 2 (2010): 236–67; Matt Evenden, "Aluminum, Commodity Chains, and the Environmental History of the Second World War," *Environmental History* 16 (April 2011): 69–93; Judith A. Bennett, *Natives and Exotics: World War II and Environment in the Southern Pacific* (Honolulu: University of Hawaii Press, 2009); Chris Pearson, *Scarred Landscapes: War and Nature in Vichy France* (London: Palgrave Macmillan, 2008); Chris Pearson, "A 'Watery Desert' in Vichy France: The Environmental History of the Camargue Wetlands, 1940–1944," *French Historical Studies* 33(4) (2009): 479–509; Chris Pearson, *Mobilizing Nature: The Environmental History of War and Militarization in Modern France* (Manchester: Manchester University Press, 2012); Jacob Darwin Hamblin, "Environmental Diplomacy in the Cold War: the Disposal of Radioactive Wastes at Sea during the 1960s," *The International History Review* 24 (June 2002): 348–75; Jacob Darwin Hamblin, "Gods and Devils in the Details: Marine Pollution, Radioactive Waste, and an Environmental Regime circa 1972," *Diplomatic History* 32 (2008): 539–60; Andrew Jenks, "Model City USA: The Environmental Cost of Victory in World War II and the Cold War," *Environmental History* 12 (July 2007): 552–77; Mark Fiege, "Atomic Scientists, the Sense of Wonder, and the Bomb," *Environmental History* 12 (July 2007): 578–613; John R. McNeill and Corinna R. Unger, eds. *Environmental Histories of the Cold War* (Cambridge: Cambridge University Press, 2010); Jacob Darwin Hamblin, "Environmentalism for the Atlantic Alliance: NATO's Experiment with the Challenges of Modern Society," *Environmental History* 15 (January 2010): 54–75; Peter Coates, Tim Cole, Marianna Dudley, and Chris Pearson, "Defending Nation, Defending Nature? Militarized Landscapes and Military Environmentalism in Britain, France, and the United States," *Environmental History* 16 (July 2011): 456–91; Charles R. Closmann, ed., *War and the Environment: Military Destruction in the Modern Age* (College Station: Texas A&M University Press, 2009); David Biggs, *Quagmire: Nation-Building and Nature in the Mekong Delta* (Seattle: University of Washington Press, 2012).

7. The conference website is http://wsw.uga.edu/files/2011UnCivilWars.pdf, accessed October 23, 2013.

8. Arthur F. McEvoy, "Toward an Interactive Theory of Nature and Culture: Ecology, Production, and Cognition in the California Fishing Industry," *Environmental Review* 11 (Winter 1987): 289–305; Donald Worster, "Appendix: Doing Environmental History," in *The Ends of the Earth: Perspectives on Modern Environmental History*, ed. Donald Worster, 289–308 (Cambridge: Cambridge University Press, 1988). Worster makes a similar argument in "Transformations of the Earth: Toward an Agroecological Perspective in History," *Journal of American History* 76 (March 1990): 1087–106. See also John R. McNeill, "The State of the Field of Environmental History," *Annual Review of Environmental Resources* (2010): 345–74; Sutter, "The World With Us," 96.

9. For Berry's comment, see "Forum: The Future of Civil War Era Studies," *Journal of the Civil War Era*, February 2012, http://journalofthecivilwarera.com/forum-the-future-of-civil-war-era-studies/.

10. On the meanings and history of "wilderness," see Roderick Nash, *Wilderness and the American Mind*, 4th ed. (New Haven: Yale University Press, 2001); William

Cronon, "The Trouble with Wilderness; Or, getting Back to the Wrong Nature," in *Uncommon Ground: Rethinking the Human Place in Nature*, ed. William Cronon, 69–90 (New York: Norton, 1996); J. Baird Callicott and Michael P. Nelson, *The Great New Wilderness Debate* (Athens: University of Georgia Press, 1998); Paul Sutter, *Driven Wild: How the Fight Against Automobiles Launched the Modern Wilderness Movement* (Seattle: University of Washington Press, 2002); and James Morton Turner, *The Promise of Wilderness: American Environmental Politics Since 1964* (Seattle: University of Washington Press, 2012).

11. Stephen Berry, introduction to *Weirding the War: Stories from the Civil War's Ragged Edges*, ed. Stephen Berry (Athens: University of Georgia Press, 2011), 6; Amy Murrell Taylor, "How a Cold Snap in Kentucky Led to Freedom for Thousands: An Environmental Story of Emancipation," in Berry, *Weirding the War*, 191–214; Joan Cashin, "Hungry People in the Wartime South: Civilians, Armies, and the Food Supply," in Berry, *Weirding the War*, 160–75.

12. Lisa Brady, *War upon the Land: Military Strategy and the Transformation of Southern Landscapes during the American Civil War* (Athens: University of Georgia Press, 2012); Megan Kate Nelson, *Ruin Nation: Destruction and the American Civil War* (Athens: University of Georgia Press, 2012); Kathryn Meier Shively, *Nature's Civil War: Common Soldiers and the Environment in 1862 Virginia* (Chapel Hill: University of North Carolina Press, 2013); Jim Downs, *Sick from Freedom: African-American Illness and Suffering During the Civil War and Reconstruction* (New York: Oxford University Press, 2012); Andrew Bell, *Mosquito Soldiers: Malaria, Yellow Fever, and the Course of the American Civil War* (Baton Rouge: Louisiana State University Press, 2012).

ONE

Fateful Lightning

The Significance of Weather and Climate to Civil War History

KENNETH W. NOE

The American Civil War was largely fought outdoors. Despite this obvious fact, the war's historians have been loath to examine, in any systematic, analytical way at least, the effects of day-to-day weather and longer-term climactic patterns on the course of the conflict. To be sure, classic studies of the soldier experience starting with Bell Wiley's relate how soldiers marched and fought in bad weather, stood guard in the rain, and survived cold Virginia winters in jerry-built shanties. Likewise, the authors of battle narratives usually discuss the specific conditions that affected particular fights, be they the drought that shaped Braxton Bragg's Kentucky campaign or the torrential downpours that made the slugfest at Spotsylvania's Mule Shoe so horrendously bestial. Civil War popular culture acknowledges the effect of weather and climate in ways as diverse as the memorably moving scene of Morgan Freeman's character John Rawlins in the film *Glory* stoically walking his beat in a driving rain, and in battlefield park novices' daily question for the living historian, "Aren't those wool uniforms hot?" In 2011 Hurricane Irene brought forth a brief flurry of blog entries on the lack of analytical studies of meteorological effects on the war, which were answered in the comments sections largely with factoids about specific battles and assertions of the hoary but completely spurious notion that artillery fire always produced storms after battles.[1]

All of these manifestations of Civil War weather ultimately are specific and narrow, however, and in many cases function as little more than the sort of interesting trivia that remains a traditional part of Civil War roundtable meetings. There is no overarching narrative. Indeed, Robert K. Krick's *Civil War Weather in Virginia* still remains the only book-length study in the field solely devoted to the subject. Based largely on the meticulous meteorological records of a Georgetown minister and supplemented with observations from a limited number of additional soldier and civilian records, Krick's annotated historical almanac provides a vital daily record that historians of the northern Virginia theater long needed.[2] Yet as Krick himself acknowledges, his volume is "designed for reference purposes, not analytical ones," and he never looks beyond the relatively limited terrain trod by Lee's army to the war beyond.[3]

At least pointing in the right direction is Harold Winters's seminal volume, *Battling the Elements*, a collaborative work on military geography, incubated at West Point, that seeks to explain "how seemingly evident factors such as weather, climate, terrain, soil, and vegetation are important, cogent, and sometimes decisive in combat."[4] In one essay Winters notably compares the effect of mud in World War I Flanders with Ambrose Burnside's ill-fated Mud March of January 1863. But while a pathbreaking book chock full of useful cues for period historians, *Battling the Elements* nonetheless remains a broad introductory text of military history that deals only in part with weather and climate, and one that includes relatively little specific to the American Civil War.[5]

The impact of climate and weather on the Civil War, then, has an incredibly limited and patchwork secondary bibliography, especially when divorced from specific battles and campaigns. The end result, as Kathryn Meier convincingly argues, is that our understanding of the soldier experience – and one might add, the civilian experience – will remain incomplete until scholars have "adequately analyzed environment as an interactive force in the Civil War."[6] This essay accordingly points toward what such an analysis devoted to the elements might look like, and speculates about the significance of wartime weather and climate, partially using ongoing research as a tentative guide.[7]

First, two definitions are in order. The National Oceanic and Atmospheric Administration (NOAA) defines "weather" as "the state of the atmosphere at a given point in time and geographic location." Daily temperatures, precipitation, wind, and clouds are all functions of weather.[8] For example, on April 12, 1861, the day the war began at Fort Sumter, the temperature in Greensboro, Alabama, was 58 degrees at 7 a.m., rising to a high of 72 at 2 p.m. The morning was cloudy but the sky increasingly cleared as the day progressed.[9] "Climate," in contrast, "is the long-term prevailing pattern of temperature, precipitation and other weather variables at a given location, described by statistics, such as means and extreme."[10] More than any other factors, temperature and precipitation categorize the earth's climates, while altitude, latitude, and location to land masses and large bodies of water shape those longer-term conditions. Certain local conditions might lead a Civil War recruit to record cool *weather* on a specific July day in western Alabama, that is to say, but the overall summer *climate* of the South Atlantic states was hot and muggy.[11] Or, as the schoolboy quoted by Mark Twain memorably wrote, "climate lasts all the time, and weather only a few days."[12]

Any evaluation of Civil War weather or climate additionally, and immediately, demands attention to the interdisciplinary and intradisciplinary approaches of other scholars. Historians most clearly have much to learn from meteorologists, but geotechnical engineers, geographers, and others offer insights as well. No analytic consideration of soldiers' accounts of marching in mud, for example, can proceed without a basic understanding of the different soils and varying muds that made up the battle zones. Union soldiers consistently marveled especially at eastern Virginia's sticky, poorly drained, and seemingly bottomless red clay mud, for example, and the soil around Richmond even confounded men born elsewhere in the state.[13] For its power to stall federal advances, environmental historian Ted Steinberg has gone so far as to call Virginia mud the Confederacy's "secret weapon" and "public enemy number one for the Union forces," yet no definitive exploration of mud and the Civil War exists.[14]

Civil War scholars also must look to other subdisciplines within the broader field of history that already have embraced climate history. As Jack Temple Kirby wrote a decade ago in his largely unheeded call for an environmental history of the war, we now have three generations of model environmental history available within the so-called "New Western History." Yet those scholars largely have ignored the Civil War even as Civil War historians have almost completely shunned them. The war merits a single short if provocative chapter in Steinberg's standard environmental history of the United States, for example.[15] Echoing Kirby's assertion that "military historians preoccupied with combat on specific landscapes *almost* do environmental history," Lisa Brady meanwhile affirms the growing interest in environmental history in the military history community over the last decade and has embodied those concerns in her own work. None concentrate on weather, however, largely focusing instead on the relationship between modern warfare on the natural environment and, in Brady's specific case, Union commanders' strategic and tactical assaults on the landscape as a way to crush the Confederacy by rendering it a wilderness in the eyes of its population.[16]

Historian Mike Davis's bold if admittedly controversial book *Late Victorian Holocausts*, which begins with U. S. Grant's world tour of 1877–79, also offers other lessons from historians of different times and places. The Grants' celebrated around-the-world trip, for example, landed them precisely in the midst of one of the worst world famines of the nineteenth century. Two more great droughts were to follow, so that by 1902 at least 30 million and perhaps as many as 50 million people had died of starvation in parts of Africa, Asia, and South America. In part, famine deaths resulted directly from the effects of the El Niño–Southern Oscillation (ENSO), which closed the heavens in some parts of the world and brought torrential monsoons and floods to others. Climate and weather were not the only culprits, however. Stressing that past local regimes had been able to effectively minimize the effects of earlier ENSO phenomena, Davis blames the new imperialist powers for much of the death toll. European imperial governments undermined older coping mechanisms, such as flood control and governmental food distribution, in favor of the market and laissez faire. Food was always available during famines, but instead of being distributed locally, European overlords sold it on the world market and shipped it away on the new railroads. At the turn of the century, local peoples reacted to famine and foreign rule with desperate millenarian revolutions. The failures of those revolts led not only to further repression, Davis concludes, but the emergence of the modern "Third World." Davis's main point for the Civil War historian is that it is not just climate, but human interactions with it, that shape historical events, sometimes decisively.[17]

Other examples can be found closer to home. Rainfall decreased on the southern Great Plains, for example, beginning in 1845 at the tail end of the Little Ice Age and continuing with minor interruptions through the Civil War years. Combined with various aspects of Euro-American expansion as well as the traditional practices and beliefs of native peoples, the drought devastated bison herds. Nations dependent on those herds, such as the Arapaho, Cheyenne, and Comanche, starved until ample rainfall revived the herds after 1865. Even then, Pekka Hämäläinen makes a strong case that Comanche society never recovered from the starvation and poverty that followed the twin assaults of American expansion and buffalo grass left dead on the plains. Again, it was not a climactic shift that brought hunger, but rather the combination of drought and various peoples' response to it that set the stage for the triumph of a different sort of empire.[18]

Notably, ENSO also was a factor in North America during the Civil War years starting in 1862, as Cary Mock and Dorian Burnette assert.[19] There is no doubt that climactic patterns during the war years were unusual. The 1860s, for example, were one of the least active hurricane decades of the last 160 years, with no hurricanes making landfall between a category 1 storm that struck eastern North Carolina in November 1861 and another category 1 hurricane that came ashore in Texas in September 1865. Four years without facing hurricanes surely were boons to blockade runners and naval squadrons alike.[20]

Accounts of the Civil War Era further reveal other manifestations of unusual and often extreme weather, especially beginning in 1862. Much of it decisively shaped the home front, yet Paul Gates was one of very few scholars to notice. Fifty years ago, in his centennial volume on Civil War agriculture, Gates not only signaled in particular the importance of home-front weather but pointed to excesses that he argued helped shape and in some ways ultimately doomed the newborn Southern nation.[21] At one juncture Gates wrote that

> nature seemed unkindly disposed to the Confederacy.... In 1862 a widespread drought sharply reduced the corn crop throughout the South, except for southern and southwestern Georgia.... Earlier that year the warm and rainy weather in Georgia had caused rust to develop on wheat, lowering output to one sixth of the lower South. Elsewhere in Virginia, eastern Tennessee, and the lower South, wheat was badly damaged by rust or ruined by drought. The Montgomery *Advertiser* even declared that wheat was almost a complete failure throughout the South. Yet in Mississippi the highest flood on the Mississippi River to that time breached the levees in the Delta and did great damage to growing crops.[22]

More bad weather was to come in 1863. "Droughts and too much rain plagued Virginia," Gates continued. "A severe summer frost did damage in Tennessee, extraordinarily heavy and long-continued rains in Georgia held back the corn and spoiled much of the promising wheat crop." During the following year, "excessive spring rains were followed in Georgia by another destructive drought. In the early part of the growing season of 1864, sections of Virginia had a drought of six to eight weeks, which materially shortened the corn crop." Ironically, the dry weather at least brought an early wheat harvest. "In Texas," Gates added, "the harsh winter of 1863–64 was reported to have killed from one half to nine tenths of the cattle on many farms. Elsewhere the cold winter killed many farm animals, cut fruit production heavily, injured gardens, and damaged the wheat crop. Drought also parched the growing crops in Alabama and Mississippi, further reducing output." The end results of alternating droughts and heavy rains, as well as early onsets of winter, were hunger, destitution, and heightened demands for relief.[23]

The newborn Confederacy, in other words, found itself grappling for life at one of the worst possible moments in the nineteenth century to launch an agricultural republic in the American Southeast. Drought struck the Confederacy over three successive summers. Yet Gates's observations about the Civil War taking place in the midst of an extended southern drought are as routinely ignored as they are vastly significant. The food shortages, inflation, and other hardships the Confederate plain folk suffered, as well as a goodly part of the disillusionment, anger, and loss of will that grew out of those issues – the entire litany of the "internalist" interpretation of Confederate defeat – in fact can be traced back at least in part to the weather, its negative effect on southern food production, and the choices the Davis Administration made when confronting a worsening situation.[24] But with the notable modern exception of Armistead Robinson, whose explorations sadly remained incomplete at the time of his untimely death, as well as a few briefer discussions from William Blair, Mark Fiege, Ted Steinberg, and Emory Thomas, historians have failed to pursue Gates's insights about drought's role in undermining the Confederacy from within. The internalists instead privilege a "rich man's war, poor man's fight" narrative that silently and incorrectly presumes stable growing weather, good crops, planter greed, and governmental incompetence.[25]

Here, one must add that unusual climactic conditions also played a role in the North. Better known to scholars than the extended Confederate drought are the bumper crops of the American Midwest, usually depicted within the trope of the diplomatic triumph of King Wheat over King Cotton. Ted Steinberg asserts that while Confederate soldiers and civilians flirted with starvation, Federal soldiers on average "received more food per person than any other army in the history of warfare." While mechanization usually receives the lion's share of the credit for record yields, favorable weather played a role as well.[26] Yet it bears noting that at times the North too had it share of unusually bad conditions. For example, at the end of August 1863, "an early and severe frost" swept through the Great Lakes states and turned eastward. Minnesota farmers woke up on

August 29 to find their field covered in ice an eighth of an inch thick. The effects were far reaching. Regional sorghum crops were destroyed, while attempts in southern Illinois to grow cotton were stymied. Midwestern corn producers suffered such losses that many farmers immediately slaughtered their hogs and sent their cattle to market, unable to feed them. Early in September, a heat wave crossed the region from the Great Plains, but then on September 18 an even more crippling frost struck from Kansas to Indiana. It snowed as early as October 22, with the ensuing storm sweeping from the Rocky Mountains to the Ohio River.[27] North and South, the winter that followed west of the Appalachians was the coldest of the war, and according to historian David Ludlum was "the outstanding weather event of the Civil War." Midwesterners remembered January 1, 1864, for decades as "the Cold New Year's Day."[28]

More than civilians, who at least had proper shelter in most cases, soldiers down south suffered due to extreme weather during that late summer of 1863. The great cold wave of mid-September not only destroyed crops in the Midwest but soon stretched as far south as north Georgia, where Union and Confederate armies were massing to do battle. Soldiers in the armies of Gens. William Rosecrans and Braxton Bragg, who had complained constantly of extreme heat and dust, now recorded in their letters and diaries a dramatic change in the weather on the night of September 17–18, one marked by a cold north wind and near freezing temperatures. Two nights later, as survivors tried to recover from the first day of the Battle of Chickamauga, frost covered the ground, the wounded, and the dead. Most of the men preparing to fight another day had no blankets.[29]

Extreme weather such as this additionally affected all kinds of horses and mules, the motive power of Civil War armies. Aside from a few famous horses, such as Traveler and Little Sorrell, horses and mules rarely are considered in a scholarly fashion. A climactic perspective suggests a new approach. Heat, rain, and winter operations especially, coupled with an increasing lack of drought-ravaged forage, ill use, neglect, and finally a devastatingly massive outbreak of equine glanders that appeared in Virginia in the spring of 1862, clearly killed army and civilian horses and mules by the tens of thousands. That death toll created a constant demand for replacement animals that totaled nearly a million purchases in the Union army alone by the end of the war, at a cost of over $100 million.[30] The cost in humane treatment was equally high. Remembering Joe Johnston's retreat from Manassas toward Richmond in March 1862, for example, Cpl. Napier Bartlett of the 3rd Battery, Washington Artillery, wrote that "one of the dreary sights about camp, especially during the winter season and on a long march, that is by the number of dead horses who perish from hunger, cold, bad treatment or exhaustion. In this and other marches it was sometimes said that we could have walked all day upon the prostrate bodies of the horses which fell by the wayside.... A horse once down was like Lucifer—he fell to rise no more. A smooth place would be worn in the mid by his moving to and fro of his head and neck, or where he had been thrown out convulsively his legs; and then a lingering death."[31] Especially in winter weather and the heat of summer, we must imagine such scenes as commonplace.

At Chickamauga, an early cold snap brought shivering temperatures to exhausted men and animals, but it did not materially affect the course of the battle. Other battles and campaigns were more dramatically shaped by weather conditions. At times, favorable conditions certainly played a positive role. David Ludlum, for example, described dry "'Yankee weather'" during Sherman's March to the Sea, conditions that "proved exceptionally favorable for the enterprise."[32]

When soldiers wrote about the weather, however, they usually meant bad weather. In an effort to consider the broader linkage between combat and such inclement conditions, I have constructed a rather basic database, using standard secondary narratives of the major battles and campaigns as well as a growing number of primary accounts. Using local weather patterns as the main criterion sometimes necessitated the separation of battles from the wider campaigns, or the division of long campaigns such as Sherman's march into weather-based phases. This leaves eighty-two discrete events. Those events are categorized using one of four broad headings: no effect, minimal effect, significant effect, and maximum effect. "Significant effect" refers to events during which bad weather played a noticeable role among several others in determining the outcome, such as the heat waves that helped exhaust raw recruits at First Manassas and Wilson's Creek, or the freezing and thawing winter roads that slowed but ultimately did not stop Samuel Curtis's winter campaign in Missouri and Arkansas during January and February 1862. "Maximum effect," in contrast, points to extreme conditions that decisively shaped battles and campaigns as the most significant factor (see appendix).

Thirteen battles and campaigns (16 percent) appear in the "maximum effect" column: Cheat Mountain, Stonewall Jackson's Bath/Romney Campaign, Forts Henry and Donelson, Williamsburg, the Valley Campaign's Front Royal, the Seven Days, Ox Hill, Fredericksburg's Mud March, the

Tullahoma Campaign, the Retreat from Gettysburg, Chattanooga (notably Lookout Mountain), Spotsylvania Court House (notably including the Mule Shoe), and Nashville. With the exception of Bath/Romney, all involved torrential rain, flooding, and mud that determined commanders' decisions in decisive ways; teaching the war's history in the first half of 1862 especially sometimes strikes one as a recitation of one decisively flooded creek or river after another. Stressing the way weather influenced these particular battles and campaigns would not be a stretch to any students of Civil War military history. More surprising is that thirty-three battles and campaigns (40 percent) ended up on the "significant" list, ultimately the largest of the four categories. Almost exactly half involved rain, high water, and mud, but winter weather forged a dozen more, and severe heat and choking road dust affected five. Heat and dust initially sound less dangerous than hypothermia, but the historian confronting them in soldiers' accounts soon comes face-to-face with the reality of men collapsing and dying of sunstroke daily along every line of summer marching. To be sure, the categories are broad if not crude, and one might well quibble over whether a given campaign belongs in one or another category. The broader lesson, however, is that bad weather played an important if not decisive role in more than half of Civil War battles and campaigns, using the groupings and subdivisions explained above. Roughly four out of ten were shaped significantly by inclement conditions.[33]

Even this cursory study of weather's effects on battles and campaigns across the war years immediately produces a vague sense of wider climactic patterns sweeping across the divided nation, patterns that soldiers and commanders confronted in similar ways. May 12, 1864, for example, not only brought fog and heavy rain to the Mule Shoe at Spotsylvania but also saw the sun emerge after two inches of rain fell on the night of May 10–11 at Snake Creek Gap, Georgia, a decisive moment at the beginning of Sherman's march through Georgia. Delineating those wider patterns requires more hard information, however. Soldiers frequently wrote about being hot or cold, but rare indeed was the fighting man who regularly recorded time and temperature. "Torrents" of rain, a favorite phrase, could mean widely varying amounts of rainfall depending upon the observer and his shelter. What is required for translation is essentially a more voluminous version of Krick's Virginia book that takes into account all the major fronts as well as home-front backwaters and major cities. Accounts of daily weather written by soldiers and civilians alike are crucial but cannot stand alone. They must be supplemented by more regular, scientific observations, notably those that exist within National Archives' Records of the Smithsonian Meteorological Project. These records relate to a massive undertaking initiated in 1847 that sought to establish scientifically the causes of storms by placing volunteer observers, including Krick's Georgetown minister, across North America and equipping them with modern tools and standardized procedures.[34]

Unfortunately, with the exceptions of a dogged but fascinating handful of individuals who somehow continued to collect data and eventually send their monthly reports to Washington — and their story demands telling — Smithsonian-commissioned weather observations ceased in the Confederacy in 1861, limiting to an extent the collection's usefulness. The overarching demands of war, the blockade, and perhaps even different sectional patterns of thinking about the environment, to echo Brian Allen Drake in the introduction to this volume, precluded substitute data collection in Dixie. Certainly, initial pleas in 1861 to continue the work with the new government fell largely on deaf ears. Writing on a bitterly cold January 28, 1865, War Department clerk John B. Jones even lamented that he could not find a single thermometer anywhere in Richmond with which to determine the temperature.[35] Observers within the Federal army, especially the Medical Corps, as well as data from the Southern nation's fringes did provide additional records. Other supplemental sources, such as naval ship logs, could be used as well to provide additional data. While the result will be imperfect, in theory scholars should be able to amass enough information to broadly chart, map, and interpret the larger weather patterns that affected the war, and thus further decipher the weather-related writings of soldiers and civilians.

Echoing Mike Davis, however, a thorough study of Civil War meteorology additionally must move beyond the effects of the elements to the question of how people and institutions shaped their responses to them. At one level this involves generals' decision making, but at another, it means the day-to-day coping mechanisms of individuals. Successful veterans learned over time how to cope with bad weather, as Kathryn Meier recently averred. Soldiers made choices when dealing with the weather, she concludes, and the sum of those personal choices, how they were able to sleep warmly or keep themselves dry, played a significant role in their physical and mental health.[36] Clearly, something of a learning curve also was in effect when it came to the main business of soldiering. Capt. Jeremiah Donahower of the 2nd Minnesota Infantry, for example, discussed how experience in moving troops on muddy roads during bad weather made the arduous Tullahoma Campaign of June–July 1863 at least easier than the Mill Springs Campaign of January 1862. Soldiers traveled lighter, he observed, trains were smaller, and the column corduroyed roads in advance of wagons. Contrasting accounts of earlier campaigns with Sherman's march through the Carolinas in early 1865 likewise demonstrates that in technology, technique, and attitude, veteran Civil War soldiers learned how to deal with bad weather, making it less of an issue when accomplishing a mission. Through flood and cold, their uniforms and shoes rotting, Sherman's columns kept moving through rainy swamps that would have stymied them two years earlier, building roads and bridges as they went.[37]

Accommodations occurred in camp as well. Civil War soldiers routinely described their winter shelters and encampments, for example, often proudly and in minute detail. Soldiers blue and gray debated the best form of construction; championed the choices of tents, cabins, or hybrid structures; and regaled readers with tales of chimneys, fire pits, and camp-made beds. Every year seemingly brought new ideas and better structures. Recent historians of the soldier experience generally have ignored these mundane descriptions of huts and "shebangs" in favor of issues such as motivation, but historical archaeologists increasingly have turned to the study of encampments.[38] Describing the site of a Confederate cantonment along the Potomac River, for example, Joseph Balicki notes the wide variety of shelter styles and concludes that Civil War camps contained a wide array of American "vernacular architecture" that has been too easily ignored.[39] While such sites increasingly compel attention, however, there has been relatively little scholarly work in comparison when it comes to less dramatic adaptations such as the ponchos, India rubber blankets, and oilcloths that functioned at times as both apparel and shelter. When it comes to such items, as well as regular woolen blankets and shelter, historians largely still abandon the field to reenactors and collectors. This must change. One fruitful study would be an examination of the all-but-ignored Union India Rubber Company, which recorded millions in profits while operating what Mark Wilson calls a "near-monopoly" in supplying rubber rainwear to the Union army and, as battlefield contraband, to Confederates as well. The business and technology of dealing with fighting outdoors, as well as the industries that devoted themselves to keeping soldiers warm and dry, must compose another crucial part of the war's meteorological history.[40]

To summarize, Civil War historians sometimes have talked about the weather, narrowly, but have neglected to pursue its study through analytical accounts of how climate shaped the Civil War. Such studies are necessary for a better understanding of the soldier experience, the process of arms, the lives of civilians on the home front, and the collapse of the Confederacy. Ideally, such histories of the war would draw from interdisciplinary and intradisciplinary bases of information and models, consider the effects of weather and climate on both soldiers and civilians as well as their livestock, and examine how those soldiers and civilians responded in everything from battle plans to building winter quarters, and from producing crops to shelter halves. To paraphrase Julia Ward Howe's familiar lyrics, in other words, we must consider the "fateful lightning" that accompanied the "terrible swift sword."[41]

Appendix

INCLEMENT WEATHER AND CIVIL WAR CAMPAIGNS

No Effect (13–16 percent)
  Fort Sumter (April 1861)
  Valley Campaign: Winchester (May 1862)
  Valley Campaign: Harpers Ferry (May 1862)
  Valley Campaign: Cross Keys and Port Republic (June 1862)
  Second Bull Run/Manassas: Battle (August 1862)
  Antietam (September 1862)
  Port Hudson (May–July 1863)
  Gettysburg: Battle (July 1863)
  Olustee (February 1864)
  The Wilderness (May 1864)
  Bermuda Hundred (May–June 1864)
  March to the Sea (November–December 1864)
  Fort Fisher: Second Battle (January 1865)

Minimal Effect (23–28 percent)
  Belmont (November 1861)
  Valverde (February 1862)
  Pea Ridge (Battle) (March 1862)
  Kernstown (March 1862)
  Glorieta Pass (March 1862)
  New Orleans (April 1862)

Seven Pines (May 1862)
Richmond, Kentucky (August 1862)
Iuka (September 1862)
Prairie Grove: Battle (December 1862)
Chancellorsville (May 1863)
Vicksburg (May–July 1863)
Charleston (July–September 1863)
Chickamauga (September 1863)
Chattanooga: Orchard Knob (November 1863)
Chattanooga: Missionary Ridge (November 1863)
Meridian Campaign (February 1864)
Atlanta Campaign: Dalton to Cassville (May 1864)
Cold Harbor (June 1864)
Battles of Atlanta (July 1864)
Siege of Atlanta (July–September 1864)
Sheridan's Shenandoah Campaign (August–October 1864)
Petersburg (November 1864–March 1865)

Significant Effect (33–40 percent)
First Bull Run/Manassas (July 1861)
Wilson's Creek (August 1861)
Curtis's Winter Campaign in Arkansas and Missouri (January–February 1862)
Pea Ridge Campaign (March 1862)
Island No. 10 (March–April 1862)
Shiloh (April 1862)
Yorktown (April–May 1862)
Valley Campaign: McDowell (May 1862)
Valley Campaign: Jackson's Retreat (June 1862)
Cedar Mountain (August 1862)
Second Bull Run/Manassas: Campaign (August 1862)
Corinth (September 1862)
Perryville (October 1862)
Prairie Grove: Campaign (December 1862)
Fredericksburg (December 1862)
Stones River/Murfreesboro (December 1862–January 1863)
Chattanooga: Siege (September–November 1863)
Red River Campaign (March–May 1864)
Camden Expedition (March–May 1864)
Spotsylvania: Post-Mule Shoe (May 1864)

Yellow Tavern (May 1864)
New Market (May 1864)
North Anna Campaign (May 1864)
Atlanta Campaign: New Hope Church to Dallas (May–June 1864)
Atlanta Campaign: Dallas to Kennesaw (June 1864)
Sheridan's Second Raid (June 1864)
Early's Washington Raid (June–July 1864)
Petersburg: First Stage (June–July 1864)
Franklin (November 1864)
Fort Fisher: First Battle (December 1864)
Sherman's Carolinas Campaign (January–March 1865)
Bentonville (March 1865)
Lee's Retreat to Appomattox (April 1865)

Maximum Effect (13–16 percent)
Cheat Mountain (July–September 1861)
Bath/Romney (January 1862)
Forts Henry and Donelson (February 1862)
Williamsburg (May 1862)
Valley Campaign: Front Royal (May 1862)
Seven Days Campaign (June–July 1862)
Chantilly/Ox Hill (September 1862)
Fredericksburg: "Mud March" (January 1863)
Tullahoma Campaign (June–July 1863)
Gettysburg: Retreat (July 1863)
Chattanooga: Lookout Mountain (November 1863)
Spotsylvania: Mule Shoe (May 1864)
Nashville (December 1864)

Notes

1. Bell Irvin Wiley, *The Life of Billy Yank: The Common Soldier of the Union* (Indianapolis: Bobbs-Merrill, 1952; repr., Baton Rouge: Louisiana State University Press, 1978), 55–58, 76–77, 127; Bell Irvin Wiley, *The Life of Johnny Reb: The Common Soldier of the Confederacy* (Indianapolis: Bobbs-Merrill, 1943; repr., Baton Rouge: Louisiana State University Press, 1978), 59–67, 74–75, 79, 244–45; Kenneth W. Noe, *Perryville: This Grand Havoc of Battle* (Lexington: University Press of Kentucky, 2001); Gordon C. Rhea, *The Battles for Spotsylvania Court House and the Road to Yellow Tavern, May 7–12, 1864* (Baton Rouge: Louisiana State University Press, 1997); *Glory*, dir. Edward Zwick, Tri-Star Pictures, 1989; Darryl Black, Chattanooga, Tenn., e-mail to Kenneth W. Noe, August 24, 2011, author's pos-

session; "Civil War Weather," *Civil War Memory*, Aug. 28, 2011, http://cwmemory.com/2011/08/28/civil-war-weather/#comments; "Irene as Retribution," *Crossroads*, Aug. 27, 2011, http://cwcrossroads.wordpress.com/2011/08/27/irene-as-retribution/.

2. Robert K. Krick, *Civil War Weather in Virginia* (Tuscaloosa: University of Alabama Press, 2007), esp. 1–6, 80.

3. Ibid., 6.

4. Harold A. Winters et al., *Battling the Elements: Weather and Terrain in the Conduct of War* (Baltimore: Johns Hopkins University Press, 1998), 1.

5. Ibid., esp. 1–4, 33–44.

6. Kathryn Shively Meier, review of Clarence R. Geier, David G. Orr, and Matthew B. Reeves, eds., *Huts and History: The Historical Archaeology of Military Encampment during the American Civil War* (Gainesville: University of Florida Press, 2006), and Robert K. Krick, *Civil War Weather in Virginia* (Tuscaloosa: University of Alabama Press, 2007), H-CivWar, December 2009, http://www.h-net.org/reviews/showrev.php?id=25633.

7. Here the obvious model is Maris A. Vinovskis, "Have Social Historians Lost the Civil War? Some Preliminary Demographic Speculations," *Journal of American History* 76 (June 1989): 34–58.

8. "Weather and Atmosphere," NOAA (National Oceanic and Atmospheric Administration): Education Resources, http://www.education.noaa.gov/Weather_and_Atmosphere/.

9. Greensboro, Ala., February 1861, Records of the Smithsonian Meteorological Project, RG 27.3, MT907, National Archives and College Park, College Park, Md.

10. "Climate," NOAA (National Oceanic and Atmospheric Administration): Education Resources, http://www.education.noaa.gov/Climate/.

11. Harold A. Winters, et al. *Battling the Elements: Weather and Terrain in the Conduct of War* (Baltimore: Johns Hopkins University Press, 1998), 75.

12. Mark Twain, *English as She Is Taught*, biographical sketch by Matthew Irving Lans (Boston: Mutual, 1900), 16.

13. See for example Sandie Pendleton's letter in Susan P. Lee, ed., *Memoirs of William Nelson Pendleton, D.D.* (Philadelphia: J. B. Lippincott, 1893; repr., Harrisburg, Va.: Sprinkle, 1991), 252–53.

14. Ted Steinberg, *Down to Earth: Nature's Role in American History*, 2nd ed. (New York: Oxford University Press, 2009), 90–91.

15. Jack Temple Kirby, "The American Civil War: An Environmental View," National Humanities Center, http://nationalhumanitiescenter.org/tserve/nattrans/ntuseland/essays/amcwar.htm; Steinberg, *Down to Earth*, 89–98. While not a Civil War specialist, Steinberg did anticipate important themes that scholars of the war regularly overlooked, notably the military significance of mud and the effect of drought on food and forage.

16. Lisa M. Brady, "The Wilderness of War: Nature and Strategy in the American Civil War," *Environmental History* 10 (2005): 423–25. Brady expands on this essay in *War upon the Land: Military Strategy and the Transformation of Southern Landscapes during the Civil War* (Athens: University of Georgia Press, 2012).

17. Mike Davis, *Late Victorian Holocausts: El Niño Famines and the Making of the*

Third World (London: Verso, 2001). I am grateful to Rupali Mishra for first pointing me to Davis's volume.

18. Dan Flores, "Bison Ecology and Bison Diplomacy: The Southern Plains from 1800 to 1850," *Journal of American History* 78 (September 1991): 479–82; Pekka Hämäläinen, *The Comanche Empire* (New Haven: Yale University Press, 2008), 292–319, 339–40, 431n9.

19. Cary Mock and Dorian J. Burnette, "Meteorological Conditions during the CSS Hunley Event of February 1864: A Civil War Example of Climate Reconstruction," The Blue, the Gray, and the Green Conference, University of Georgia, October 21, 2011.

20. Ibid., 234–35; "El Niño Theme Page," National Oceanic and Atmospheric Administration, http://www.pmel.noaa.gov/tao/elnino/la-nina-story.html; "La Niña," http://www.publicaffairs.noaa.gov/lanina.html; Colin J. McAdie et al., *Tropical Cyclones of the North Atlantic Ocean, 1851–2006*, Historical Climatology Series 6-2 (Asheville N.C.: National Climactic Data Center, 2009), 11, 16, 20, 31, 46, 58; Mock and Burnette, "Meteorological Conditions."

21. Paul W. Gates, *Agriculture and the Civil War* (New York: Alfred A. Knopf, 1965), 16, 29, 86.

22. Ibid., 86.

23. Ibid., 85–90, 113–16, 86.

24. Ibid., 34–40, 85–90.

25. Armstead L. Robinson, *Bitter Fruits of Bondage: The Demise of Slavery and the Collapse of the Confederacy, 1861–1865* (Charlottesville: University of Virginia Press, 2005), esp. 121, 126–30, 307n30; William Blair, *Virginia's Private War: Feeding Body and Soul in the Confederacy, 1861–1865* (New York: Oxford University Press, 1998), 118; Mark Fiege, "Gettysburg and the Organic Nature of the American Civil War," in *Natural Enemy, Natural Ally: Toward an Environmental History of War*, ed. Richard P. Tucker and Edmund Russell (Corvallis: Oregon State University Press, 2004), 95–96; Steinberg, *Down to Earth*, 89, 93, 95–97; Emory M. Thomas, *The Confederate Nation: 1861–1865* (New York: Harper and Row, 1977), 202.

At the time of his death in 1995, Robinson's manuscript remained incomplete. One important missing section was a promised appendix that would have provided weather statistics and crop forecasts for 1862. The author clearly had made use of the Center for Polar and Scientific Archives, RG 106, National Archives and Records Administration, Washington D.C., see xv, 307n30, 308n42. Thomas notes the Richmond bread riot followed on the heels of a heavy snowfall that made food transportation into the city all but impossible. For examples of leading internalist accounts that all but ignore the significant role of bad weather in producing the Confederacy's food shortages, see Stephanie McCurry, *Confederate Reckoning: Power and Politics in the Civil War South* (Cambridge, Mass.: Harvard University Press, 2010), which only notes drought and resultant corn shortages once, and only in North Carolina (see 206); and David Williams, *A People's History of the United States: Struggles for the Meaning of Freedom* (New York: New Press, 2005), which blames greedy cotton and tobacco planters, speculators, inept government officials, and transportation collapse for shortages of corn. Williams does cite a Georgia woman who lamented her bad crop in the autumn of 1863 but does not otherwise comment; see esp. 93–95, 171, 183, 203–4. Steinberg, *Down to Earth*, ix, points out that American historians in general automatically assume a "stable environmental backdrop" to historical events.

26. Steinberg, *Down to Earth*, 95.

27. Gates, *Agriculture*, 148, 153, 177–78, 183–84 (quotation, 148); Glenn Tucker, *Chickamauga: Bloody Battle in the West* (Indianapolis: Bobbs-Merrill, 1961; repr., Dayton, Ohio: Morningside, 1984), 411, 411–12n2.

28. David M. Ludlum, *Early American Winters II, 1821–1870* (Boston: American Meteorological Society, 1968), 133, 169; Steinberg, *Down to Earth*, 97.

29. Tucker, *Chickamauga*, 411–12; Peter Cozzens, *This Terrible Sound: The Battle of Chickamauga* (Urbana: University of Illinois Press, 1992), 97, 118, 280, 305, 319, 511, 569n63.

30. Mark R. Wilson, *The Business of Civil War: Military Mobilization and the State, 1861–1865* (Baltimore: Johns Hopkins University Press, 2006), 140–47; Kirby, "The American Civil War: An Environmental View"; Fiege, "Gettysburg," 98, 104–5; G. Terry Sharrer, "The Great Glanders Epizootic, 1861–1866: A Civil War Legacy," *Agricultural History* 69 (1995): 79–97; G. Terry Sharrer, *A Kind of Fate: Agricultural Change in Virginia, 1861–1920* (Ames: Iowa State University Press, 2000), 9–18; Steinberg, *Down to Earth*, 93.

31. Napier Bartlett, *Military Record of Louisiana, Including Biographical and Historical Papers Relating to the Military Organizations of the State* (New Orleans: L. Graham, 1875; repr., Baton Rouge: Louisiana State University Press, 1964), 73–74.

32. Ludlum, *Early American Winters*, 134.

33. Database, author's possession, Auburn, Ala.

34. Lewis J. Darter Jr., *List of Climatological Records in the National Archives* (Washington, D.C.: National Archives, 1942).

35. J. B. Jones, *A Rebel War Clerk's Diary at the Confederate States Capital*, ed. with and introduction by Howard Swiggett (New York: Old Hickory Bookshop, 1935), v. 2, 401. See also Ludlum, *Early American Winters*, 121.

36. Kathryn S. Meier, "'No Place for the Sick': Nature's War on Civil War Soldier Mental and Physical Health in the 1862 Peninsula and Shenandoah Valley Campaigns," *Journal of the Civil War Era* 1 (June 2011): 176–206.

37. J. C. Donahower, "Narrative of the Civil War," 1:195, Jeremiah Chester Donahower papers, 1853–1919, M561, Minnesota Historical Society, St. Paul. For Sherman's march, see for example K. Jack Bauer, ed., *Soldiering: The Civil War Diary of Rice C. Bull, 123rd New York Volunteer Infantry* (San Rafael, Calif.: Presidio, 1977), 2022–38; Wilfred W. Black, "Marching with Sherman through Georgia and the Carolinas: Civil War Diary of Jesse L. Dozer," *Georgia Historical* Quarterly 52 (1968): 460–73; Olynthus B. Clark, ed., *Downing's Civil War Diary, by Sergeant Alexander G. Downing, Company E, Eleventh Iowa Infantry, Third Brigade, "Crocker's Brigade," Sixth Division of the Seventeenth Corps, Army of the Tennessee. August 15, 1861–July 31, 1865* (Des Moines: Historical Department of Iowa, 1916), 244–70; W. B. Hazen, *A Narrative of Military Service* (Boston: Ticknor, 1885; repr., Huntington, W.V.: Blue Acorn Press, 1993), 336–69.

38. Note several essays in Clarence R. Geier Jr. and Susan E. Winter, eds. *Look to the Earth: Historical Archaeology and the American Civil War* (Knoxville: University

of Tennessee Press, 1994); as well as Clarence R. Geier, David G. Orr, and Matthew B. Reeves, eds., *Huts and History: The Historical Archaeology of Military Encampment during the American Civil War* (Gainesville: University of Florida Press, 2006).

39. Joseph F. Balicki, "'Masterly Inactivity': The Confederate Cantonment Supporting the 1861–1862 Blockade of the Potomac River, Evansport, Virginia," in Geier, Orr, and Reeves, *Huts and History*, 127. For a recent exception, see Megan Kate Nelson, *Ruin Nation: Destruction and the American Civil War* (Athens: University of Georgia Press, 2012), 119–35.

40. Wilson, *Business of Civil War*, 17–18, 117. For more on the rubber industry, see Richard P. Tucker, *Insatiable Appetite: The United States and Ecological Degradation of the Tropical World* (Berkeley: University of California Press, 2000), 226–30.

41. Julia Ward Howe, "Battle Hymn of the Republic," 1861.

TWO

"The Difficulties and Seductions of the Desert"

Landscapes of War in 1861 New Mexico

MEGAN KATE NELSON

The express rider galloped through the dusty streets of Santa Fe on the last day of July 1861, dismounting in front of Union army headquarters. He handed lieutenant colonel Edward R. S. Canby a dispatch and the Mexican War veteran quickly scanned the report. Canby then penned a note to William Chapman, the commander at Fort Union. "The express has just been received from Major Lynde," he wrote, "reporting an engagement with the Texans near Fort Fillmore." The dispatch bore the news that "Lynde has abandoned and burned Fort Fillmore and was moving in the direction of Fort Stanton. I do not consider this rumor reliable, but it is given for your information."[1] Canby's suspicion of this report was not unwarranted; in the far western territories in 1861, half-truths and lies whipped through Union camps and forts like dust devils. Fort Fillmore was the Union's southernmost military installation in New Mexico, just outside of Las Cruces. Canby had sent men, cattle, and provisions to Fort Fillmore several weeks before, in an effort to concentrate Union forces and prepare them to defend the territory against Confederate incursions. Maj. Isaac Lynde, another Mexican War veteran, was in command, and had seven companies of the 7th U.S. Infantry (regulars) and three companies of Mounted Rifles under his authority. Lynde had reported in late June that he did not anticipate "a force from Texas will pass Fort Fillmore to attack any Post west of that point." Everything seemed under control.[2]

When around four hundred paroled Union soldiers staggered into Fort Craig on August 6, the rumors proved true and Canby realized that the Union army was about to lose southern New Mexico to the Confederates. Lynde's men, desperate for food and water, ate and drank their fill and then told their stories. The week before they had skirmished with Confederate lieutenant colonel John Baylor's 2nd Texas in the tiny town of Mesilla. The engagement was brief and indecisive; Lynde withdrew to Fort Fillmore but then gave the order to retreat. Sometime after 1:00 a.m. on July 27, around six hundred soldiers, women, and children left Fillmore, moving northward along the Rio Grande toward Fort Craig, more than one hundred miles away. As they neared the town of Las Cruces, however, Lynde ordered the column to take the road to Fort Stanton, which headed off across the high desert valley to the east. When the sun rose, they were clearly visible to Baylor, who then pursued, catching up with the stragglers at a pass in the Organ Mountains and driving them into the mining town of San Augustin Springs. Lynde was already there, trying to rally his exhausted men. When he could only form one company in defense, Lynde sent word to Baylor, asking for the terms of surrender.[3]

After their arrival at Fort Craig, Lynde's subordinate officers filed irate reports attesting to the major's cowardice, his apparent fear of the mounted Texans, his tolerance of women and children at Fillmore (who slowed the pace of the march), and his mercurial behavior in the moments before the surrender. Both his men and other officers in the Union army—in addition to Union politicians in Washington—deemed Lynde's actions "unaccountable" and potentially treasonous.[4] They could not believe that he would capitulate to Baylor when his soldiers outnumbered the Texans three to one. "It was not possible to conceive of such a disgraceful surrender," one officer reported in disgust, "than was made at San Augustin Springs."[5] After several months of accusations and affidavits, Union general-in-chief George McClellan, in a rare moment of agreement with President Lincoln, dropped Isaac Lynde from the rolls of the army for "abandoning his post—Fort Fillmore, N. Mex.—on the 27th of July, 1861, and subsequently surrendering his command to an inferior force of insurgents."[6]

However, the official reports of the retreat, Union and Confederate officers' letters and memoirs, and testimony regarding Lynde's dismissal all reveal that it was not the major's cowardice that had led to the federals' surrender. Instead, from the moment Lynde decided to abandon Fort Fillmore to the last, limping steps his soldiers took into Fort Craig ten days later, what Edward Canby later termed the "difficulties and seductions of the desert"—the excessive heat, intensive solar radiation, and lack of water sources—brought about this Union disaster in the far western theater.[7] By tracking Lynde's column along their thirty-mile retreat we can see how both the military landscapes already in place in New Mexico and the nature of the desert—its topography, hydrology and climate—shaped the course of the Civil War in the southwestern territories.

Civil War historians rarely discuss the conflict in the far West. Relatively small armies (around twenty-five hundred to three thousand regulars and volunteers on each side) fought in only three major battles here; by the spring of 1862 the war between the Union and the Confederacy in the desert Southwest was functionally over. Thus, military historians have not paid much attention to this theater; to most of them "The West" is the Trans-Mississippi West. Social and cultural historians of the Civil War have not turned to this region either, despite its ethnically and socioeconomically diverse populations.[8] Environmental historians, on the other hand, have lavished a great deal of attention on southwestern deserts. Indeed, "environmental history" as a field was forged in studies of the Great Plains and the mountain West; its scholars have examined the clashes of Mexican, Native American, and Anglo cultures in the southwestern borderlands in addition to the effects of aridity and elevation on agricultural development and urbanization, and growing movements for conservation and preservation. But they almost never include discussions of the Civil War in their analyses. Only recently have such historians as Ari Kelman begun to call for an integrated approach to studies of the desert Southwest, one that brings together its (very much interrelated) histories of warfare, environment, community formation, and nationalism.[9]

The marginalization of the far Western theater in Civil War histories can also be attributed to its location on the geographic margins of the United States. New Mexico and Arizona (as well as Colorado and Utah) were new territories with relatively few Anglo inhabitants in 1861. But for antebellum Americans, this huge land mass and its denizens were a central concern in national politics, and in the arguments that brought about the war to come.

The territories acquired from Mexico by military conquest (1846–48) and diplomatic negotiation (1853) were at the center of both American dreams of Manifest Destiny and sectionalist rancor in the 1850s. Expansionist Southerners envisioned New Mexico and Arizona as landscapes of mobility and a crossroads of empire, a vast region through which Anglo Southerners would travel quickly and in all seasons, from eastern Texas to the Pacific coast of California or southward into Mexico.[10] Enslaved men and women would construct the Southern Route, a transcontinental railroad following the 32nd parallel, which would connect the Southeast to the Pacific and the Gulf of California; slaves would also labor in the copper and silver mines of the desert Southwest. Free Soilers objected to this vision, arguing for the abolition of slavery in the far West and a northern railroad route through Kansas and the Colorado territory.[11]

While Northern and Southern congressmen argued bitterly over the future of the far West, the U.S. Army went about creating landscapes of expansion in New Mexico and Arizona. They constructed eight forts along the Rio Grande in New Mexico, each about one hundred miles apart and each located within water-hauling distance of the Rio Grande. In so doing, the U.S. Army inscribed a kind of palimpsest of empire; many of these forts were located near the ruins of ancient pueblos and the gridded streets and plazas of northern Mexican towns, and along *el camino real de tierra adentro*, the "royal road" pounded out by Mexican soldiers pushing northward in the early seventeenth century. These outposts were manned by U.S. Army regulars and offered protection for American traders and migrants as they moved westward in the 1850s. On *el camino real* and on roads winding through high deserts, river valleys, and jagged mountains, these travelers often fell victim to Mexican bandits and Native American raiders. As Brian DeLay has argued, in the 1830s Comanches, Kiowas, Apaches, and Navajos abandoned long-held peace agreements with northern Mexicans and began to fight a continuous war against farmers and ranchers in the region. And when Anglo-American wagon trains appeared on the horizon, Native groups saw this development as both a threat and an opportunity.[12] Raiders rode off with supplies of grain, weapons, preserved meat, and live cattle. The U.S. regulars garrisoned at each fort pursued attackers into the surrounding mesas and mountain ranges and protected travelers and local residents within the adobe walls of their military compounds.

In the spring and summer of 1861 these forts became active targets in the American Civil War. Each army had to feed thousands of men, horses, mules, and cattle; the large quantities of government supplies in forts' storage rooms were vital to the success of long-term campaigns in the desert. New Mexico's military infrastructure was therefore the centerpiece of Confederate general Henry H. Sibley's plan to take the far West for his new nation. The plan, he explained to Jefferson Davis in the spring of 1861, was to recruit Texans, arm them with rifles and artillery taken from federal arsenals in the Lone Star State, and easily conquer New Mexico by overrunning the territory's forts and living off of their provisions. Once both New Mexico and Arizona were theirs, the Confederates would move on. "California had to be conquered, so that there would be an outlet for slavery," Sibley argued, for "with New Mexico, Arizona, California, and Utah there would be plenty of room for the extension of slavery, which would greatly strengthen the Confederate States."[13] Confederates would also use California's ports to reestablish international trade and subvert the Union blockade. And most important, the gold extracted from California's Sierra Nevada mountains—in addition to the silver deposits buried deep in New Mexico's Piños Altos mines—would fund the Confederate government and its war effort. Through the instruments of empire (military presence, government structure, and extractive industry) Confederates would ensure the survival of their new nation. Davis was not difficult to convince; Sibley's plan articulated the central tenets of Southern (now Confederate) Manifest Destiny, offering a military blueprint for fulfilling "long-cherished Southern dreams."[14]

To make these visions a reality, Confederates needed to gain control of the military landscapes along the Rio Grande. The closest installation to the Confederate base at Fort Bliss was Fort Fillmore, just over the Texas–New Mexico border. Construction of Fillmore began in 1851, and three years later the fort contained nine buildings: two of them larger storehouses for weapons and provisions, and seven smaller structures containing barracks and a hospital. All were built of a mixture of adobe (the sand-clay-straw-water mixture used for thousands of years in the American Southwest) and small stones pulled from the desert sands. These structures were cheap to build and strong defenses against small bands of Native American or Mexican raiders armed with rifles.

But when Isaac Lynde arrived at Fillmore from Fort McLane in June 1861, several things worried him. First, the fort did not have an exterior wall as a first line of protection. Second, while adobe was a resilient building material, it was no match for the more sophisticated weaponry carried by Confederate troops: six-pound cannon shot would have punched huge holes in the fort's buildings. Third, "the Fort was so placed as to be indefensible against artillery," Lynde wrote, "being commanded on three sides by sand hills within easy range of a six-pounder."[15] The U.S. Army had likely built Fillmore in this particular location in order to shield it from the region's frequent sandstorms. But in the context of the Civil War's larger armies and mobile artillery, the fort's siting made it vulnerable. Lynde was not the only one to notice this. Capt. F. J. Crilly, an assistant quartermaster stationed at the fort, felt that "Fillmore was an untenable position," as it was "surrounded by hills which were within easy cannon range of every spot in the garrison."[16]

Also worrisome was the fact that Fillmore was located more than a mile from the Rio Grande, its only source of fresh water. The path to the river meandered through the sand hills abutting the installation before descending through thick groves of cottonwood trees into the river valley.[17] Soldiers equipped with wagons for hauling water had to make a three-mile round trip to fetch water on a daily basis. This in itself was not a problem; but the coming war would be fought with long-range and accurate artillery, weapons that made siege warfare possible. Without on-site access to water, Fort Fillmore's denizens could survive a siege for only a few days at most. Crilly considered the fort's position to be so unfavorable in all of these respects that its soldiers would be better off fighting outside of its walls, from "strong defensive points along the river ... from which four times their number could not have driven them."[18]

While Lynde pondered the weaknesses of his fortifications, Confederate lieutenant colonel John Baylor planned his attack. He knew that Canby had concentrated men and materiel at Fillmore over the preceding months; the larger numbers of Union soldiers would be inconvenient, but the cache of provisions for men and beasts was alluring. With his eye on Fillmore, Baylor left Fort Bliss on July 24 and moved northward with three hundred men to make the move in the Civil War for New Mexico. Baylor was apparently unaware of Fillmore's vulnerabilities; his plan was to establish a strong position on the riverbank and provoke the federals to attack him; this strategy was thwarted when a deserter snuck out of Baylor's camp and informed Lynde that the Texans had arrived. Baylor withdrew to the nearby town of Mesilla; the next day, July 25, Union and Confederate troops exchanged gunfire between the houses and corrals of the town, and after an hour or two of "half-hearted assaults," Lynde pulled his men back to Fillmore.[19]

When they returned Lynde set his soldiers to work digging trenches around Fillmore's buildings. By nightfall, however, the major concluded that even these improved defenses could not stand up to the Confederates' weapons.[20] He knew the abandonment of Fillmore would be controversial; despite its physical and environmental weaknesses, the fort was an important salient in the Union's military strategy to hold New Mexico. But Fort Fillmore clearly could not be defended against a Confederate charge or a siege. In his order of evacuation, issued at 10:00 p.m. the night of July 26, Lynde determined that "all property, of whatever description, public and private, that cannot be transported will be destroyed as far as practicable." Soldiers were to take only what they could carry, five days' rations, and one blanket.[21] Lynde knew that the fort's excess supplies were a liability; he could not take them with him on the retreat, and he could not leave them for the Confederates.

Among the stores to be destroyed were medical supplies. Assistant surgeon J. Cooper McKee asked Lynde for permission to use fire to destroy them, but Lynde refused, for reasons that are unclear. McKee subsequently "made the destruction as complete as possible without the aid of fire."[22] Therefore, the hospital stores were only "partially destroyed" and much of what was saved (accidentally or not) was whiskey. This and other medicinal liquors "got among the men and there were a few cases of intoxication."[23] Several months after the surrender, Union lieutenant colonel Benjamin S. Roberts was still outraged about this element of the debacle. "I am merciless enough to charge all our misfortunes in this Territory to drunkness [sic]," he wrote angrily to Canby in October, "Lynde's surrender was, I believe, consequential upon whiskey!"[24] Many commentators—including *New York Tribune* editor Horace Greeley—also blamed liquor for the weakened state of Union soldiers on the march from Fort Fillmore.[25] This may have been the case, not because soldiers were drunk and therefore disorganized but because they were dehydrated even as they began the retreat. And as they turned away from the cool, swift Rio Grande and entered the high desert on the Fort Stanton Road, heat and lack of water would exacerbate their dehydration and lead, in many cases, to their deaths.

Fort Fillmore, Las Cruces, and San Augustin Springs all sat in the northernmost reaches of the Chihuahuan Desert, a high-altitude zone of aridity and semi-aridity that extends from southern Mexico into central New Mexico. This ecosystem is about eight thousand years old, and by the 1860s it exhibited features associated with the "shrub-steppe": sandy, rocky soil anchored by dispersed clumps of sagebrush, low shrubs, and intermixed grasses. The Rio Grande Valley in this part of New Mexico is wide and mostly level, with rolling desert land along its borders (such as the sand hills bordering Fort Fillmore); its elevation varies, but averages more than three thousand feet. The climate is characterized by low relative humidity, abundant sunshine, an average annual precipitation of around eight inches, and large swings in daily temperatures (more than twenty-five degrees). Excepting the Rio Grande, water sources are few and far between; only a handful of small water holes betray the presence of underground aquifers. Twelve miles east of Las Cruces, the volcanic Organ Mountain range rises up in jagged peaks more than eighty-five hundred feet above sea level.[26]

In 1861 the Fort Stanton Road crossed the southern edge of the Jornada del Muerto, a legendary stretch of desert that is one of the hottest and most arid habitats in New Mexico, and then wound precipitously upward into the Organ Mountains, gaining more than 2,000 feet before reaching San Augustin Pass at 5,719 feet. The road continued on to the northeast for 5 more miles to San Augustin Springs; beyond the town lay the Tularosa Basin and 275 square miles of towering gypsum dunes, which from the heights of the pass looked like a huge, white, inland sea. It was into this "wholly mineral landscape," with its alkaline soils, infrequent shade, and lack of water sources, that Lynde's column retreated in late July.[27]

Lynde admitted later that he "had not personal knowledge of the road" to Fort Stanton. "It was reported to me that the first day's march would be 20 miles to San Augustin Springs."[28] The distance was closer to twenty-five or thirty miles, and around five of those were steep vertical ascents up the western face of the Organ Mountains, with little to no water along the route. Lynde's officers had packed containers of water in the supply wagons, most of which brought up the rear of the train. As they swung onto the Fort Stanton Road, the federals followed a narrow path carved through fine particles of desert soil and small rocks. The soil was parched; only about one and a half inches of rain had fallen in the preceding month.[29] Therefore, as they trudged along the road, Lynde's followers created huge plumes of dust in their wake. Because summertime winds are usually light (especially with clear skies) in this region, the dust clouds hovered in the air above them, marking their path for everyone to see. And unluckily for them, John Baylor was looking.

After confirming Lynde's location from a rooftop in Mesilla, Baylor and about 150 of his cavalrymen gathered water supplies, found and saddled up a local guide named Barnes, and set off in pursuit of the retreating federals. They rapidly closed the distance not only because they were on horseback (a small percentage of Lynde's men were mounted, and almost none of the civilians) but also because the marchers were slowing down considerably as the day wore on. The participants who recorded their experiences of the retreat remembered that the march was proceeding fairly briskly and in an organized fashion until sunrise, when it became "excessively" and "intensely" hot.[30] It was likely a pleasant seventy degrees during the first five or six miles of their walk, but the temperature would have risen rapidly once the sun came up. By 10:00 a.m. it was probably in the mid-90s.[31] And as the sun began to beat down on the open road, the air temperature was "made doubly hot reflected by the sand."[32]

There was not much respite from the sun's scorching rays along the Fort Stanton Road. F. J. Crilly remembered that men fell out of the ranks in droves, "each man trying to save himself from the terrible heat," seeking "the shade of the bushes, which were so small as to cover scarcely their heads." These bushes were likely creosotes, the dominant shrub in the deserts of the American Southwest and the most drought-tolerant perennial plant in North America. Creosotes have small, shiny leaves (their waxy coating prevents water loss) and their branches grow out low to the ground to protect their roots and then curve upward into a cone shape. The men seeking relief along the Fort Stanton Road would have had to crawl under these low branches to obtain even a modicum of shade.[33] Union commissary Alfred Gibbs, who had galloped "off the road and across the country" from Point of Rocks when he heard about the retreat, reached the column as it wound its way up to San Augustin Pass. There was more shade at these higher elevations; oaks, junipers, and piñon pines would have given the federals some shelter from the sun.[34] But to his dismay, Gibbs found "under the bushes by the side of the road over 150 men" who were lying there helpless, "unable to rise or carry their muskets and useless and disorganized in every way." Even those who made it to San Augustin Springs collapsed upon arrival; when the Confederates approached and Lynde looked around to gather his soldiers, "many were lying under the bushes near the Spring, totally unable to rise."[35]

People walking on foot – or even riding on horseback at a walking pace – cannot hope to withstand the desert's summer temperatures for very long. For reasons that physiologists still do not entirely understand, the human body can survive large drops in internal temperature but not even the smallest of increases. Although lying down and ceasing muscular contractions helps, if you do not rest in a cool spot, out of direct sunlight, the benefits are moot. The sun's rays absorbing into bare skin (in the event a person has shed some of his clothes, which often happened on such marches) can produce as much heat in the body as the exertion of walking. And if a person's body generates more heat than it can disperse through sweating, his body temperature will increase rapidly. On a day like July 27, 1861, with an air temperature over 95 degrees, a person lying partially in the shade without a means of cooling down would have grown hotter by 2 degrees per hour. And when his body temperature reached 105 degrees, convulsions, unconsciousness, and death would have resulted. For those soldiers and civilians in advanced stages of heatstroke, drinking water would not have helped. However, dehydration would have made things worse, weakening a body that was already suffering from temperature fluctuations. Heatstroke often strikes those who are exerting themselves in excessively warm weather without adequate water supplies—and those who have replaced the water in their bodies with alcohol.[36]

As the horses and mules began to struggle in the sands of the Fort Stanton Road, most of the supply wagons carrying water lagged far behind the column. To make matters worse, once Lynde reached San Augustin Springs at the head of his column, he found "the supply of water so small as to be insufficient for my command."[37] As men and women fell by the wayside the "whole Infantry Command can hardly be said to have had an organization; it was stretched for miles along the line of march." F. J. Crilly attempted to organize the men to face the Confederate pursuit but gave up, and decided to ride for San Augustin Springs and bring water back to the column. He "pushed forward into Camp to get the mules from the wagons that had already reached there, and had been watered. I started them back, and also had all the canteens and kegs filled that I could carry, which I took back with me in a light wagon to give to the men lying along the road." Crilly was shocked to see the state of his friend George Ryan, who was struggling toward the pass. "I had great fears for his recovery," he remembered. He dispensed canteens to Ryan and "to what men I met," continuing at his task until he saw the first of the Confederates reach the summit.[38]

When Baylor and his men caught up to the column they found at its rear "famished stragglers, endeavoring to make their way to water." The Confederate commander was moved to help. "Finding most of them dying of thirst," he wrote in September, "we gave them the water we had, and were compelled ourselves to go to a spring in the mountain for water." Barnes—Baylor's guide—led him to the spring; there they found twenty-four Union men, collapsed around the pool. As they reached the summit of the pass, the Confederates had a full view of the five miles of road between them and the town of San Augustin Springs. Along its entire length were "fainting, famished soldiers, who threw down their arms as we passed and begged for water."[39]

It is unclear how many men and women died along the Fort Stanton Road on July 27. Lynde surrendered 410 soldiers to Baylor that afternoon, and according to participants around 500 had started from the fort that morning.[40] If this is true, then the Union soldiers' mortality rate on this retreat was 18 percent, an incredibly high rate even for the bloody Civil

War battles to come. There is no data accounting for the more than one hundred women and children who marched and rode along; those who may have staggered off into the brush and perished are unknown.

It is likely that those who died during the retreat succumbed to a combination of heatstroke and thirst. Dying of thirst is a terrible ordeal, coming on slowly but steadily in five phases, each phase corresponding to increasing amounts of water depletion. In the early twentieth century, an American naturalist and museum director named W. J. McGee began to study the phenomenon of desert thirst after meeting a Mexican man who had lost a quarter of his body weight traveling more than 150 miles through the Gila Desert in Arizona. McGee noted that "desert rats" in the Southwest had colorful yet physiologically accurate names for each phase: "Clamorous, Cotton-mouth, Shriveled tongue, Blood sweat, and Living death." The first three phases were survivable but in the final two phases, "there is no alleviation but the end."[41] A person walking in the hot sun without water could progress through these phases in as few as seven hours; the loss of water and sodium through sweating causes blood volume loss and brain cell swelling. Sufferers who have reached the "shriveled tongue" stage begin to stumble as they walk, have intense headaches and hallucinations, and ultimately begin to experience seizures. They will drink just about anything to wet their mouths, including urine and blood—human or animal.[42] F. J. Crilly came to this horrible realization when he encountered several dehydrated soldiers at high noon on the 27th: "It was beyond anything that it was possible to imagine; many of the men became absolutely insane. Some wandered off the road and died; one party killed a dog and drank his blood."[43]

The high desert's climate and summer temperatures—and the federals' slow, straggling march through it—explain why the retreat from Fort Fillmore disintegrated along the Fort Stanton Road. The evidence also suggests that Lynde was suffering from desert-induced afflictions that hampered his ability to lead his troops effectively. The major reported that when he arrived at San Augustin Springs he "became so much exhausted that I could not sit upon my horse, and the command proceeded without me."[44] After he rested for a bit, Lynde headed back toward San Augustin Pass with water for his men, but "became so much exhausted from fatigue and excessive heat that I could sit on my horse no longer, and I had to stop and dismount." He sat on the roadside for what he characterized as "some time," returning to the town only slowly, and on foot. He claimed to be "suffering from such intense pain in my head as to be almost blind."[45]

Many of his officers were chagrined at Lynde's seemingly bizarre behavior. When Alfred Gibbs arrived after his sweaty ride from Point of Rocks, Lynde ordered him to take seventy men and use the two companies of infantry still on the Fort Stanton Road to hold off the pursuing Confederates. To Gibbs, this plan made no sense. "It will be well here to mention that the infantry had been marched up to noon 20 miles without water," he protested, "This was the rear guard on which I was ordered to rely. Major Lynde had not seen it for several hours."[46] Throughout the day Lynde continued to send Gibbs confusing and contradictory orders: "He told me that I might water my command and horses[;] . . . while I was doing so, Major Lynde sent me an order not to move. While watering, Major Lynde sent me word that I could leave for Fort Stanton if I chose. Before I could mount I received another order not to move from camp."[47] J. Cooper McKee's report was even more damning. When the surgeon told Lynde that Texans were in their rear, Lynde "grinned in an imbecile way and said, 'Ah, indeed!'" McKee also noted with disgust that he watched Lynde walk back to town after dismounting, and it was "the d – dest kind of slow walk."[48] These accounts suggest that Lynde was nearing the third stage of desert thirst. His symptoms – the intense headache, the lack of coordination, the exhaustion, and the confused and contradictory orders – all point to dehydration and heatstroke.

In his account of the fiasco, Crilly argued that after he gave his fellow soldiers water, they were "refreshed" and "eager and ready for a fight."[49] But the days after the surrender belie this assertion. The already low supplies of water at San Augustin Springs gave out entirely, and Alfred Gibbs reported "a great suffering for want of water."[50] In a letter to a fellow Confederate officer, John Baylor complained that he had been "delayed at the place of surrender for two days on account of the condition of the enemy."[51] It took the Fort Fillmore men that long to recover enough strength to march back over San Augustin Pass and to Las Cruces as prisoners of war. During this time, the Texans became the Union soldiers' water carriers.

For the 410 soldiers who survived the Fort Stanton Road, their desert walk was not over. After they arrived in Las Cruces, Baylor paroled them because he did not think he could guard them and simultaneously turn to face fresh Union troops, whom he thought would arrive at any moment (an erroneous assumption).[52] What horses the federals had were now in the hands of the Confederates, and so the paroled soldiers who left Las Cruces on August 2 walked more than one hundred miles to Fort Craig in four days. Although they marched northward along the Rio Grande and therefore had supplies of fresh water, they had very few provisions. There were reports of insanity and blood drinking on this march as well.[53] The Confederates, for their part, triumphed in the wake of the Union surrender. By the fall of 1861 they had seized Fillmore's remaining supplies and then Fort Stanton, which Union troops abandoned after the news of San Augustin Springs came by express. They confiscated horses and men in addition to federal drafts totaling $17,000, which Lynde's commissary Lt. Augustus H. Plummer had been holding.[54] Because of these developments, and the toll that the desert had taken on Union troops, the Confederates were nicely situated for their successful assault on Fort Craig in February 1862.

These developments were humiliating for the Union army in the far West. However, the surrender provoked Canby to prepare more intensively for the Confederate invasion; he began to harass the governors of the New Mexico and Colorado territories for volunteers. He also ordered the commanders of New Mexico's remaining Union forts to augment their military landscapes by building stronger earthworks for successful defense against Confederate light artillery. Canby even went so far as to order Fort Union be moved "from its old location under the mesa" further east into the plains "and converted into a fieldwork." Ultimately, Canby hoped that, for Union soldiers and citizens, "San Augustin[e] be remembered only as a watchword and an incentive to renewed exertions for the honor of their country and their flag."[55]

The evacuation of Fort Fillmore, the deadly march on the Fort Stanton Road, and the Confederate pursuit and Union surrender at San Augustin Springs were the opening salvos in the Civil War Southwest – the Bull Run of the Desert. This Union disaster did not determine the outcome of the war in New Mexico, however. The federals ultimately regained control of the territory as the result of one significant maneuver eight months later: Maj. John Chivington's destruction of the Confederate wagon train outside Glorieta in late March 1862. Without a steady supply of provisions, the Southerners were unable to sustain themselves in the desert; they then made their own disastrous retreat, marching from Santa Fe to San Antonio over the course of two months. Along the way, they lost 30 percent of their men to heatstroke and dehydration.

So what do we learn by tracking Lynde and his column through the Jornada del Muerto on that exceedingly hot day in July 1861? In most accounts of the retreat from Fillmore and the surrender at San Augustin Springs, Isaac Lynde has taken the bulk of the blame. Historians have argued that his decisions were unaccountable, especially in light of his experiences with desert fighting in the Mexican-American War, and his years as the commander of Fort McLane. But Lynde's decision to abandon Fort Fillmore seems reasonable when we consider – as he did – its environmental history: the fort's low-lying site, its adobe construction, and its distance from the only water source in the area. Fillmore and the other U.S. military landscapes built in the 1850s were vulnerable in a Civil War context. These adobe fortifications were no match for artillery; and they were so far apart that they could not sustain large armies on the move. While Lynde probably should have known how the sandy and exposed conditions of the Fort Stanton Road would affect his column, the high desert's summer climate explains the slowness of the march, the uselessness of the water wagons, and the large numbers of federals who succumbed to heatstroke and dehydration. Understanding these conditions and their effects on the human body also helps us to comprehend the large death toll, and Lynde's inability to lead his troops effectively during the march and after his arrival in San Augustin Springs. Environmental conditions shaped every decision that Lynde made in late July 1861; and they would continue to determine the way that both Union and Confederate forces fought in the New Mexico campaigns of 1861–62.

This may seem to some like an argument for nature's "agency," an assertion that the desert exerted a malevolent power over the men and animals attempting to move through it in the summer of 1861. Such an argument is admittedly extreme, and it would be absurd to assert that the forces of nature act with "intent." But it is in the southwestern territories that we see the power of the landscape to shape human action in its most extreme form. The temperature fluctuations, solar radiation, lack of water sources, vast and uncultivated distances between towns and forts, scrubby and spiky vegetation: all of these elements of the desert climate and ecosystem reveal it to be a uniquely unsuitable place to fight a conventional, large-scale war. Such conditions demanded adaptive responses from soldiers. As Kenneth Noe, Katy Meier, and Lisa Brady have shown, the health of armies and military victories depend on soldiers' abilities to react to environmental conditions in meaningful ways. During the retreat to San Augustin, Lynde and his officers did not adjust their plans to enable the large column to move quickly through the Jornada del Muerto. Baylor and his men had the advantage of fewer men and nimble, rested horses;

each Texan carried his own water supply. What looked to military personnel in the East (and to some of Lynde's subordinates) like surrender to "an inferior force of insurgents" was actually a moment in which environmental conditions favored small numbers and mobility.[56]

These are the kinds of insights we gain when we approach the history of the Civil War with careful, analytical attention to landscapes and climate. As Ken Noe observes in his essay for this collection, these are not just interesting bits of trivia, although this is often how they appear in scholarly work.[57] An environmental history of the Union retreat and surrender at San Augustin Springs shows us that war may be waged in the name of politics and ideology, but it is fought by bodies moving through space. War is boots trudging through drifting sand, a hot sun rising in the eastern sky, tongues swelling in parched mouths. It is men and women and children falling by the wayside on a little-known road, and dreams of martial glory dying on the soft and drifting sands of the desert Southwest.

Notes

1. E. R. S. Canby to William Chapman from Santa Fe, July 31, 1861, in John P. Wilson, *When the Texans Came: Missing Records from the Civil War in the Southwest, 1861–1862* (Albuquerque: University of New Mexico Press, 2001), 66.

2. Ray C. Colton, *The Civil War in the Western Territories: Arizona, Colorado, New Mexico, and Utah* (Norman: University of Oklahoma Press, 1959), 13–14; George Henry Pettis, "The Confederate Invasion of New Mexico and Arizona," in *Battles and Leaders of the Civil War* (New York: Century Co., 1887), 2:103; Isaac Lynde to E. R. S. Canby, from Fort McLane, N.M., June 24, 1861, in Wilson, *When the Texans Came*, 29.

3. Colton, *The Civil War in the Western Territories*; George Henry Pettis, *The California Column: Its Campaigns and Services in New Mexico, Arizona, and Texas during the Civil War* (Santa Fe, 1908), 8–9; Statement of F. J. Crilly, [1865], in Wilson, *When the Texans Came*, 41–46; Statement of Major Isaac Lynde, n.d., in Wilson, *When the Texans Came*, 46–50; John R. Baylor to Captain T. A. Washington, September 21, 1861, in U.S. War Department, *The War of Rebellion: A Compilation of the Official Records of the Union and Confederate Armies* (Washington, D.C.: Government Printing Office, 1880–1901) (hereafter cited as OR) I: 4, pp. 17–20.

4. Pettis, "The Confederate Invasion," 2:103; W. B. Lane to Mrs. (Alfred) Gibbs, July 30, 1861, in Wilson, *When the Texans Came*, 41; Crilly in Wilson, *When the Texans Came*, 46; Alfred Gibbs to E. R. S. Canby, August 6, 1861, OR I: 4, pp. 7–8; Statement of J. C. McKee, August 1861, OR I: 4, p. 11; I. N. Moore to Adjt. General's Office, September 1, 1861, in Wilson, *When the Texans Came*, 109.

5. Moore to AGO, September 1, 1861, in Wilson, *When the Texans Came*, 109.

6. L. Thomas (by order of Major-General McClellan), November 25, 1861, OR I: 4, pp. 16.

7. Canby, General Orders No. 31, August 27, 1861, OR I: 4, p. 3.
8. The notable exceptions are Colton, *The Civil War in the Western Territories*; Alvin Josephy Jr., *The Civil War in the American West* (New York: Vintage, 1993); Martin Hardwick Hall, *Sibley's New Mexico Campaign* (Albuquerque: University of New Mexico Press, 2000); Donald Frazier, *Blood and Treasure: Confederate Empire in the Southwest* (College Station: Texas A&M University Press, 1996); Wilson, *When the Texans Came*; and Jerry Thompson, *Confederate General in the West: Henry Hopkins Sibley* (College Station: Texas A&M University Press, 1996), and *Civil War in the Southwest: Recollections of the Sibley Brigade* (College Station: Texas A&M University Press, 2001).
9. There are too many studies of western and southwestern environmental history to list here but the major works are Patricia Nelson Limerick, *The Legacy of Conquest: The Unbroken Past of the American West* (New York: W. W. Norton, 1987); Donald Worster, *Rivers of Empire: Water, Aridity, and the Growth of the American West* (Oxford: Oxford University Press, 1985); Richard Wright, *"It's Your Misfortune and None of My Own": A New History of the American West* (Norman: University of Oklahoma Press, 1993); Elliott West, *The Contested Plains: Indians, Goldseekers, and the Rush to Colorado* (Lawrence: University Press of Kansas, 1998); Karl Jacoby, *Shadows at Dawn: An Apache Massacre and the Violence of History* (New York: Penguin, 2009); Sam Truett, *Fugitive Landscapes: The Forgotten History of the U.S.–Mexico Borderlands* (New Haven: Yale University Press, 2006); Brian DeLay, *War of a Thousand Deserts: Indian Raids and the U.S. Mexican War* (New Haven: Yale University Press, 2009); Pekka Hämäläinen, *The Comanche Empire* (New Haven: Yale University Press, 2009); Ari Kelman, *A Misplaced Massacre: Struggling over the Memory of Sand Creek* (Cambridge, Mass.: Harvard University Press, 2013).
10. Hall, *Sibley's New Mexico Campaign*, 8; Frazier, *Blood and Treasure*, 13, 36, 75.
11. Jefferson Davis's interest in solving the problem of crossing the vast lands of the far West also led him to argue for a more adaptive strategy in the Southwest: the use of camels for military transportation and in campaigns against Comanches and Apaches. In March 1855 Davis convinced Congress to appropriate $30,000 for the purchase of camels in the Middle East and North Africa, and their transportation to the United States. By 1859 there were more than eighty camels lodged at forts in Texas and California. William J. Cooper Jr., *Jefferson Davis, American* (New York: Vintage, 2001), 277; *Los Angeles Times*, November 23, 1857, reprinted in *Portland Oregonian*, December 26, 1857, as quoted in Fred S. Perrine, "Uncle Sam's Camel Corps," *New Mexico Historical Review*, no. 4 (October 1926): 442; Henry C. Wayne to Jefferson Davis, April 10, 1856, in Jefferson Davis, *Report of the Secretary of War [. . . regarding] The Purchase of Camels for the Purposes of Military Transportation* (Washington: D.C.: A. O. P. Nicholson, 1857), 54, front matter.
12. Pettis, "The Confederate Invasion," 2:103; "Fort Craig National Historic Site [History]"; Brian DeLay, *War of a Thousand Deserts: Indian Raids and the U.S.–Mexican War* (New Haven: Yale University Press, 2008), xv, xix.
13. T. T. Teel, "Sibley's New Mexican Campaign – Its Objects and the Causes of its Failure," in *Battles and Leaders*, 2:700.
14. Hall, *Sibley's New Mexico Campaign*, 21–22; Thompson, introduction to *Civil War in the Southwest*, xiv; Frazier, *Blood and Treasure*, 75; Theophilus Noel, *Auto-*

biography and Reminiscences of Theophilus Noel (Chicago: Theo. Noel Co., 1904), 56; Teel, "Sibley's New Mexican Campaign," 2:700.

15. Lynde in Wilson, *When the Texans Came*, 46; Lynde to Asst. Adjt. General, August 7, 1861, OR I: 4, p. 5.

16. Crilly in Wilson, *When the Texans Came*, 45.

17. Lynde in Wilson, *When the Texans Came*, 46; Lynde to AAG, August 7, 1861, OR I: 4, p. 5.

18. Crilly in Wilson, *When the Texans Came*, 45.

19. Latham Anderson, "Canby's Services in the New Mexican Campaign," in *Battles and Leaders*, 698; Colton, *The Civil War in the Western Territories*, 3–4; Lynde in Wilson, *When the Texans Came*, 46; Gibbs to Canby, August 6, 1861, OR I: 4, p. 7; Martin Hardwick Hall, *Sibley's New Mexico Campaign* (1960; Albuquerque: University of New Mexico Press, 2000), 18, 19.

20. Lynde to AAG, August 7, 1861, OR I: 4, p. 5.

21. General Orders No. 37, July 26, 1861, in Wilson, *When the Texans Came*, 40; Colton, *The Civil War in the Western Territories*, 15.

22. McKee to the S-G, August 16, 1861, OR I: 4, p. 11–12.

23. Crilly in Wilson, *When the Texans Came*, 43.

24. Benjamin S. Roberts to Canby, October 5, 1861, in Wilson, *When the Texans Came*, 130.

25. Greeley quoted in Colton, *The Civil War in the Territories*, 15.

26. Norman R. Malm, *Climate Guide, Las Cruces, 1892–2000* (Las Cruces, N.M., 2003), 1; Charles G. Scalet, Lester D. Flake, and David W. Willis, *Introduction to Wildlife and Fisheries: An Integrated Approach* (New York: W. H. Freeman and Co., 1996), 266; Janice Emily Bowers, *Shrubs and Trees of the Southwest Deserts* (Tucson: Western National Parks Association, 1993), 3; G. E. Griffith, J. M. Omernik, M. M. McGraw, G. Z. Jacobi, C. M. Canavan, T. S. Schrader, D. Mercer, R. Hill, and B. C. Moran, *Ecoregions of New Mexico*, color poster with map, descriptive text, summary tables, and photographs (Reston, Va.: U.S. Geological Survey, 2006).

27. Peter Stark, *Last Breath: The Limits of Adventure* (New York: Ballantine, 2002), 256.

28. Lynde to AAG, August 7, 1861, OR I: 4, p. 5; Lynde in Wilson, *When the Texans Came*, 48.

29. This rainfall amount is about average for the Las Cruces area in July (Malm, "Climate Guide, Las Cruces," tables 1 and 4, pp. 1, 3, 4, 9).

30. Malm, "Climate Guide, Las Cruces," table 6, pp. 2, 12; Crilly in Wilson, *When the Texans Came*, 43; Lynde in Wilson, *When the Texans Came*, 48; Lynde to AAG, August 7, 1861, OR I: 4, p. 5; "The Surrender of Fort Fillmore, New Mexico – The Treason of the Officers," *Leavenworth Daily Conservative*, (October 19, 1861, 2, in Wilson, *When the Texans Came*, 50.

31. Malm, "Climate Guide, Las Cruces," table 1, pp. 1, 4.

32. Crilly in Wilson, *When the Texans Came*, 43.

33. Jonathan DuHamel, "The Creosote Bush, a Desert Survivor," *Tucson Citizen*, March 6, 2010, http://tucsoncitizen.com/wryheat/2010/03/06/the-creosote-bush-a-desert-survivor/.

34. Griffith et al., *Ecoregions of New Mexico*.

35. Crilly in Wilson, *When the Texans Came*, 43; Lane to Mrs. Gibbs, July 30, 1861, in Wilson, *When the Texans Came*, 41; Gibbs to Canby, August 6, 1861, OR I: 4, p. 7; Lynde in Wilson, *When the Texans Came*, 49.

36. Stark, *Last Breath*, 139–47.

37. Lynde to AAG, August 7, 1861, OR I: 4, p. 6.

38. Crilly in Wilson, *When the Texans Came*, 44.

39. Baylor to Washington, September 21, 1861, OR I: 4, p. 18.

40. J. H. Potter, *Recapitulation of Troops Surrendered at San Augustine Springs, N. Mex., July 27, 1861*, OR I: 4, p. 15.

41. W. J. McGee, "[The Phenomena of Desert Thirst]" (1906), as synopsized in "Desert Thirst as a Disease," *American Medicine* 12 (May 1906): 51–52.

42. Stark, *Last Breath*, 254–56, 259, 267, 274, 283.

43. Crilly in Wilson, *When the Texans Came*, 43–44.

44. Lynde to AAG, August 7, 1861, OR I: 4, p. 6.

45. Lynde in Wilson, *When the Texans Came*, 48; Lynde to AAG, August 7, 1861, OR I: 4, p. 6.

46. Gibbs to Canby, August 6, 1861, OR I: 4, p. 7.

47. Gibbs to the AAG, November 7, 1861, OR I: 4, p. 10.

48. McKee, August 16, 1861, OR I: 4, p. 13.

49. Crilly in Wilson, *When the Texans Came*, 45.

50. Gibbs to Canby, August 6, 1861, OR I: 4, p. 8.

51. Baylor to Washington, September 21, 1861, OR I: 4, p. 19.

52. Baylor Report, August 3, 1861, OR I: 4, p. 17.

53. Colton, *The Civil War in the Western Territories*, 17.

54. Ibid., 16–18; Baylor to Washington, September 21, 1861, OR I: 4, p. 19.

55. Pettis, "The Confederate Invasion," 2:104; Colton, *The Civil War in the Western Territories*, 19–20; Canby to AAG, August 4, 1861, OR I: 4, p. 2; Canby, General Orders No. 31, August 27, 1861, OR I: 4, p. 3.

56. Kenneth Noe, "Fateful Lightning: The Significance of Weather and Climate to Civil War History," in this volume; Kathryn Shively Meier, *Nature's Civil War: Common Soldiers and the Environment in 1862 Virginia* (Chapel Hill: University of North Carolina Press, 2013); Lisa M. Brady, *War upon the Land: Military Strategy and the Transformation of Southern Landscapes during the American Civil War* (Athens: University of Georgia Press, 2012).

57. Noe, "Fateful Lightning."

THREE

Yancey County Goes to War
A Case Study of People and Nature on Home Front and Battlefield, 1861–1865

TIMOTHY SILVER

On May 1, 1861, 112 men and boys from the far reaches of western North Carolina signed up to fight for the Confederacy. They hailed from Yancey County, a 313-square-mile tract of upland that included a range of tall, evergreen-draped peaks known as the Black Mountains. Calling on nature for inspiration, the new soldiers christened themselves the Black Mountain Boys and soon became part of Company C, 16th North Carolina Regiment (originally known as the 6th North Carolina). Additional enlistments brought the total number of Yancey men in the company to about 130 by late summer. Over the next four years those soldiers fought and died in some of the Civil War's most celebrated battles. On the home front the conflict spawned violence and lawlessness that left local people struggling for survival in a place where they had once prospered. Before the war ended, many residents of the southern mountains faced similar troubles, owing in part to the "social, economic and political complexities" of life in Confederate Appalachia.[1]

Though historians have been slow to acknowledge it, many of the problems plaguing mountain communities resulted directly from the ways in which war reshaped the natural world. Alfred Crosby reminded us long ago that people are never really alone in nature. They live alongside what Crosby calls the "portmanteau biota," that conglomeration of microorganisms, crops, and domestic and wild animals that reside in their bodies, on their farms, and in the woods and fields around them.[2] Local environmental history—including that of Yancey County—provides an opportunity to look closely at the ways in which the Civil War altered established relationships between southern people and their fellow organisms. One way to tell that story — and to ensure that the portmanteau biota get equal time with humans — is to follow the Black Mountain Boys into and out of the war, paying particular attention to the ways in which their absence from the home front and their presence on the battlefield reshaped the natural world. Narrated in this fashion, the history of a single small place can illuminate the effects of the wartime environment on soldiers and civilians in Appalachia and across the South.

In 1860 some 8,293 white people inhabited the coves and hollows of Yancey County. Due to the rugged forested terrain, arable land was scarce and most residents farmed relatively small bottomland tracts along the county's major rivers. In addition to supplying their own needs, local people sold surplus grain, spirits, and livestock to merchants and factors in Asheville, who then sent the goods to planters in the eastern Carolinas. To combat soil exhaustion, county farmers used a loosely organized system of field rotation. They initially opened the dense hardwood forests by girdling trees and burning off underbrush. These semicleared plots, known as "deadenings," could be tended for several years until erosion and declining fertility decreased yields. At that point, additional forest had to be opened while the old fields lay fallow and recovered some of their fertility, a process that might take two decades or more. The system was labor intensive, but sustainable — as long as mountain residents had fresh woodland and a sufficient work force.[3]

Like the majority of Appalachian people — indeed the majority of southerners — most county farmers did not own slaves. In 1860 roughly 362 slaves resided in Yancey, and the federal census listed only 3.8 percent of heads of households as slaveholders. Even so, slavery was deeply entrenched in the county's economy and agriculture, especially among its more prominent citizens. As Kevin Young's careful analysis of Yancey slavery has demonstrated, many of the county's largest slaveholders occupied the best farmland or were engaged in some of the larger livestock and farming operations. In Burnsville, the county seat and the region's only substantial town, roughly one third of the eighteen households had slaves, some of whom worked on outlying farms owned by town residents. Burnsville slaveholders also rented bound labor to other landowners during the busiest agricultural seasons. By 1860 Milton Penland, a politically well-connected merchant and hotel owner in Burnsville, was one of the county's richest men and the town's largest slaveholder with thirty-one slaves at his disposal.[4]

In Yancey, as elsewhere in Appalachia, slaves were part of a varied and shifting agricultural work force that included white farm families, white day laborers, and white tenants. Due to the importance of black labor and the region's economic ties to the eastern Carolinas, most local political leaders supported slavery, though they often differed sharply over secession. Indeed, Union sentiment ran so strong in Yancey's northern reaches that a new county, Mitchell, had to be carved out in 1861, in part to placate antisecessionists. That delineation reduced Yancey's size from more than 500 square miles to its current 313 square miles.[5]

In the years before secession, other events shaped the local economy. In 1857 Elisha Mitchell, a University of North Carolina science professor, fell to his death while trying to settle an argument with a former student, Thomas Clingman, over which of them had been first to measure the East's highest peak (now called Mount Mitchell). As a result, the region garnered national publicity, and by the late 1850s it became an important tourist destination, especially for Lowcountry planters who sought respite from summer heat. A number of local farmers supplemented their incomes by guiding visitors around and to the East's tallest mountain.[6]

The war's most immediate effect on the Yancey environment was to empty county fields of some of their most visible organisms, namely white men. Though the Black Mountain Boys ranged in age from sixteen to forty-nine, 80 percent of them (104) were between the ages of twenty and thirty-nine. Some 1,034 males of that age lived in the county, so in that single enlistment, about 10 percent (allowing for some who returned home early for various reasons) of Yancey's most able-bodied white men left for war. Two months later, on July 3, 1861, at least another 132 men ages twenty to thirty-nine enlisted in Company B of the 29th North Carolina. Nearly all of those who listed their civilian occupations described themselves as "farmers" or "farm laborers." (Two teachers and a hatter, both members of the Black Mountain Boys, were notable exceptions.) For the most part, military service took the men straight from county fields at the beginning of the agricultural season.[7]

Many of those first recruits signed on for a year, leaving families to manage their lands until they returned. Evidence from local sources is sparse, but many wives and daughters skillfully tended such farms elsewhere in Appalachia. Women not only toiled behind the plow but also bartered for seed and implements, supervised farmhands, acquired real estate, and bought and sold slaves. When it came to the more arduous work of clearing new fields, however, women usually needed male labor, occasionally from slaves, but more frequently from hired white farmhands.[8]

More of that work force disappeared after April 1862 when the Confederate Congress passed the Conscription Act. That summer, approximately 172 more Yancey farmers, ages twenty to thirty-nine, went into Companies C and G of the 58th North Carolina regiment, bringing the documented number of Yancey recruits from that age group to more than 400. Sporadic enlistments in other units (including the 6th North Carolina Cavalry) and an unknown, but much smaller, contingent that joined Federal forces, pushed the total higher. Due to the varied makeup of the agricultural work force, it is difficult to determine exactly what percentage of total laborers (male and female, free and slave) the new soldiers represented or the exact number of men still available to clear new fields. What does seem certain, though, is that at least 40 to 50 percent of Yancey's most productive farmhands left home for an extended period, many for the duration of the war.[9]

Even under the best of circumstances, the absence of so many laborers could easily have stymied food production in the sparsely populated county, especially as the clearing of fresh land slowed and the fertility of old fields declined. Between 1862 and 1864, however, the labor shortage was not the only problem farmers encountered. For three straight years, heavy spring rains gave way to clear skies and extraordinarily dry weather during June, July, and August. As Ken Noe's essay for this volume makes clear, conditions in Yancey County were part of a larger weather pattern across the South, trends overlooked by all but a handful of Civil War historians. Yancey County provides an opportunity to observe those effects at a local level and to show how weather became "a defining factor" for one mountain community.[10]

Summer droughts in Appalachia left corn and other mountain crops shriveled in the fields. Each autumn, even as the rain returned, unseasonable cold and early frosts eliminated any chance for recovery.[11] The catastrophic effects of depleted fields, bad weather, and men gone off to war can be read in letters sent to North Carolina governor Zebulon Vance. A Burnsville man complained that "the absence of the labouring class, together with the early frost in the Fall has cut us short . . . of at least five thousand bushels of corn." From nearby Mitchell County a citizen's group worried that the "hard freezes that visited this country much earlier this season than heretofore" had left local people with less than "half enough grain to bread their own families" and none "to let their neighbors."[12]

In times past, when crops failed, cattle and hogs had helped mountain families fend off famine. Slaughtered in winter, even a few head of poorly nourished livestock might see a family through a lean season. However, to preserve beef and pork, farmers needed salt, a staple now in critically short supply. By the summer of 1862, as the first crops began to fail, war and encroaching Union troops had choked off the usual salt supply from several sites in West Virginia. In time, the Federal blockade curtailed salt imports to many southern ports as well. Mountain roads, barely passable in peacetime, fell into disrepair as the conflict wore on, making it difficult to transport any staples into the region. Farmers did have the option of keeping animals alive through winter, slaughtering them one at a time, and selling any meat they could not immediately use. But without salt as a preservative, livestock no longer provided as much insurance against hunger.[13]

Beginning in 1861 the Confederate government instituted a policy of "impressment" that allowed military commanders to appropriate food, fodder, and materiel needed to supply their troops, horses, and mules. Two years later, the "tax-in-kind" permitted officials to take one-tenth of numerous crops, including such mountain staples as "wheat, corn, oats, rye, and buckwheat." By law, farmers received compensation or "certificates of credit" redeemable for fair value of crops and livestock. But with food scarce and inflation rampant, merchants and speculators frequently offered better prices than the government, creating a thriving black market that also pulled resources from county farms.[14]

The scramble to feed hungry troops occasionally turned Confederate military leaders against one another. In autumn 1863, beef grew so scarce in and around Burnsville that the head of the Home Guard (a loosely organized militia charged with keeping order in and around the town) told Governor Vance that he "would suffer no [more] cattle drives out of [Yancey and surrounding] counties." Instead, available cattle were to be slaughtered for use by the Home Guard. "It would," he explained, "take all the provisions that wane here to support [his] troops." He did not say whether or how other townsfolk might survive. As scarcity became a way of life, Governor Vance initiated a massive program of poor relief. From all accounts, though, even unprecedented government largesse did little to alleviate local shortages.[15]

The men who left their fields for battle fared little better in the wartime environment. To understand their plight, we need look no further than the experiences of the Black Mountain Boys and the 16th North Carolina. Before their enlistment, the Black Mountain Boys (like most southern soldiers) had lived in relative isolation from common viruses and bacteria that flourished in larger human populations. Over time, without enough human hosts to sustain and spread them, common childhood diseases had all but disappeared from the local community. When would-be soldiers mustered in large groups, as in the Raleigh organization of the 16th (where 1,200 new recruits gathered), a few men who carried dangerous microorganisms set off devastating epidemics in the crowded camps.

In the summer of 1861, as the 16th moved out to join Robert E. Lee in what is now West Virginia (by way of Richmond), sickness dogged them every step of the way. One Yancey recruit died of measles at Huntersville, (West) Virginia, in early August. As on the home front, weather compounded the problems. A month later, at Valley Mountain, a heavy rainstorm left roads knee-deep in mud and water "bubbling up" in the tents. Half the regiment came down with rash and fever. Three Yancey men died in a local hospital, probably from measles complicated by typhoid, exposure, and pneumonia. The company lost no one during Lee's unsuccessful efforts at Cheat Mountain, but four more died from measles and exposure on the return trip.[16]

Winter brought little relief. An unidentified Yancey County soldier who wrote home in January from Prince William County, Virginia, noted that a comrade had suffered "a very bad cough" that had put him in the "horsepittle." The writer happily reported that he had "bin for the last three weeks stouter" than at any time since he left Raleigh, but also noted that, "There is right smart of illness in our regiment, now they have the mumps." Another member of the 16th who witnessed the early epidemics put it more simply. "Disease," he said, "caused greater mortality among us than any battle of the war."[17]

In early 1862 the 16th moved farther south to defend Richmond against Union general George Brinton McClellan during his Peninsula Campaign. Those operations are well known among military historians for McClellan's paranoia about rebel numbers, Lee's replacement of Gen. Joseph E. Johnston as Confederate leader, and some of the bloodiest battles of the war. The Black Mountain Boys were in the thick of it. Fighting in William Dorsey Pender's brigade, the Yancey men had seven wounded at Seven Pines, two killed at Mechanicsville, and four killed and five wounded during the bloody assault at Gaines Mill during the Seven Days campaign.[18]

On a daily basis, however, the men of the 16th spent far more time battling the rigors of camp life than fighting Yankees. As the childhood maladies ran their course, the crowded unsanitary conditions of the battlefield gave rise to other ailments. Heavy spring rains overflowed trench lines, filled wagon ruts, and flooded latrines and drainage ditches. A Georgia lieutenant who fought and traveled over the same ground as the Black Mountain Boys remembered that he "had to drink water out of the road where the wagons, horses and men would wade through. It was muddy," he said, "and tasted very badly." Small wonder that typhoid, dysentery, and chronic diarrhea ran rampant in Confederate camps. The average Confederate soldier deployed on the peninsula (including, one can infer, those from the 16th North Carolina and Yancey County) had likely endured at least three extended bouts with some combination of those diseases by the spring and summer of 1862.[19]

By midsummer, malaria was also a problem. Mosquito-borne parasites responsible for the malady had been present in Tidewater Virginia for at least two hundred years, and malaria had become endemic in many locales throughout the South. But during the first decades of the 1800s, the disease had been less visible on the peninsula as the local population acquired some immunity to common parasites and increased settlement eliminated mosquito-breeding sites. Those conditions changed abruptly in 1862 as war reshaped local ecology and the rain left acres of mud and standing water in which anopheline mosquitoes proliferated. Soldiers in the converging armies provided thousands of fresh non-immune hosts for parasites carried by the winged pests. As mosquito populations peaked in summer, troops already battling dysentery, fatigue, and camp diseases could expect to fall victim to spiking fevers and debilitating chills. As in colonial times, summer became a sickly season on the peninsula.[20]

For the most part, though, the Black Mountain Boys might have fared better in their new environment than McClellan's men. Although many Southern soldiers (including those from Yancey County) probably lacked acquired immunity to malaria, Confederate forces remained close to Richmond with hospitals and private homes to nurse the sick. At that early stage of the war, Southern soldiers also occasionally drew fresh provisions from the city and the surrounding countryside. Moreover, proximity to the capital afforded them campsites on some of the region's highest and healthiest ground.[21]

Union forces were not so fortunate. Slowed by the rain, McClellan's men slogged through the muck and mire of the Chickahominy River floodplain, camping anywhere they could find dry ground. Indeed, after the

Battle of Seven Pines, thousands of Northern soldiers remained camped on the battlefield (known in Union circles as Fair Oaks), not far from three thousand partially buried corpses. According to a British newspaperman, "myriads of flies enjoyed a banquet of putrescent vileness," human nostrils "filled with odors too foul" and feet "slipped upon carrion grease" as the Union men went about their daily duties. No doubt the various viruses, protozoa, and bacteria responsible for dysentery and typhoid flourished there, as did anopheline mosquitoes.[22]

As if those conditions were not bad enough, by late June 1862, a diet rich in salt beef and pork led to an outbreak of scurvy among the Union soldiers, a nutritional malady that Confederate troops, for the moment, had avoided. Though McClellan moved quickly to remedy the problems with fresh provisions, scurvy only added to the mélange of diseases that Federal troops called "Chickahominy Fever" or, with special reference to dysentery, "The Virginia Quickstep." By early July, when McClellan arrived back at Harrison's Landing after the retreat from Richmond, the summer heat was stifling, his men suffered from battle fatigue, and his army's health was at its nadir. Union surgeons also had reason to suspect that things might get worse. Typically malarial outbreaks peaked in August and September as the parasites injected by mosquitoes in early summer multiplied in human livers and bloodstreams. (McClellan himself suffered periodic bouts of malaria and perhaps other camp diseases during the Peninsula Campaign.) Reinforcements who had little experience with camp life would also be especially vulnerable to typhoid and dysentery, something that might have been a consideration as Union leaders contemplated another assault on Richmond.[23]

The two armies brought more than men and microorganisms to Virginia. Thousands of animals accompanied the troops into battle. Some historians estimate that McClellan employed no fewer than thirty-five thousand horses to move his men, artillery, and supply wagons. Horses and mules were essential to Southern defenses as well. After the carnage at Gaines Mill in late June, the 16th's regimental historian ventured onto part of the battlefield where, lying among the fallen soldiers, he saw "hundreds of horses ... some not dead, some with legs shot off trying to get up, moaning and crying like children begging for help, as if begging someone to shoot them and end their pain." Across the peninsula, the rotting corpses (many of which were partially burned, but never buried) only added to the contamination in Confederate and Federal camps.[24]

Like the soldiers, horses and mules that survived battle faced new threats from epidemic disease. In early 1862 an outbreak of glanders, a highly contagious and deadly equine infection, began to afflict animals in both armies. Confederates thought a sick Union mount was the source of the contagion; a Union officer blamed it on Joseph E. Johnston, claiming that the Confederate general had intentionally left diseased horses at Manassas to infect the Federal herds (a kind of equine biological warfare). Passed on by contact at corrals, hayracks, and watering troughs, glanders spread quickly through horses on the peninsula, adding to the daily attrition from the battlefield. Though both armies suffered serious losses from glanders over the next three years, the South – with its horse supply from Kentucky and Tennessee cut off by invading federal forces – bore the brunt of the epidemic. When the war ended, Grant had more horses in the field than Lee had men. Glanders also "broke out from the military herds" and "followed the trails of war" to infect animals on southern farms. The disease remained a significant problem in the South well into the 1870s.[25]

To provide troops with at least some fresh food, Confederate officials shipped cattle and hogs from across the South to holding pens and packing plants in and around Richmond. Some of those animals carried deadly disease organisms, including the virus responsible for hog cholera and the protozoan (spread by ticks) that caused cattle fever. Cholera killed nearly three-quarters of the swine in some Virginia counties by 1866; cattle fever devastated herds in the southern and southwestern parts of the state.[26] The gathering of horses, mules, hogs, and cattle for the Peninsula Campaign – like the mustering of men – created a new disease environment that affected southern animals and agricultural life for years to come.

Meanwhile the Black Mountain Boys fought on. One can follow their trail simply by counting casualties: J. Wilburn Silver wounded at Second Manassas; another recruit dead of wounds at Fredericksburg; two killed and five wounded at Chancellorsville; a soldier who lost a right arm and another who lost a leg at Gettysburg, along with several more who fell during Pickett's Charge; two more wounded at the Wilderness. It is also possible to follow (albeit with less precision) the environmental chaos that swirled around them: a man dead in a Charlottesville hospital from "febris typhoides"; another discharged due to a "hemorrahage of the lungs;" one dead of "chronic diarrheoea" in Maryland; others "reported sick" for long periods. Of the original 1,200 recruits, the 16th North Carolina surrendered just 12 officers and 83 enlisted men. Today a monument outside the courthouse in Burnsville notes that 148 Yancey men (about 25 percent of those who enlisted or were conscripted into the Confederate Army) lost their lives in the war.[27]

For some, the strain of the new battlefield environment was too much. At least twenty men from Yancey County abandoned the 16th before the fighting ended. Officials identified only two that returned to duty. Five deserted to the enemy, while the rest apparently just walked away. Exactly how many of those men made their way back home is difficult to determine (the January 1862 letter from Prince William County, Virginia, mentions one soldier who had "got home"), but Yancey County had its share of deserters, draft dodgers, and Union sympathizers, known as "Tories." They roamed the countryside in small guerrilla bands, bushwhacking Confederate troops and skirmishing with the Home Guard.[28]

As the guerrilla war escalated and travel became dangerous, tourist traffic in and around the Black Mountains disappeared. As a result, local people found themselves without another traditional source of income. Of more immediate concern, however, were guerilla raids on local farms. Yancey farmers routinely lost livestock and other provisions to the roving outlaws. Marauding soldiers ripped apart fencing and farm buildings for firewood and occasionally burned unoccupied homes. A man who was watching property for an absentee owner (the wartime equivalent of house sitting) lived in chronic fear of the raiders. As he later told the owner, "I have gotten up often [at night], imagining that I heard the fire roaring, when it would be [the wind in] the pine trees below the house . . . the fences were all down and rails burnt, a good many by the soldiers." Even wild animals seem to have disappeared amid the hunger and lawlessness. As a relative of one Civil War survivor remembered, "By the time of the surrender almost all the game, even to the squirrels had been shot, snared or trapped."[29]

In mid-April 1864 countywide famine spawned violence in Burnsville. In an incident reminiscent of food riots elsewhere in the Confederacy a year earlier, fifty Yancey women marched into town and walked out with sixty bushels of army wheat. Twenty-four hours later, an armed band of seventy-five Tories plundered a town storehouse, taking a hundred guns and five hundred pounds of bacon, while members of the dispirited Home Guard fled into the countryside. The Tory leader was Montreville Ray, a deserter from Company C of the 16th North Carolina. He abandoned the 16th during the Peninsula Campaign.[30]

During the assault on the town cache, Ray's men apparently grabbed Milton Penland (the town's largest slaveholder, who had assets of more than fifty thousand dollars) "and swore that they would hang him" unless he paid their price and promised to "move from the county." That incident is rife with class issues, but from an environmental standpoint it is intriguing for what the raiders demanded in exchange for Penland's freedom: "8 head of beaves, 100 pounds of bacon, and 50 bushels of wheat." In the desperate search for sustenance, food literally became a king's (or at least a local elite's) ransom. Penland forked over the provisions, though he did not leave Burnsville until 1870.[31]

With the return of the deserters and the raids on Burnsville we come full circle, from the ecology of the battlefield back to the ecology of the home front and, ultimately, to the question that haunts any historian who undertakes this type of community study: So what? What can we glean from the story of Yancey County that might be useful in an environmental interpretation of the Civil War?

First, the troubles on Yancey County farms prompt us to ponder a broader question: Why did soldiers and civilians go hungry in the South, one of the world's foremost agricultural economies? Our story points to the paucity of labor on mountain farms, a local manifestation of a much larger trend in the South. The mustering of troops for the Confederate cause took more than half a million white men—roughly a third of the white labor force—out of the fields. War also broke down the plantation system as slaves were put to work in the military, ran away to Union lines, or simply refused to obey masters. Other factors contributed to the food crisis, notably distribution problems, impressment, and southerners' reluctance to abandon cash crops for corn, wheat, and field peas. But a lack of farm labor goes a long way toward explaining why the South failed to feed itself.[32]

Second, military historians have long known that for every Civil War soldier killed in battle, two more died of disease. However, until recently, the exchange of microorganisms has usually been subordinated to the exchange of Minie balls and rifled artillery shells. Much scholarly work still focuses on the quality of medical care that, while abysmal by modern standards, proved far better than the aid offered European soldiers in the Crimean War or American troops in the Mexican War.[33]

If we rethink the Civil War battlefield on Crosby's terms—as a site where large groups of people and their associated organisms encountered one another for the first time—then disease is not just an ancillary story. It is *the* story. Indeed, when it comes to the Peninsula Campaign, we might agree with medical and agricultural historian G. Terry Sharrer that "the fighting was actually a secondary terror, happening in the midst of an unprecedented pandemic—not of one disease widely spread, but of many, all at once." In terms of human pathogens, the South enjoyed some advantages by waging war on familiar soil. But when it came to diseases of domestic animals, fighting on home turf proved a distinct liability as glanders, hog cholera, and cattle fever spread from the battlefield to wreak long-term havoc. In the confrontation of the portmanteau biota, the South (as so often seems to have been the case militarily) won the battle, but lost the war.[34]

Finally, a fundamental tenet of environmental history is that nature is an active agent in history, not as a hard and fast determinant of events, but as a significant and often overlooked participant in the human story. Many environmental historians now see nature as inherently unstable, a realm in which occurrences can be explained, but not predicted.[35] To find the unruly element in our story, we need only look to the weather. Summer drought and early frosts compounded difficulties created by lost labor on the home front. On the peninsula, heavy spring rain slowed McClellan's progress and left his troops exposed to malaria and other diseases.

To what extent did nature influence the outcome of the Peninsula Campaign? Given McClellan's personality, we may never come up with a completely satisfactory answer. The Union commander's indecisiveness and penchant for overestimating opposing forces have baffled generations of military historians. Even as President Lincoln pondered removing McClellan from the peninsula, the general doggedly insisted that he could succeed if provided with still more reinforcements. McClellan eventually requested sixty thousand more troops for a second assault on Richmond.[36] Without question, such equivocation and Lincoln's eventual determination that his commander would not fight were major factors in the decision to remove Union forces from the peninsula. Still one wonders: What if it had not rained so much that spring? What if McClellan's men had not been so sick? Would the general have retreated to Harrison's Landing? Or would he have taken Richmond? Ended the war before the Emancipation Proclamation?

Venturing into counterfactual history is as dangerous as it is appealing. However, for environmental historians, there remains the nagging feeling that nature, perhaps as much as human nature, not only helped starve the South, but also contributed—at least in some measure—to McClellan's retreat and eventual departure from Union ranks. For now, suffice it to say that as historians of people *and* nature we should look forward to a day when rain and mud, horses, mules, hogs, cattle, mosquitoes and measles are as much a part of Civil War history as Johnston, Pender, Lee, and McClellan. As on the Yancey home front and the peninsula battlefield, our understanding of the war will be the richer for it.

Notes

1. John C. Inscoe and Gordon B. McKinney, *The Heart of Confederate Appalachia: Western North Carolina in the Civil War* (Chapel Hill: University of North Carolina Press, 2000), 9; *Common Times of Yancey County* (Burnsville, N.C.: Yancey Graphics, 1981), 26; Yancey County, North Carolina, *U.S. Census Bureau: State and County Quick Facts,* http://quickfacts.census.gov/qfd/states/37/37199.html. I calculated the total number of recruits by counting enlistees from Yancey County in "16th Regiment N.C. Troops," in Weymoth T. Jordan Jr. and Louis H. Manarin, *North Carolina Troops 1861–1865: A Roster* (Raleigh: N.C. Department of Archives and History, 1997), 6:29–37 (hereafter cited as *N.C. Troop Roster*).

2. Alfred Crosby, *Ecological Imperialism: The Biological Expansion of Europe* (New York: Cambridge University Press, 1986).

3. *Population of the United States in 1860, Compiled from the Original Returns or Eighth Census* (Washington, D.C.: Government Printing Office, 1864), 250–51; Timothy Silver, *Mount Mitchell and the Black Mountains: An Environmental History of the Highest Peaks in Eastern America* (Chapel Hill: University of North Carolina Press, 2003), 66–75, 117–19.

4. John C. Inscoe, *Mountain Masters: Slavery and the Sectional Crisis in Western North Carolina* (Knoxville: University Press of Tennessee, 1989), 66; Kevin W. Young, "A Family Affair: Slaveholding Kinship Networks in Western North Carolina's Toe Valley," University of Georgia, paper presented at the annual conference of the Society of Appalachian Historians, Morgantown, W.V., May 21, 2012. I am indebted to Mr. Young for permission to read and cite his paper in advance of publication.

5. Inscoe, *Mountain Masters,* 66; Silver, *Mount Mitchell,* 92–93; *Common Times of Yancey County* (Burnsville, N.C.: Yancey Graphics, 1981), 26.

6. Silver, *Mount Mitchell,* chap. 3.

7. *Population of the United States in 1860,* 250–51; *N.C. Troop Roster,* 6:29–37, 8:246–55. Kevin Young and Michael C. Hardy directed me to these sources by providing information about companies in which Yancey County recruits served.

8. Gordon B. McKinney, "Women's Role in Civil War Western North Carolina," *North Carolina Historical Review* 69 (January 1992): 36–46; John C. Inscoe, "Coping in Confederate Appalachia: Portrait of a Mountain Woman and Her Community at War," *North Carolina Historical Review* 69 (January 1992): 388–413.

9. *N.C. Troop Roster,* 14:300–311, 358–74, 2:354–59.

10. Kenneth W. Noe, "Fateful Lightning: The Significance of Weather and Climate to Civil War History," this volume.

11. Ted Steinberg, *Down to Earth: Nature's Role in American History* (New York: Oxford University Press, 2002), 96; Lloyd Richard Bailey, ed., *The Heritage of the*

Toe River Valley (Durham, N.C.: L. R. Bailey, 1994), 2:47; Silver, *Mount Mitchell*, 123.

12. A. D. Childs to Zebulon Baird Vance, November 29, 1863, and S. J. Westall to Vance, January 17, 1864, in *The Papers of Zebulon Baird Vance*, ed. Gordon B. McKinney and Richard M. McMurray (Frederick, Md.: University Publications of America, 1987), microfilm, reels 20, 21.

13. Mary Elizabeth Massey, *Ersatz in the Confederacy* (Columbia: University of South Carolina Press, 1952), 63–64; John Solomon Otto, *Southern Agriculture During the Civil War Era, 1860–1880* (Westport, Conn.: Greenwood Press, 1994), 23–30, 36; Silver, *Mount Mitchell*, 124.

14. Paul D. Escott, *After Secession: Jefferson Davis and the Failure of Confederate Nationalism* (Baton Rouge: Louisiana State University Press, 1978), 68–69.

15. J. W. McElroy to Zebulon Baird Vance, October 23, 1863, in McKinney and McMurray, *Papers of Zebulon Baird Vance*, reel 20. Paul D. Escott, "Poverty and Governmental Aid for the Poor in Confederate North Carolina," *North Carolina Historical Review* 61 (October 1984): 465–66; Philip Shaw Paludan, *Victims: A True Story of the Civil War* (Knoxville: University of Tennessee Press, 1981), 68–69.

16. George Henry Mills, *History of the Sixteenth North Carolina Regiment* (N.p.: John C. Mills, 1901), 2–6, http://digital.ncdcr.gov/cdm4/document.php?CISOROOT=/p15012coll8&CISOPTR=1923&REC=1. The deaths of Yancey County recruits are recorded in the *N.C. Troop Roster*, 6:29–37.

17. *Common Times of Yancey County*, 31; Lawson Harrill, *Reminisces, 1861–1865* (Brady the Printer, 1910), 7, http://digital.ncdcr.gov/cdm4/document.php?CISOROOT=/p15012coll8&CISOPTR=2087&CISOSHOW=2921.

18. Casualties from *N.C. Troop Roster*, 6:29–37; Stephen W. Sears, *To the Gates of Richmond: The Peninsula Campaign* (New York: Ticknor & Fields, 1992), see esp. chaps. 3–9; Brian K. Burton, *Extraordinary Circumstances: The Seven Days Battles* (Bloomington: Indiana University Press, 2001), 72, 96; Mills, *History of the Sixteenth*, 16–19.

19. Entry for June [n.d.] 1862, "Diary of Captain John H. Harris," in *Confederate Stamps, Old Letters, and History*, ed. Raynor Hubbell (Griffin, Ga.: n.p., n.d). I am indebted to Professor Judkin Browning, Department of History, Appalachian State University, for this source. On the prevalence of camp diseases among Confederate troops, see Paul E. Steiner, *Disease in the Civil War: Natural Biological Warfare in 1861–1865* (Springfield, Ill.: Charles C. Thomas, 1968), 139.

20. Timothy Silver, *A New Face on the Countryside: Indians, Colonists, and Slaves in South Atlantic Forests, 1500–1800* (New York: Cambridge University Press, 1990), 155–58; G. Terry Sharrer, *A Kind of Fate: Agricultural Change in Virginia, 1861–1921* (Ames Iowa: Iowa State University Press, 2000), 8; Steiner, *Disease in the Civil War*, 139; Andrew McIlwaine Bell, *Mosquito Soldiers: Malaria, Yellow Fever and the Course of the American Civil War* (Baton Rouge: Louisiana State University Press, 2010), 72–76.

21. Sharrer, *A Kind of Fate*, 7–8; Steiner, *Disease in the Civil War*, 138–40.

22. F. M. Edge, quoted in Steiner, *Disease in the Civil War*, 135; Clifford Dowdey, *The Seven Days: The Emergence of Lee* (Lincoln, University of Nebraska Press, 1993), 86–87; Bell, *Mosquito Soldiers*, 76–77.

23. James W. McPherson, *Battle Cry of Freedom: The Civil War Era* (New York:

Oxford University Press, 1988), 461; Bell, *Mosquito Soldiers*, 74; Steiner, *Disease in the Civil War*, 134–42; Stephen W. Sears, *To the Gates of Richmond: The Peninsula Campaign* (1992; repr., New York: Mariner Books 2001), 163–64.

24. Mills, *History of the Sixteenth North Carolina*, 18; Sharrer, *A Kind of Fate*, 9–10; Jack Temple Kirby, "The Civil War: An Environmental View," http://www.nhc.rtp.nc.us/tserve/nattrans/ntuseland/essays/amcwar.htm, 2.

25. G. Terry Sharer, "The Great Glanders Epizootic, 1861–1866: A Civil War Legacy," *Agricultural History* 69, no. 1 (1995), 83–84; Sharrer, *A Kind of Fate*, 10–16.

26. Otto, *Southern Agriculture*, 29–30; Sharrer, *A Kind of Fate*, 18–21.

27. Casualties from *N.C. Troop Roster*, 6:29–37; *Common Times of Yancey County*, 26. Thanks to Jason Robinson, Clerk of the Board of County Commissioners in Yancey County, for the information on the monument to Confederate war dead.

28. *Common Times of Yancey County*, 31; *N.C. Troop Roster*, 6:29–37; Richard Randolph, "North Carolina Troops and the Deserter Problem," *North Carolina Historical Review* 66 (January 1989): 61; Peter S. Bearman, "Desertion as Localism: Army Unit Solidarity and Group Norms in the U.S. Civil War," *Social Forces* 70 (December 1991): 329.

29. Mc [McDaniel?] William Horton to Dr. Abraham Job, January 12, 1867, in *Heritage of the Toe River Valley*, 2:47; Fred M. Burnett, *This Was My Valley* (Charlotte, N.C.: Heritage Printers, 1960), 73.

30. J. W. McElroy to Governor Z. B. Vance, April 12, 1864, in U.S. War Department, *War of the Rebellion: A Compilation of the Official Records of the Union and Confederate Armies* (Washington, D.C.: U.S. Government Printing Office, 1898), 53:326–27. I first encountered this incident in John C. Inscoe and Gordon B. McKinney, *The Heart of Confederate Appalachia: Western North Carolina in the Civil War* (Chapel Hill: University of North Carolina Press, 2000), 133. On Ray's desertion, see *N.C. Troop Roster*, 6:35, s.v. "Ray, Montreville."

31. Robert Vance to Governor Zebulon Vance, April 18, 1864, in *Heritage of the Toe River Valley*, 2:48.

32. James L. Roark, "Behind the Lines: Confederate Economy and Society," in *Writing the Civil War: The Quest to Understand*, ed. James M. McPherson and William J. Cooper Jr. (Columbia: University of South Carolina Press, 1998), 205, 207–9; Otto *Southern Agriculture*, 32–34.

33. Steiner, *Disease in the Civil War*, and Bell, *Mosquito Soldiers*, are notable exceptions. See also Katherine Meier's essay in this volume, "'The Man Who Has Nothing to Lose': Environmental Impacts on Civil War Straggling in 1862 Virginia."

34. Sharrer, *A Kind of Fate*, 8.

35. Donald Worster, *Nature's Economy: A History of Ecological Ideas*, 2nd ed. (New York: Cambridge University Press, 1994), 411.

36. Judkin Browning, *The Seven Days' Battles: The War Begins Anew*, Battles and Leaders of the American Civil War, ed. John David Smith (Santa Barbara: Praeger, 2012), 156.

FOUR

"The Man Who Has Nothing to Lose"
Environmental Impacts on Civil War Straggling in 1862 Virginia

KATHRYN SHIVELY MEIER

Henry E. Handerson was a southerner in spirit if not by birth. Originally from Ohio, he ventured to Virginia and Louisiana to tutor and briefly try his hand at a New Orleans medical school until his money ran out. When Civil War demanded that even the itinerant choose their geographical allegiances, Handerson joined the 9th Louisiana and was stationed in Virginia. He quickly found soldiering to be his most challenging occupation yet. In his memoir, he recalled an incident from March 11, 1862. "The rain had fallen almost incessantly during our march, and our camps . . . were converted into shallow lakes by the standing water, which prevented comfortable rest by night or day. After a week or more of such experience, thoroughly worn out by want of sleep, I determined one rainy evening to slip quietly out of camp and seek some shelter where I might rest comfortably for one night at least."[1]

Though treading lightly in his memoirs for the sake of his readers (his children), Handerson's euphemism is clear: the private was straggling, a punishable offense. Straggling, one of the most common disciplinary infractions of the war, was defined as being absent from camp or roll call without leave, as every enlisted man who wished to leave the ranks was required to obtain a pass from his commander.[2] The duration of straggling could range from a few hours to a night or even several weeks, the latter often termed French Leave or French Furlough. Unlike in the case of desertion, the straggling soldier's intent was to return to his unit.

Wishing to avoid the stigma of cowardice, Handerson explained, "I felt desperate enough to face almost anything for the chance of securing shelter."[3] Handerson knew that if caught, he could face a number of humiliating punishments as a straggler or worse yet, be falsely accused of desertion, court-martialed, and executed. But desperation was born of experience. The previous October, he had suffered a prolonged bout of typhoid fever, resulting in weeks at a Charlottesville hospital and subsequent convalescence in a civilian home. By March he was with his unit but was serving in a reduced capacity as bookkeeper to preserve his strength.

Handerson's understanding of disease causation prompted his risky pursuit of lodging. Conventional belief among Civil War common soldiers held that nature—weather, miasmas, the southern climate, seasonal shifts, flora, and fauna—was a major cause of disease and mental unfitness. This experiential understanding of health was popular among laypeople before the war but decidedly flourished among the men who now camped, marched, and fought solely outside.[4] To counteract perceived environmental threats, soldiers developed a set of habits that often prevented and sometimes treated ailments. For instance, soldiers sought out clean water for drinking or washing their clothes and bodies; they creatively eradicated insects; they foraged for fruits, vegetables, and medicinal herbs; and they constructed or located shelters to protect against Virginia's variable elements.[5] Straggling became not only a form of self-care used to avoid environmental exposure, but it also enabled other self-care techniques, which could not be effectively practiced without pushing the limits of army discipline. Because the majority of common soldiers in Civil War armies were volunteers (citizen soldiers), they were often permitted looser discipline by regimental officers than were regular units composed of professional soldiers.[6] Those soldiers who straggled for instrumental reasons often returned to the ranks with improved morale and physical health.

Straggling, however, also had serious consequences for military campaigns in 1862 Virginia, as sometimes upwards of 20 percent of the soldiers in a given army were absent without permission.[7] Manpower was vital to waging successful battles, and commanders and government officials lamented the pervasive absenteeism for good reason; however, rather than identifying and correcting the causes underlying straggling, military and medical command increasingly employed punishment as a deterrent, often conflating straggling and desertion. This is a conflation that historians have preserved. As the case of environmental impacts on absenteeism elucidates, straggling should be studied separately from desertion, because it was sometimes a deliberate survival technique that allowed men to improve their performance as soldiers.[8] Desertion, in contrast, was a decision to abandon soldiering altogether. In short, despite its appearance to commanders, straggling could actually improve army effectiveness, while desertion necessarily harmed it. While some scholars have looked at absenteeism caused by environmental exposure, illness, or low morale, too often this type of straggling is lumped in with desertion.[9] Scholars have not looked at straggling as an intentional survival technique, as it has been difficult to do so without the lens of environmental history.[10]

Not all straggling was instrumental and therefore advantageous to soldier health, but it did present a sensible solution for the volunteer soldier faced with tremendous odds against remaining well in 1862 Virginia. While the best surviving official sources have calculated that 20 to 30 percent of armies were sick in 1862 (with deplorably unreliable numbers on mental health), my recent study of the Peninsula and Shenandoah Valley Campaigns estimates that 42 percent of Union and Confederate soldiers were sick and 20 percent suffered from low morale.[11] Furthermore, most soldiers complained bitterly about environmental exposure, while commanders confirmed that they could not adequately protect their troops from their natural enemy.[12] Because some soldiers regarded straggling as a self-care technique (or at the very least, a reprieve from suffering on par with the military furlough), and volunteers were more willing and able to defy army discipline than regulars, common soldiers could simultaneously straggle and remain very much devoted to cause.

Returning to Handerson's case, his quest for reprieve from these elements he deemed dangerous to health eventually led him to a church. "Opening the door carefully and peering within, a novel sight met my eye. Most of the pews were already occupied by soldiers who had fled to the sacred building for shelter, each of them having preempted his own position and spread his blanket upon the seat." To add to the gathering's comfort, "A large fire had been started in the stove, upon the surface of which numerous slices of bacon were cooking and diffusing an appetizing odor throughout the building." Handerson was quick to assure the reader that "in the morning, refreshed and strengthened by a comfortable night's rest, I returned to my command, where, so far as I know, I had not been missed."[13]

Only in the private's memoirs did he admit to his transgression, omitting the incident from his letters, which speaks to the difficulty scholars face in analyzing straggling. Many soldiers were reticent about the practice for fear of appearing cowardly or incurring embarrassing punishments from their officers. Thus, direct references to straggling in eyewitness accounts are rare. Locating absenteeism requires a careful combing of the most quotidian eyewitness accounts augmented by serious attention to memoirs. Further, in order to distinguish soldiers who straggled in pursuit of better health from those who malingered, it is important to spend significant time with each soldier's collection. Research for this piece, for instance, is anchored by a close reading of two hundred complete collections of Confederate and Union soldiers' letters, diaries, and memoirs from winter of 1861–62 through mid-August 1862 during the Shenandoah Valley and Peninsula Campaigns.[14]

The most dramatic battle over straggling in 1862 Virginia, and certainly the best documented, occurred in Maj. Gen. Thomas "Stonewall" Jackson's ranks in the Shenandoah Valley. At times in the early part of the year, certain Rebel valley regiments lost over 20 percent of their forces to straggling.[15] Brig. Gen. Turner Ashby's cavalry was particularly notorious for employing the lengthier French Furlough – illicit sojourns at soldiers' nearby homes that could extend up to four weeks. Such longer stays were risky, as they smacked of permanence and might be punished as desertion. As Lt. Albert C. Lincoln, a subordinate of Ashby, complained on February 18, 1862, "That portion of the [7th Virginia Cavalry] that are now at home have left three or four times in the same manner. . . . Some of them had not been back more than three weeks since the retreat from Romney."[16]

Jackson's men recorded good cause for defying discipline. As Pvt. Charles W. Trueheart explained of the Romney campaign (which directly preceded the Shenandoah Valley campaign in January and February 1862), "We made [our first day's march] through a cloud of dust, and a perfect gale of wind." Conditions worsened from there. "On our second days march, it began blowing, and was extremely cold. On the 3rd day it began snowing." Then, "The roads were so slippery with sleet, that the poor [horses] could not keep their feet in pulling the cannon & wagons, but fell continually – sometimes 3 out of 4 of a team would be down at once. Splotches and puddles of blood frequently marked the places where they fell. . . . Many of us got our feet and hands frostbitten. My feet were so badly bitten that I could scarcely walk."[17] When most troops were wintering, Jackson's men were suffering on a campaign that would return no long-term gains.[18]

The Shenandoah Valley campaign commenced in March not long before the passage of the Confederate Conscript Act on April 16, 1862. In response to the first national draft in American history, Rebel desertion picked up considerably, drawing more attention to any person who strayed from the ranks and prodigious ire from Jackson.[19] And yet spring weather conditions in the valley remained horribly taxing on the undersupplied Confederates. Meanwhile, Jackson enforced an exhausting marching pace back and forth across mountain passes that pushed his men to their physical limits. Maj. Frank B. Jones explained that in April, "it soon commenced raining and for three days it has hailed and rained and snowed in the most unaccountable manner. Our encampment is worse than any barnyard for in many places there seems no bottom." As a result, his and fellow soldiers' spirits sank: "I laid in bed a long while rather than expose myself to the bitter dawn and cold. My heart was very sad. Our great discomfort and our cause weighed down upon me."[20] By June, Jackson's army appeared to some observers to be self-destructing from exhaustion and exposure. Confederate stragglers scattered the Valley Turnpike, the main thoroughfare in the region, and were plucked up by Federals.

By the time Jackson's troops were ordered to quit the valley and join the Peninsula Campaign in June, they had marched more than 650 miles. The appropriately termed "foot cavalry" (Jackson's infantry) remembered disembarking from the valley on June 17 and scarcely pausing again until July 8 to rest. By then, "some of the men had not washed their hands and faces for five or six days."[21] Sanitation gravely suffered, and men were sick as dogs. Desertion and straggling spiked again.[22] Jackson had learned perhaps better than any commander that extended marching in combination with severe environmental exposure resulted in straggling. And yet the more stagnant Army of Northern Virginia, to which Jackson's men were headed, had been experiencing its own discipline problems that spring.

Gen. Joseph E. Johnston, in command of Confederates on the peninsula, had for months watched his ranks melt away. These soldiers spent far more time in camp than on the march; while less exhausting, camping in the swamps of Virginia carried its own environmental burdens. Lt. William H. Morgan described "service on the Peninsula [as] arduous and disagreeable; in the muddy trenches, or back in the woods, lying on the rain-soaked ground, or marching along the cut-up and muddy roads, was trying indeed, and caused no little sickness among the troops." Even native Virginians were shocked by the weather conditions they endured. Virginian Pvt. Edgar Warfield wrote, "We returned to the camp at midnight in the midst of a terrible storm of wind, rain, and vivid lightening, thunderbolts, and rain, as severe as ever known to any climate." Other men feared the swamp miasmas they believed to be causing fevers: "This country is extremely unhealthy, being exposed to the malarious and miasmatic winds which every day blow between the rivers. Fever and ague and cholera, especially abound in this part of the world, and yellow-fever has always loved it." Indeed, encampment tended to heighten certain types of exposure that marching soldiers could avoid. For instance, the high population density of army life and aftermath of battle fouled water sources, making it difficult to find a proper drink. Pvt. Kinchen Jahu Carpenter wrote, "It is impossible for me to describe what our troops have gone through. Hunger, thirst and fatigue was awful. We would drink water from a stream that had dead horses in it. When you are so very thirsty, any kind of water is good."[23] Correspondingly high rates of Confederate straggling followed.

By June, when Gen. Robert E. Lee took command of the Confederate army on the peninsula after the wounding of Johnston, Lee could scarcely believe its disarray. Stationed near Richmond on July 1, the Army of Northern Virginia disintegrated into "hordes of stragglers [turning] the city into a veritable resort town." Local newspapers lambasted army discipline, calling for the death penalty. Approximately fifty stragglers per day were arrested in Stanton in the month of July as they poured in from the east.[24] The addition of Stonewall Jackson's troops from the valley only worsened matters. Historian Joseph Harsh has provided detailed evidence that by August and September of 1862, Lee became obsessed with identifying stragglers, rebuking them as "cowards of the army."[25]

Straggling in the Union armies in 1862 Virginia was also a considerable problem, though Federals did not often have the temptation of being as close to their families, as did some Virginian units. Union straggling was particularly bad in the valley, where Gens. John C. Frémont, Nathaniel P. Banks, and James Shields were frightfully limited in rations, equipment, and medical supplies.[26] Frémont's troops endured the worst circumstances. The general lamented that "as late as April 19, . . . so illy provided in other respects were the coming re-enforcements that thirty-eight days had been passed by them without tents or other shelter, and this during the inclemencies of a spring seldom paralleled for severity in the history of the Virginia Valley."[27] *Frank Leslie's Illustrated Newspaper* famously pictured General Frémont's army as "ragged," hunched, and straggling as a result of these conditions.

Union troops' accounts from the valley lent credence to this illustration. Lt. Charles Fessenden Morse wrote from the aptly named "Camp Misery" near New Market, "The name of our camp did not originate at headquarters, but it is the most appropriate one I can think of for it. The reg-

"The Man Who Has Nothing to Lose" 73

Figure 4.1. *The Army of General Fremont on Its March up the Shenandoah Valley – Wounded and Ragged Soldiers*, Frank Leslie's Illustrated Newspaper, War Supplement, July 5, 1862.

iment has been here for three days without tents. . . . The rain has been pouring down in torrents most of the time, making the whole surface of the ground a perfect mire." He continued, "We are lying around, like pigs, in straw, with wet blankets, wet feet, wet everything, and a fair prospect of nothing for dinner." Morale sank under the weight of the spring rain. Lt. Col. David Strother wrote: "Warm rain. Have suffered all day with dullness and discouragement arising doubtless from physical exhaustion. The wet weather and the fact of our retreat to this place seem to have cowed and irritated everybody."[28]

The Peninsula Campaign, being the larger endeavor focused on conquering the Rebel capital, drew even more criticism from Union command because of its stragglers. U.S. peninsula medical director Charles S. Tripler complained, "Whenever a march was undertaken straggling was permitted to go on unrestrained, and I fear was sometimes even encouraged by officers whose duty it was to have prevented it." As the director implied, upper-level command often blamed regimental officers for failing to enforce discipline. Indeed, Tripler witnessed men charging the hospital boats to flee the field, leading him to announce, "I . . . determined to send no more men from the Peninsula on account of sickness if there were any means of avoiding it."[29] As a means to curb straggling, Maj. Gen.

George B. McClellan, Federal commander on the peninsula and onetime general-in-chief, issued a new whiskey ration in mid-May, but this paltry nod to the men's comfort had limited effect.[30] McClellan, too, grew increasingly impatient with what he interpreted as malingering and shirking of duty. "Absentees tell such exaggerated stories of the hardships and sufferings of campaign life . . . that they deter troops from enlisting. . . . There are two well men absent to one really sick man."[31]

The Union troops were vocally complaining, but it appears they did so with good reason. As usual, rain with inadequate shelter drove their discomfort: "We have had a verry bad time of it for the last ten days it rained constantly our tents are no acount the rain pours through them and I have not had a dry stick on me till yesterday for six days and I have a verry severe cold my head is completely stopped up and I am afraid that I will lose my hearing," explained Pvt. Thomas Ellis to his sister. Pvt. James T. Miller linked the rain to declining bowel health: "Between the hard watter the marching and sleeping in the rain and rob[b]ing us of our rations it made plump [plumb] one half of our regiment sick with the dysentery." The threat of swamp miasma also loomed over the peninsula camps. Pvt. Robert G. Carter noted, "A short distance to the rear was a large swamp, reeking with malaria." Other men lamented the incessant pestering of insects even without realizing that the pests transmitted disease. "The greatest annoyance we have . . . is the flies which stay about and include their unwelcome presence at all times of day & threaten to devour one 'sans ceremonie.' It is difficult to eat without swallowing more or less of the [saucy?] insects," spat one man. A common refrain involved torment from the lice: "One night I was troubled a good deal by something running about on my neck all night long; I suspected that it was an army of lice, and in the morning I found outside my tent, by my corner (and I sleep close, for there were five in the tent) an old dirty shirt, all covered over with body lice, and they had been marching at close quarters all night."[32] Other complaints bemoaned the ticks and mosquitoes common to Virginia swamps and forests. McClellan's men grew desperate for even a short reprieve from such environmental harassment.

By July 13 United States president Abraham Lincoln took notice of the mass absenteeism in McClellan's ranks and warned him, "45,000 of your Army [are] still alive, and not with it. I believe half, or two thirds of them are fit for duty to-day. . . . How can they be got to you? and how can they be prevented from getting away in such numbers for the future?" While McClellan haggled with Lincoln's numbers, he admitted, "The number . . . really absent is thirty eight thousand two hundred fifty. . . . I quite agree with you that more than one half these men are probably fit for duty to-day. I have frequently called the attention lately of the War Dept to the evil of absenteeism."[33] Both focused on the result rather than the cause of the problem.

As Union and Confederate absenteeism escalated in 1862, the Virginia-based commanders and War Departments redoubled their efforts to punish the offense. Official army regulations stipulated no particular chastisement, and so officers had traditionally punished as they saw fit. Early on, penalties included being forced to "ride a wooden horse, . . . wear a barrel shirt," dig latrines, or bury dead horses.[34] Jackson censured one of his own, Brig. Gen. Charles S. Winder, for relying too heavily on the painful practice of bucking and gagging – binding the wrists together and slipping them over the knees, while gagging the mouth with a bayonet.[35]

Yet Jackson himself resorted to executing four deserters on July 18, some of whom argued that they had only been straggling in search of shoes.[36] The situation in the Confederate army prompted Adj. Gen. Samuel Cooper to first issue General Order 16 on March 21, 1862, abolishing furloughs for men except those on medical leave.[37] By May, Cooper added Special Order 107, arresting all absentees for prompt court-martial. If stragglers refused arrest, they would be automatically punished as deserters: death by firing squad. By December, Confederate General Order 137 institutionalized a slew of new convictions for stragglers and deserters, ranging from having a twelve-pound iron strapped to one's legs, forfeiting a year of pay, and receiving lashes.[38]

The United States took longer to implement a slightly less punitive approach, in part because of an advantage in manpower and also because Lincoln favored a more moderate approach to appease a scrutinizing public. The August U.S. General Order Number 18 required that all commanders of regiments and companies march continually in the rear collecting absentees. There was only one excuse for a laggard: "written permit from the medical officer of the regiment that they are too sick to perform the march, and therefore must ride in ambulances."[39] This put the walking sick at considerable peril. The order also made little progress toward correcting the offense, and Lincoln continued to survey the problem from Washington, urging McClellan to action. He was aghast that those on furlough plus those absent from the ranks without permission outnumbered the new recruits. But Lincoln also remained reluctant to conflate straggling and desertion, fearing public backlash to the army's practice of capital punishment.⁴⁰ Americans had historically criticized military discipline they deemed too harsh.

Under considerable pressure from their respective War Departments, commanders, in turn, put pressure on their medical departments to eliminate straggling by keenly scrutinizing the sick. Surgeons were instructed to be skeptical of sickness that lacked outward symptoms as potential cases of malingering. In this vein, Confederate surgeon general Samuel P. Moore warned his surgeons "that the pains of Chronic Rheumatism are easily feigned and that Medical officers should be very careful in their examinations of such cases, and approve of the discharge of such as show in their person, evident marks of this disease."⁴¹ No doubt, some soldiers feigned illness to escape their duties; however, many soldiers complained of being increasingly turned away from morning sick call without care. Slow-developing diseases, such as scurvy, which took months to manifest, were marked by a gradual onslaught of debilitating aches and pains, in addition to depressed spirits. These diseases could easily be missed or misdiagnosed. In another misguided interpretation, Union medical director Tripler appeared to believe that healthy soldiers were straggling away from the ranks only to succumb to illness outside of the care and comfort of army infrastructures. "Hundreds were collected in the woods and in houses and huts and in our old position at Camp Winfield Scott who were borne not upon the surgeon's reports." The stragglers were allegedly brought in "after days of privation had brought on actual disease."⁴² More likely, the men had straggled because of illness in the first place.

In short, high command and their medical directors began to devote an increasing amount of energy to preventing absenteeism over the course of 1862, while failing to adequately address the conditions men complained about. Leaders too often assumed the men were feigning their discomfort, low spirits, and ailments and lacked dedication to cause. Tension over army disciplined resulted, not only between common soldiers and high command but also between officers, as those at the regimental level more directly empathized with their men. Generals suffered significantly less exposure than the ranks, because of their access to superior quarters, rations, water quality, and medical care. Furthermore, they traveled on horseback, avoiding the strain of heavy marches. Commanders therefore believed that the volunteers had failed to be acculturated into the army, when, in fact, the men argued the opposite: "How did we stand those long, tiresome marches, through the rain and the mud of spring, through the dust and heat of summer, and midst snow and ice of winter, often poorly shod, scantily clothed, and on short, very short rations.... It took men to do these things—men with muscles, sinews, and nerves in their bodies."[43] Men who occasionally straggled.

High command regulated straggling rather than attempting to manage underlying environmental and health problems for other reasons as well. In the 1860s, there was a genuine lack of clarity on the role environment played in shaping human physical and mental health, with many competing scientific theories afloat. Medical officers maintained belief in humor-based medicine (the idea that imbalance in bodily fluids made one ill), in constitutional theory (the idea that body types corresponded to certain predilections to disease and mental illness), in hereditarianism (the idea that one's parents shaped health at conception and other sensitive stages, such as at birth or during breast feeding), and in personal volition.[44] In the last case, a positive attitude and judicious personal habits could improve wellbeing. Class bias held that the middle- and upper-classes enjoyed better health because of more refined behavior.[45] A U.S. Sanitary Commission nurse, Katherine Wormeley, encapsulated this viewpoint when she chided a Pennsylvanian soldier, "What a terribly long face ... you will never get well till you learn to laugh."[46] Specific class critiques of soldier behavior in 1862 included overindulgence in alcohol, self-pity, and "delicacies"—nonregulation food sent from home or purchased from sutlers, all of which appeared to render a man more vulnerable to disease. Medical personnel and the military leaders they advised saw little contradiction in simultaneously subscribing to any number of these theories in addition to believing in a concept of disease environment similar to that of the men. This final assumption maintained that hot, humid climates like that of the South were potentially virulent. For instance, the widely accepted Miasma Theory attributed malaria to miasmas wafting off the southern swamps.

If the so-called experts embraced such chaos, it is perhaps unsurprising that commanders approached soldier health with a kind of fatalism and even distaste. It was, for instance, nearly impossible to avoid stationing army camps in swampy terrain on the peninsula, and so malaria appeared inevitable. Even if an army could avoid the lowlands, it could hardly avoid the entire South in the heat of summer—the height of campaign season. Furthermore, as Frémont's case demonstrated, even commanders who were savvy about environment's impacts on troops based on their past military experiences believed their hands tied by logistical limitations.[47] As the men increasingly complained about exposure and illness, some commanders and their medical staffs encouraged them to bear up under hardship and embrace the suffering endemic to soldiering. Frémont lauded his army's acceptance of their fate: "The heroism, the uncomplaining patience, with which the soldiers of my command endured the starvation and other bodily sufferings of their extended marches ... entitle them to my gratitude and respect."[48] Leaders instead chose to focus on a problem with a much simpler solution than managing the environment of war: straggling. Straggling could be curbed with stricter army discipline.

A final point of contention over straggling between common soldiers and their superiors had to do with their different roles in waging war. Generals shouldered the responsibility for winning battles and needed a critical mass of soldiers to accomplish their plans. Obtaining sufficient manpower was indeed one of the weightiest concerns of the war. While commanders had to absolve the sick dismissed to hospital, they clung desperately to the able-bodied men who remained in the ranks, even if those men needed rest. The 1862 Confederate debate over the furlough, the army-sanctioned alternative to straggling, revealed a controversy over the very idea of resting healthy troops. When Judah Benjamin was still Confederate secretary of war in January of 1862, he pushed for General Order Number 1, which granted furloughs to all men who had been in the service for twelve months who agreed to reenlist. Peninsula commander Johnston stridently protested, arguing, "To grant [furloughs] in such numbers I deem incompatible with the safety of this command. The men here now are as few as we can safely meet the enemy with; yet there is no saying how soon he may attack us." Benjamin urged Johnston to consider "that the eager desire for a furlough during the inclement season will form the strongest inducement for your men, and thus afford the best guarantee of your having under your orders a large force of veteran troops when active operations recommence."[49] The secretary of war feared that men who were not given legitimate leave would take matters into their own hands and straggle. Winter months were the most environmentally taxing and tended to be devoid of active campaigning (except, for instance, in the case of Jackson's Romney campaign). December through February appeared the perfect time to offer furloughs, so that men would not slip away when they were needed most. Johnston, however, remained unconvinced by this logic.

Regimental officers tended to agree with Benjamin, having observed and experienced firsthand the hardships driving men from the ranks. For instance, Confederate colonel Samuel V. Fulkerson in the valley explained to his local congressmen, "We are willing to endure all that men can bear when our cause requires it; but where there is a discretion, that discretion should be exercised in favor of men who have seen such hard and continued service." In other words, "With the benefit of a short furlough for the men, I am satisfied that at Winchester I could have enlisted 500 of my regiment.... With the present prospect before them, I do not know that I could get a single man."[50] The debate over the necessity of leave would continue for the duration of the war. Ultimately, argues historian Joseph Glatthaar, an expert on the Army of Northern Virginia, more liberal granting of furloughs might have improved morale and health and, no doubt, lessened straggling.[51]

Despite increasing warnings from the top, common soldiers like Private Handerson continued to risk punishment and humiliation to straggle, because they believed they could not rely on medical staff to help them survive. Many feared they would fail to convince the regimental surgeons at morning sick call that their poor health warranted a break from the ranks. Others feared the lack of skills and experience among Civil War surgeons even if they were identified as in need of care. Only a limited number of Civil War surgeons had army experience; some were still medical students, and some were even political appointments with no medical backgrounds whatsoever.[52] Medicine was also rudimentary, often as dangerous as the disease it was meant to treat. As Confederate surgeon William Taylor illuminated, "Diagnosis was rapidly made, usually by intuition, and treatment was with such drugs as we chanced to have in the knap-sack and were handiest to obtain." For instance, one day he had a ball of blue mass (a preparation of mercury and often licorice, herbs, and sugar) in one pocket and a ball of opium in the other. He asked the soldiers how their bowels fared; if they had diarrhea he would administer the opium, if constipated the mercury.[53] The soldiers were well aware of the inadequacies of this haphazard care. When Pvt. Aaron E. Bachman took sick with "swamp fever," he complained that the surgeon "gave me ten or fifteen grains of quinine and a lump of bluemass as big as a cherry, and required me to take it in his presence." As a result, "The intense heat, the fever, and the doctor's 'dope' fixed me completely, so I gave my blacksmith's tools away and was taken to the hospital." By the time Bachman reached the hospital, he was almost dead from exposure.[54] If the soldier had malaria (very likely given his symptoms), he had actually received one of the more useful treatments available during the Civil War: quinine for malaria. Even so, he mistrusted the surgeon's cure. Another soldier, Sgt. Henry Keiser from Pennsylvania, similarly complained of the available quality of treatment. On June 22, 1862, his surgeon gave him "two pills and a dose of vil ... which made me very sick all day."[55]

As much as the deficient remedies and lack of medical expertise inspired loathing, soldiers dreaded even more being removed from their regiments to the cold, impersonal hospitals. Chaplain A. M. Stewart explained, "A serious business, usually, it is to be sick at home, where all its unnumbered sympathies unite to comfort, to soothe, and to relieve that member.... A very different matter, however, is it to become sick in camp, and forced to enter [the] hospital." Musician Lewis Shepard succumbed to that fate and lay in the hospital for more than two weeks, "not getting any better." Like many in his circumstances, "I have been in hopes that the Authorities would discharge me or send me home till I got fit for service again. One thing is certain I cannot get well here."[56] As suggested by these men, antebellum care for the sick had traditionally been conducted at home by a loved one or neighbor. Generally only impoverished Americans or those traveling in strange cities had received treatment in a hospital before the war.[57] Thus, accustoming oneself to hospital care required a shift in cultural values.

Pvt. W. H. Bird explained typical torment over the perceived callousness he encountered at a Danville, Virginia, hospital. There was an outbreak of smallpox, and the senior surgeon ordered the staff to "close the doors and not let a one go to the army that we have here. Better to let this 80 die than to send them back to camps and the disease they carry with them, kill, maybe 10,000 others." Quarantining the hospital may have saved lives, but to Bird the incident served as a cruel reminder that soldiers were mere cogs in a massive, indifferent medical machine. Chaplain Stewart again put it succinctly: "Against entering an hospital, there usually exists in the mind of the soldier a strong repugnance, even a manifest horror. Nor is this, by any means, an unnatural feeling."[58]

Soldiers were also well versed in the army's lack of supplies, staff, and hospital space in 1862. Pvt. Thomas I. Taylor suffered a severe cough for months and noted feeling "weak & nervous my mind troubled about home," revealing how persistent sickness could further lead to diminished morale. When he attempted to get help, he reported: "went to Doctors had no cough medicine have to get along Best I can." One soldier bitterly concurred that "all the falt is now in the doctors for when we get sick they do not know how to take care of us they have no medicine nor they do not intend to take care of us."[59] While the Rebel medical department has rightly been described as lacking in crucial medications, such as the Northern-manufactured quinine, and possessing limited staff, Frémont's experience in the Shenandoah Valley proved the Union could suffer equally from logistical meltdown. In April and May the general complained that his men were deprived of tents and food, because of the quartermaster department's "want of funds," while the sick and wounded ("upward of 1,000") were "brought along mainly in army wagons, owing to want of ambulances. The hospitals were full, and I was deficient in the necessary medicines, as well as the requisite number of surgeons to give attendance."[60] As Frémont outlined, hospital space was severely limited, and the rolling nature of battle casualties meant that sick patients were frequently evacuated to make way for the wounded. For most soldiers, the farther they were removed from their regiments – the friendly faces they knew from home – the more their morale plummeted.

What soldiers did not recognize was that hospital workers were often very ill themselves. Surgeon Alfred Castleman wrote, "For three nights I have not slept, and last night I had an attack of cholera morbus. This morning, being sick and worn out, I asked permission to return to Vienna.... Permission was denied me."[61] Famous Union nurses Hannah Ropes and Louisa May Alcott lasted only weeks before they contracted illnesses serious enough to inhibit their duties. If the medical staff were not granted leave to attend to their own health, then the soldiers had little hope of receiving suitable care.

This is to say nothing of mental health, which the medical establishments chronically under-supported. The Union and Confederate medical departments monitored only the most severe mental afflictions – nostalgia (potentially fatal homesickness), mania, insanity, and suicide. Yet many men suffered from frequent homesickness and depression, or what they commonly referred to as "the blues," and the accompanying behaviors of alcoholism or negligence of duty.[62] In military parlance soldiers' spirits equated to morale – a vital component of army effectiveness. The U.S. Sanitary Commission was more attentive than the medical establishment at boosting Union morale, for instance, by encouraging camp inspectors to assess recreational activities (such as regimental libraries, bands, or religious meetings); however, as middle-class reformers, commission workers often fell back on criticizing the men for their own lack of moral fortitude.[63]

The soldiers, therefore, had to analyze and counteract the reasons for declining morale on their own. Lacking a background on the complex medical debates taking place over asylum care, which weighed "mental hygiene" (personal habits geared toward brain health) against inherited characteristics, men allowed experience to inform their opinions on mental fitness.[64] Many soldiers therefore connected low spirits to environmental hardships—particularly wearisome weather. For instance, Pvt. George Perkins wrote on June 4, 1862, that it was "drizzly and rainy all day. Longed very much for home." On July 3 he incisively explained, "Rained all last night. Felt sad and thought of home." Lt. Col. David Strother scribbled: "Warm rain. Have suffered all day with dullness and discouragement arising doubtless from physical exhaustion. The wet weather and the fact of our retreat to this place seem to have cowed and irritated everybody." Other men simply became depressed by their own persistent illnesses or from watching their ailing comrades fall from disease. Pvt. Jacob Blackington grew so weary of losing friends, including his own brother, that he preferred to be captured by the enemy. He lamented to his sister, "Once more your letter found me in good health but in low spirits. I am very lonesome. There is but a few men [left] in the regiment."[65]

Without the proper infrastructures in place to protect physical and mental health, men took to straggling to bolster their own well-being. Some soldiers fell out on an individual basis, others in pairs, and still others en masse. Cavalrymen found it easiest to straggle, as they enjoyed the benefit of being on horseback, but infantrymen constantly looked for opportune moments to slip out of the ranks. Some went under cover of darkness, in the midst of a distracting storm, or during a particularly chaotic march. It was easier to quit the ranks when the armies were moving than when they were stationary in camp. When it came to straggling for environmental reasons, the soldiers self-described as straggling to seek reprieve from the environment and the associated mental and physical afflictions or to pursue self-care to prevent or treat poor health.

One of the most common reasons for straggling was excessive exposure to extreme weather. Pvt. E. Kendall told of an instance in August when "Hundreds 'fell out' some died. Glass told 106 in shade." When the dust grew intolerable on the road near Malvern Hill, Pvt. Kinchen Carpenter wrote, "Many of the soldiers stayed behind, lay down in the woods and did not get with their command until next day and, I, one of them. Under strict military rules this was an offense and no doubt many an officer would have put some hardship on us for doing so." Pvt. Randolph McKim agreed that there were certain environmental circumstances that necessitated straggling. In March, when weather was worst in the Shenandoah Valley, he described, "When we had no tents and when the weather was so inclement and our exposure so unusually severe, we would slip off to some private house whenever opportunity offered and leave could be obtained, and sometimes without leave. Only in this way, I think, could we have endured the ordeal."[66] In each of these cases, the straggling was unplanned but considered necessary to survival.

Exposure to rain and subsequent mud also prompted exoduses. One night, Cpl. Horace M. Wade tried sleeping on rails with just his coat as cover from a deluge. He fared poorly. The following evening, he slipped off into the woods to locate a broad-canopied tree. The subsequent sleep proved vastly superior. Private Patterson appeared to have little choice but to straggle given his regiment's experience near Lebanon Church, Virginia. He wrote of a march that "beggars description. The night was so dark that it was absolutely impossible to see anything and we relied entirely on the sense of hearing and feeling." It was not the dark so much as the rain that afflicted the men. "And the mud and water was literally knee deep, and the men would run against each other, strike their faces against another's back or gun without seeing anything." The result was almost comical. "Some fell in mudholes and had to be dragged out, and our regiment became scattered for a mile, and all along the road you could hear, 'This way, Co. D,' 'Here is your company A,' 'Close up Company C,' &c &c." Patterson did what he could to keep up. "I continued the march about 5 miles when I ran into a clump of bushes, and winding myself up in my wet blankets as well as I could remained there until daylight, keeping the bushes under me as much as possible to keep from drowning."[67] He found his comrades in the morning, one of whom complained that he had lost his boots in the preceding night's mud pit. Though Patterson was only gone a few hours, technically he had straggled.

Another commonly cited reason for absenteeism was falling ill from environmental causes and seeking relief. Because of soldiers' distrust in the military medical system, they would sometimes seek comfortable shelter to recover on their own or attempt to secure civilian care. In Pvt. William C. McClellan's case, he believed that mud undid his fragile health. "We had 10 miles to march and a Bad Road. We started in a few minutes it was so dark We could not see our hands before us and then I would fall into a mud hole up to my knees." As a result, "I have a very violent cold some fever." He cast off restraint and made for the nearest civilian quarters. An industrious southerner welcomed McClellan and fellow absentees into his home for the price of 1 dollar each, providing "a glorious nights rest" on the carpet. Though still a bit unwell when he returned to the ranks the next morning, McClellan was glad to have spent the height of his fever in front of a roaring fire. Lt. Elisha F. Paxton also fell ill and informally quit the ranks to stay in a nearby civilian house. "The weather is worse upon us than last winter," he wrote home. "Then the ground was frozen and we had the satisfaction at least of being dry—having dry clothes and dry blankets. But now everything is wet and we have no tents. It has had no happy effect upon my health. Yesterday I left the brigade to stay in a house a few days, but think I shall join it again to-morrow."[68] These acts of straggling were premeditated but expressly intended to be temporary sojourns.

Other soldiers chose to straggle when despair consumed them. Furloughs would have been ideal for bolstering mental health, but too few soldiers were granted leave in 1862. Instead, the men made their own furloughs. Henry Keiser described not one but three separate instances of straggling after environmental hardships chipped away at his morale on the peninsula. "At daylight it commenced raining and continued most all day. I 'played out' and could not keep up with the regiment. A miserable place." "Played out" was a typical common soldier refrain that referred to mental as well as physical fatigue as a result of exhaustion and preceded straggling. Lt. Charles Haydon was an officer on the peninsula responsible for keeping men like Keiser in the ranks and found it increasingly difficult to justify exhorting the men in their duties. "It is no exaggeration to say that I was many times in the main road in mud to my knees. It required great exertion to urge on the men & keep them in the ranks."[69] Haydon could scarcely preserve his own spirits let alone his men's.

And yet, officers were well aware that they enjoyed benefits unavailable to enlisted men. While officers were supposed to sleep by their men in camp unless given specific permission to seek other quarters, they enjoyed more freedom and less potential punishment than enlisted men.[70] Maj. Frank B. Jones explained, "the day is very cloudy and a cold rain started about 10am. It was very disagreeable. . . . We [the officers] went into a log church and slept very comfortably." Subsequently, his spirits rose: "This is a romantic spot." When he had another hard day of it, he wrote, "Sun was hot. Felt depressed and miserable. Had suffered the day before from a violent nervous headache" and fell out for a "pleasant" nap "under an apple tree." Even better, that night as the "men bivouacked on the wet ground," he "was fortunate enough to get into a carpenter shop and slept comfortably on the dry floor."[71] In such cases, the officers were modeling loose discipline by example. In sympathy for their men, many officers would simply look the other way at disciplinary infractions. For instance, when Pvt. John Casler stole off in search of whiskey to revive his spirits and was reported to his superior, the officer just laughed and released him. Casler was not so lucky later in the war when Jackson cracked down on his men. That instance of straggling caused Casler to be bucked from sun up to sun down, which almost resulted in his desertion.[72]

For many soldiers, environment, poor physical health, and sinking spirits became inseparably intertwined, overwhelming them and prompting straggling. Sgt. William West was transferred to hospital after contracting typhoid in February of 1862. He rejoined the Army of the Potomac in March, scarcely recovered. On the march, he "had to fall out and go back to the camp." West stayed behind all day and night with no permission, lamenting that he felt "real home-sick." One month later, in April, he remained troubled by illness and straggled again. "I being sick fell out and joined the wagons. I lay alongside of the road for an hour in the woods very sick joined the wagon trains when they came along. did not join the regt but Bill Merritt & I camped along side of the road." West painted an interesting portrait of an army straggler. Each time he fell out, he improved enough to rejoin the ranks but never fully recovered. Straggling was his attempted remedy, despite his status as a noncommissioned officer and role model to the lower ranks. He took sick again in May, but it wasn't until June 7 that he reported another incident. "I laid in my tent most all day for there being nothing to eat. Did not feel much like moving around. Today I *almost* wished I was at home. I knew of a certain house in the little town of M. where I could find plenty to eat."[73] The soldier's once buoyant spirits and avowed commitment to setting a good example for his unit were worn down over time. His case also illustrates the complexity that command faced in getting to the heart of the problem behind environmental-related straggling. There was often no single cause.

Besides viewing straggling as an opportunity to escape the difficulties of soldier life, the men also fell out in pursuit of self-care techniques meant to improve their chances of remaining healthy and happy. Much of this care was preventative in nature, and therefore superior to the remedial treatments offered by military surgeons. For instance, soldiers straggled in pursuit of clean water. Diarrhea, often contracted through contaminated water, was the most common wartime ailment and carried a 10 percent mortality rate.[74] Thus, when soldiers sought out water that looked, tasted, and smelled clean, they could prevent a host of bowel disorders, not to mention other diseases spread through feces, such as typhoid fever. Large army populations quickly fouled nearby water sources, forcing men to get creative in their quests for a clean drink. Some stole off to purchase water from local wells or civilians. Cavalryman Sgt. David Ashley and his companions were most inventive. They furtively laid eyes on black civilians tending to their cows. "We waited for [them] to milk and all took a good drink and left."[75]

Clean water was not just important for drinking, but for washing. Soldiers on the march were often given little time to clean their bodies, and yet sanitation was increasingly recognized as vital to health. Bathing could help detach lice, which, unbeknownst to the soldiers, could carry typhus. The men may not have understood insect-borne illness, but they certainly understood that bathing increased comfort and spirits. Pvt. Ephraim A. Wood casually mentioned slipping out after inspection for a bath every two to four days—far more often than his comrades. As a consequence, he remained in distinctly high morale, referring to the blazing temperatures of over 90 degrees as merely "warm." Considering weather was the most cited cause of poor health and spirits in the valley, straggling was vital to Wood's well-being.[76] Pvt. William Stilwell, a Georgian, sought fresh water to clean his clothes. To accomplish this end, he straggled with a buddy. "Molly, you would have been surprised to have seen me and Bob McDonald washing out shorts and drawers the other day. We did not have any clothes but what we had on for eight or ten days and we went about half mile from camp, pulled off stark naked and went out to wash like good fellows, dried and put them on again. We are very good hands at the business." As Capt. Robert G. Carter explained, the grime of soldiering took its toll on morale if one did not find a way to clean up. "There was hardly a man who did not tumble headlong [into the mud] at least once. They looked as little like human beings as any men I ever saw. All were drenched with rain to the skin & cased with mud to the waist at least."[77] Bathing was, in this sense, crucial to morale.

Some soldiers also hinted that they straggled in search of forage. Rations were sometimes dangerously short in 1862, particularly when it came to fruits and vegetables. Scurvy cases in both Union and Confederate armies in Virginia climaxed in July because of deficiency in vitamin C.[78] Scurvy not only led to physical upset—bleeding gums, joint pain, and weakness—but also lethargy and depressed spirits. Yet when, for instance, Union surgeon Jonah Franklin Dyer tried to report the need for issuing vegetables to the peninsular ranks, headquarters dismissed him. After prolonged solicitation, Dyer finally convinced headquarters to send down a surgeon, who confirmed the cases. Subsequently, the newspapers began to report upon the scurvy epidemic, assuring concerned civilians that vegetables would be administered shortly, but Dyer's regiment saw no sign of the improved rations for weeks.[79]

In the meantime, men who were desperate for relief straggled in search of vitamin C. For instance, on the peninsula Pvt. Jacob Blackington and his messmate Jake supplied themselves "every day for a week or more" with swamp berries. Those stationed in the valley had an easier time locating forage, as apple trees and various berries colored the landscape. Cavalryman Ashley wrote boldly of "foraging for my own benefit, and patroling for my own satisfaction, my duties in camp are finished about 11 O'Clock then I am at liberty to stroll; within 4 days I have picked upwards of 20 quarts of beautiful Blackberries which will make a good relish."[80] The sergeant repeatedly benefited from the mobility and extra storage his horse afforded him. Private Wood, the serial bather, was also adept at stealing off to locate cherries and apples to maintain his fine health and cheerful countenance.[81]

Other men slipped away simply to augment their meager rations, because they were hungry. They often purchased meals from local civilians or the notorious sutlers, whose quality of food was suspect. Private Fletcher remembered straggling in search of additional rations, one time to bad effect. He located oysters but grew sick from them, then straggled to find a civilian bed in which he could recover. He recalled that when a provost guard came in to examine his (nonexistent) pass, Fletcher played dead. "'Men, we are not hunting a corpse,'" the guard commented, "and turned and went out." While Fletcher implied it was illness that kept him still, more likely it was fear. He had narrowly escaped being caught as a potential deserter.[82]

Most foraging was meant to feed a man, but the rare soldier also sought out medicinal roots and herbs. Domestic Manuals, such as *Gunn's Domestic Medicine*, were popular antebellum guides that provided instruction on locating American herbs and using them to treat everything from hysteria to cancer.[83] Though no soldiers hauled such hefty manuals to the front, the do-it-yourself knowledge was diffuse. In one example, Pvt. Lorenzo N. Pratt of the 1st New York Light Artillery explained to his father that when sick in the New Market area, he "got hold of some of that spice root and sasafraz root and I chawed it and it made me well."[84]

In a final example of straggling to pursue self-care, some men simply wished to escape the toxic environment of camp with a bit of refreshing exercise. Much of soldiering engendered severe boredom, which could dampen spirits and lead to eventual sickness from contagions in camp water and crowds. Contagious diseases quickly sickened up to 50 percent of a new regiment, and the soldier who could put distance between himself and the thousands who made up his camp was lucky indeed. One lethargic soldier wrote to his brother, a fellow soldier, in March of 1862, "I can not write you but a short letter as I am so badly afflicted with the war fever as to be unable to do hardly anything." He had little distraction from his illness as he lay in camp unmoving. His condition and spirits worsened, unlike regimental Surg. James Richard Boulware, who actively practiced self-care. An officer with the added flexibility of being in the medical department, Boulware frequently quit the ranks to pursue fresh air. He explained: "I believe ... exercise is what kept me from having a spell of Typhoid Fever for I had most of the symptoms."[85]

Overall, soldiers who straggled demonstrated improved spirits and health after returning to the ranks. While straggling was certainly not a panacea, it often gave the men an edge over encroaching illness or a chance to ease suffering. Like a furlough, straggling improved morale by providing a break from the environmental challenges of soldiering. This is not to say that some men who straggled were not simply malingerers or shirkers. The fact that both the United States and the Confederacy had to resort to the first national drafts in American history confirms that soldier commitment was a serious and evolving problem as the war dragged on. It is important, however, to move beyond the command perspective to the soldiers' views that there were many good reasons to straggle in 1862. Strategic straggling was not out of spite for officers or because of cowardice, but because the men considered the practice necessary to survival. Improving health and morale also better enabled the men to complete their duties as soldiers, in turn making them more valuable to command. Given the uncertain state of scientific knowledge, the men's experiential, observation-based method of interpreting and managing disease environments may have well been superior to their leaders' understandings.

Returning to Handerson's memoir, the private's succinct explanation for why soldiers straggled perhaps best encapsulates the motivation behind instrumental absenteeism. He wrote, "We have the testimony of Horace that *Vacuus viator cantabit coram latrine.*"[86] More likely Handerson, who quite rightly had latrines on his mind, intended "cantabit vacuus coram latrone viator." This Latin phrase means "the penniless traveler will sing in the presence of the highwayman." In other words, the man who has nothing has nothing to lose. Deprived of resources and exposed to the bitter onslaughts of nature, common soldiers cast aside fears for their reputations and safety. Straggling to escape the clutches of death was well worth the risk.

Notes

The author would like to thank the participants of "The Blue, the Gray, and the Green" and Aaron Sachs and his graduate students at Cornell University for providing constructive suggestions on how to improve this article.

1. Henry E. Handerson, *Yankee in Gray: The Civil War Memoirs of Henry E. Handerson with a Selection of His Wartime Letters*, ed. Clyde Lottride Cummer (Cleveland: The Press of Western Reserve University, 1962), 39.

2. John D. Billings, *Hardtack and Coffee: The Unwritten Story of Army Life* (1887; repr., Lincoln: University of Nebraska Press, 1993), 144.

3. Handerson, *Yankee in Gray*, 39.

4. For an extended study of environmental explanations of disease in antebellum America, see Conevery Bolton Valencius, *The Health of the Country: How American Settlers Understood Themselves and Their Land* (New York: Basic Books, 2002).

5. For soldiers' perspectives on environment and health and "self-care" practices, see Kathryn Shively Meier, "'This Is No Place for the Sick': Nature's War on Civil War Soldier Mental and Physical Health in the 1862 Peninsula and Shenandoah Valley Campaigns," *Journal of the Civil War Era* 1 (June 2011): 176–206.

6. Permissiveness tended to occur at the regimental level, while many generals were West Point–educated professionals who chafed at the democratic spirit of volunteers (see Peter S. Carmichael, *The Last Generation: Young Virginians in Peace, Warm and Reunion* [Chapel Hill: University of North Carolina, 2005], 154). While Americans historically celebrated the citizen soldier, by the Civil War, they also recognized the drawbacks of looser discipline: for instance, lax regulation standards in camp could lead to worse sanitation and therefore higher rates of disease (see G. T. Strong, *Origin, Struggles and Principles of the U.S. Sanitary Commission* [Boston, 1864], 3).

7. The year 1862 is additionally a relevant case study, because early enlisters from 1861 to 1862 were less likely to desert, making it easier to distinguish stragglers from those deserters who might have claimed to be straggling after the fact. The Union and Confederate drafts were on the horizon, but the majority of soldiers in this study had chosen to be soldiers and were dedicated to Cause.

8. This chapter only investigates environmental impacts on straggling and does not explore alternate reasons for straggling, many of which do overlap with reasons for deserting: e.g., malingering, resistance to army discipline, objection to conscription, lack of dedication to soldiering, insufficient pay, desire to assist one's family at home, etc.

9. The most penetrating examination of straggling as distinct from desertion is in Joseph Harsh's *Taken at the Flood: Robert E. Lee and Confederate Strategy in the Maryland Campaign of 1862* (Kent: Kent State University Press, 1999). Harsh sys-

tematically catalogues the worsening conditions that caused soldiers to seek solace outside of army discipline. Carmichael's work is also careful not to conflate straggling and desertion, though it has typically explored other issues than soldiers' motivations for straggling; see Peter S. Carmichael, "So Far from God and So Close to Stonewall Jackson: The Executions of Three Shenandoah Valley Soldiers," *Virginia Magazine of History and Biography* 111 (2003): 33–66, and *The Last Generation*. Scholarship on desertion has accurately identified many of the reasons for straggling without distinguishing between the two disciplinary infractions; see Mark A. Weitz, *More Damning than Slaughter: Desertion in the Confederate Army* (Lincoln: University of Nebraska Press, 2005); Ella Lonn, *Desertion during the Civil War* (1928; repr., Lincoln: University of Nebraska Press, 1998); Kevin C. Ruffner, "Civil War Desertion from a Black Belt Regiment: An Examination of the 44th Virginia Infantry" in *The Edge of the South: Life in Nineteenth-Century Virginia*, ed. Edward L. Ayers and John C. Willis (Charlottesville: University of Virginia, 1991), 79–108; William Blair, *Virginia's Private War: Feeding Body and Soul in the Confederacy, 1861–1865* (New York: Oxford University Press, 1998), 55–68; Joseph T. Glatthaar's *General Lee's Army: From Victory to Collapse* (New York: Free Press, 2008); Aaron Sheehan-Dean, *Why Confederates Fought: Family and Nation in Civil War Virginia* (Chapel Hill: University of North Carolina Press, 2007); Mark V. Wetherington, *Plain Folk's Fight: The Civil War and Reconstruction in Piney Woods Georgia* (Chapel Hill: University of North Carolina Press, 2005); Peter Cozzens, *Shenandoah 1862: Stonewall Jackson's Valley Campaign* (Chapel Hill: University of North Carolina Press, 2008); and John F. Reiger, "Deprivation, Disaffection, and Desertion in Confederate Florida," *The Florida Historical Quarterly*, 48 (January 1970): 279–98.

10. Common soldier straggling related to environmental factors is an example of what Lisa Brady discusses in this volume as the Clausewitzian notion of "friction." As Brady suggests, a soldier, "no matter how insignificant his role, becomes the fulcrum upon which war hinges." Individual responses to environmental phenomena could make or break an engagement, as could a general's decision about how to counteract such problems.

11. For my estimates, see Meier, "'This Is No Place,'" 198. Official estimates for Union armies grossly underestimated the walking sick, as sick soldiers often either avoided sick call or failed to convince surgeons of illness. Confederate records burned in the 1865 fires in Richmond, and so we must piece together evidence from regimentals. Mental health categories recorded by the Union and Confederate health departments only include the most grave: nostalgia, mania, insanity, and suicide. For samples of Union and Confederate medical records respectively, see U.S. War Department, *The Medical and Surgical History of the War of the Rebellion: Prepared, in Accordance with the Acts of Congress, Under the Direction of Surgeon General Joseph K. Barnes, United States Army*, 6 vols., index and illustrations (Washington, D.C.: GPO, 1870–88), vol. 1, pt. 2:25–45, 174 (hereafter cited as MSHWR); and 25th Virginia Infantry, Medical Requisition and Sick Lists and General Orders, 25th Virginia Regiment, Medical records, 1861–1865, vol. 1861–64, Library of Virginia (hereafter cited as LVA).

12. The concept of the environment as a form of "enemy" in war was intro-

duced by Edmund Russell and Richard Tucker in *Natural Enemy, Natural Ally: Toward an Environmental History of Warfare* (Corvallis: Oregon State University Press, 2004).

13. Handerson, *Yankee in Gray*, 39–40.

14. Seventy percent of the sample is composed of enlisted men, or common soldiers; 77 percent of the collections were eyewitness, while 23 percent were retrospectives.

15. Peter S. Carmichael, "So Far from God," 43.

16. Peter S. Carmichael, "Turner Ashby's Appeal," in Gary W. Gallagher, ed., *The Shenandoah Valley Campaign of 1862* (Chapel Hill: University of North Carolina Press, 2003), 163–65.

17. Charles William Trueheart, *Rebel Brothers: The Civil War Letters of the Truehearts*, ed. Edward B. Williams (College Station: Texas A&M University Press, 1995), 41–43.

18. Cozzens, *Shenandoah 1862*, 67–69.

19. Ibid., 291. Jackson complained that his people were straggling "badly."

20. Maj. Frank B. Jones, 2nd Regiment Stonewall Brigade Infantry, diary, April 10, 1862, Frank B. Jones Diary, March–June 1862, Eleanor S. Brockenbrough Library, Museum of the Confederacy, Richmond, Virginia (hereafter cited as MOC).

21. John H. Worsham, *One of Jackson's Foot Cavalry: His experience and what he saw during the war 1861–1865: Including a history of "F Company," Richmond, Va., 21st Regiment Virginia Infantry, Second Brigade, Jackson's Division, Second Corps, A. N. Va.* (1912; repr., Alexandria, Va.: Time Life Books, 1982), 97–105.

22. Of those men arrested, 12 percent were sentenced to death; 40 percent had sentences overturned due to irregularities (Carmichael, "So Far from God," 45).

23. William H. Morgan, *Personal Reminiscences of the War 1861–5: In Camp–en Bivouac–on the March–on Picket–on the Skirmish Line–on the Battlefield–and in Prison* (Lynchburg, Va.: J. P. Bell, 1911), 98; Edgar Warfield, *Manassas to Appomattox: The Civil War Memoirs of Pvt. Edgar Warfield, 17th Infantry* (McLean, Va.: EPM Publications, Inc., 1996), 73; John Yates Beall, *Memoir of John Yates Beall: His Life, Trial, Correspondence, Diary, and Private Manuscript Found Among His Papers, Including His Own Account of the Raid on Lake Erie*, ed. Daniel Bedinger Lucas (Montreal: John Lovell, 1865), 228; Kinchen Jahu Carpenter, *War Diary of Kinchen Jahu Carpenter: Company I, Fiftieth North Carolina Regiment War Between the States 1861–5*, ed. Julie Carpenter Williams (Rutherford, N.C.: n.p., 1955), 8.

24. Weitz, *More Damning than Slaughter*, 42; Blair, *Virginia's Private War*, 67.

25. Harsh, *Taken at the Flood*, 74, 117.

26. See Cozzens, *Shenandoah 1862*, 151–52, 233, for examples.

27. U.S. War Department, *The War of the Rebellion: A Compilation of the Official Records of the Union and Confederate Armies*, 129 vols., index and atlas (Washington, D.C.: GPO, 1880–1901), ser. 1, vol. 12, 1:6 (hereafter cited as OR).

28. Charles Fessenden Morse, *Letters Written during the Civil War, 1861–1865* (Boston: Privately published, 1898), 52–53; David Hunter Strother, *A Virginia Yankee in the Civil War: The Diaries of David Hunter Strother*, ed. Cecil D. Eby Jr. (Chapel Hill: University of North Carolina Press, 1961), 35.

29. OR, ser. 1, vol. 11, 1:183–85.

30. Stephen W. Sears, *To the Gates of Richmond: The Peninsula Campaign* (New York: Ticknor and Fields, 1992), 109.

31. George B. McClellan, *The Civil War Papers of George B. McClellan: Selected Correspondences, 1860–1865*, ed. Stephen W. Sears (New York: Ticknor & Fields, 1989), 373.

32. Pvt. Thomas Ellis to sister, July 25, 1862, Ellis, John C.–HCWRTColl-Ellis-MarshallFamilyColl, U.S. Army Military Institute at Carlisle, Pa. (hereafter cited as USAMHI); James T. Miller, *Bound to Be a Soldier: The Letters of Private James T. Miller, 111th Pennsylvania Infantry, 1861–4*, ed. Jedediah Mannis and Galen R. Wilson (Knoxville: University of Tennessee Press, 2001), 26; Robert Goldthwaite Carter, *Four Brothers in Blue: Or Sunshine and Shadows of the War of the Rebellion a Story of the Great Civil War from Bull Run to Appomattox*, ed. John M. Carroll (Austin: University of Texas Press, 1978), 51; Pvt. Allen Seymour Davis, 1st Minnesota Infantry, to Angie Davis, August 1, 1862, A. S. Davis Civil War letters, Albert and Shirley Small Special Collections Library, University of Virginia, Charlottesville, Va. (hereafter cited as UVA); Carter, *Four Brothers*, 93.

33. Abraham Lincoln, *The Collected Works of Abraham Lincoln*, ed. Roy P. Basler, 9 vols. (New Brunswick: Rutgers University Press, 1953), 5:323.

34. John O. Casler, *Four Years in the Stonewall Brigade*, 2nd ed. (1906; repr., Columbia: University of South Carolina Press, 2005), 50; and John D. Billings, *Hardtack and Coffee: The Unwritten Story of Army Life* (1887; repr., Lincoln: University of Nebraska Press, 1993), 145.

35. Carmichael, "So Far from God," 48.

36. Carmichael, "So Far from God," 52, 56.

37. Medical leave was only for the severely ill and more commonly granted to officers than enlisted men.

38. Weitz, *More Damning than Slaughter*, 87; Confederate States of America, *General Orders, Confederate States of America, Army of Northern Virginia* (Richmond: Confederate States of America, 1862), No. 137, December 28, 1862.

39. OR, ser. 1, vol. 12, 2:52.

40. Lonn, *Desertion during the Civil War*, 143–44; Carmichael, "So Far from God," 45.

41. John Hunter Harrison to Surgeon General's Office, "From your Quarterly Report of Sick and Wounded for Quarter Ending June 30, 1862," July 28, 1862, Papers of John Hunter Harrison 1842–1888, UVA.

42. OR, ser. 1, vol. 11, 1:206.

43. Morgan, *Personal Reminiscences of the War*, 100.

44. Charles E. Rosenberg, *No Other Gods: On Science and American Social Thought* (Baltimore: Johns Hopkins University Press, 1961), 29.

45. Frances M. Clarke, *War Stories* (Chicago: University of Chicago Press, 2011), 10.

46. A. Potter, *Notes of Hospital life, From November 1861 to August 1863* (Philadelphia: Lippincott, 1863), 108.

47. Frémont was no stranger to environmental hardship, having served as a junior officer in the Army Corps of Engineers from 1842 to 1853 in five expedi-

tions in the American West before the Civil War (William J. Miller, "Such Men as Shields, Banks, and Frémont: Federal Command in Western Virginia, March–June 1862," in *The Shenandoah Valley Campaign of 1862*, ed. Gary W. Gallagher [Chapel Hill: University of North Carolina Press, 2003], 46).

48. OR, ser. 1, vol. 12, 1:25.

49. OR, ser. 1, vol. 5, 1037, 1045.

50. Ibid., 1041.

51. Joseph T. Glatthaar, *General Lee's Army: From Victory to Collapse* (New York: Free Press, 2008), 225.

52. George Worthington Adams, *Doctors in Blue: The Medical History of the Union Army in the Civil War* (1952; repr., Baton Rouge: Louisiana State University Press, 1996), 10.

53. W. H. Taylor, "Some Experiences of a Confederate Surgeon," *College of Physicians of Philadelphia, Transactions* 28 (1906): 105, 115.

54. Pvt. Aaron E. Bachman memoir, 10, Bachman, Aaron E. – HCWRTColl, USAMHI.

55. Sgt. Henry Keiser, *Diary of Henry Keiser of Lykens, Pennsylvania: Company G, 95th and 96th Pennsylvania Volunteers, War of the Rebellion, 1891 to 1865*, typescript, 29, USAMHI.

56. Rev. A. M. Stewart, *Camp, March and Battle-field; on Three Years and a Half with the Army of the Potomac* (Philadelphia: Jas. B. Rodgers, Printer, 1865), 74; Pvt. Lewis C. Shepard, 7th Massachusetts Infantry, diary, June 4, 1862, Lewis C. Shepard Diary, Massachusetts Historical Society, Boston (hereafter cited as MHS).

57. Charles E. Rosenberg, *The Care of Strangers: The Rise of America's Hospital System* (New York: Basic Books, 1987), 4.

58. Pvt. William H. Bird, 13th Alabama Infantry, Pvt. William H. Bird Memoir, 4, USAMHI; Stewart, *Camp, March and Battle-field*, 74.

59. Pvt. Thomas I. Taylor, 49th Pennsylvania Infantry, diary [February 14 and April 12, 1862 entries], Taylor, Thomas – HCWRTColl-GACColl, USAMHI; Pvt. Oscar Bailey, 1st Massachusetts, to mother, August 10, 1861, Bailey Family Letters, 1842–1866, MHS.

60. OR, ser. 1, vol. 12, 1:6, 25.

61. Castleman, *Diary of Alfred Lewis Castleman*, 75, 98–99.

62. For examples of official military categories of mental unfitness, see the Confederate "Reports of Sick and Wounded," Hunter Holmes McGuire Collection, MOC; and the Union MSHWR, vol. 1, pt. 2.

63. For evidence of the Sanitary Commission's focus on recreation, see United States Sanitary Commission, Camp Inspection Report, 5th New Hampshire Infantry, January 1, 1862, Series 1 Medical Committee Archives, 1861–65, and Series 7 Statistical Bureau Archives, Camp Inspection Reports, 1861–64, United States Sanitary Commission Records, NYPL. For evidence on commission views toward common soldiers, see A. Potter, *Notes of Hospital Life, From November 1861 to August 1863* (Philadelphia: Lippincott, 1863), 108.

64. See Isaac Ray, *Mental Hygiene in America* (Boston: Ticknor and Fields, 1863).

65. George Perkins, *Three Years a Soldier: The Diary and Newspaper Correspondence of Private George Perkins, Sixth New York Independent Battery, 1861–1864*, ed. Rich-

ard N. Griffin (Knoxville: University of Tennessee Press, 2006), 48, 50; David Hunter Strother, *A Virginia Yankee in the Civil War: The Diaries of David Hunter Strother*, ed. Cecil D. Eby Jr. (Chapel Hill: University of North Carolina Press, 1961), 35; Pvt. Jacob Blackington, 19th Massachusetts Infantry, to sister, July 21, 1862, Blackington, Lyman and Jacob – BlackingtonColl, USAMHI.

66. Pvt. E. Kendall Jenkins, 1st Massachusetts Heavy Artillery, diary [August 5, 1862 entry], E. Kendall Jenkins Diaries, 1862–1879, MHS; Carpenter, *War Diary of Kinchen Jahu Carpenter*, 8; Randolph McKim, *A Soldier's Recollections: Leaves from the Diary of a Young Confederate with an Oration on the Motives and Aims of the Soldiers of the South* (New York: Longmans, Green, and Co., 1910), 78–79.

67. Cpl. Horace M. Wade, 12th Virginia Cavalry, to parents, May 3, 1862, Wade, Horse M. (Letters) – Leigh Collection Bk 33A, USAMHI; Edmund DeWitt Patterson, *Yankee Rebel: The Civil War Journal of Edmund DeWitt Patterson*, ed. John G. Barrett, Voices of the Civil War (Knoxville: University of Tennessee Press, 2004), 15–16.

68. William Cowan McClellan, *Welcome the Hour of Conflict: William Cowan McClellan and the 9th Alabama*, ed. John C. Carter (Tuscaloosa: University of Alabama Press, 2007), 156; Elisha Franklin Paxton, *Memoir and Memorials: Elisha Franklin Paxton, Brigadier-General, C.S.A., Composed of His Letters from Camp and Field while an Officer in the Confederate Army*, ed. John Gallatin Paxton (New York: Neale Publishing, 1905), 58.

69. Keiser, *Diary of Henry Keiser*, 30, USAMHI; Charles B. Haydon, *For Country, Cause and Leader: The Civil War Journal of Charles B. Haydon*, ed. Stephen W. Sears (New York: Ticknor and Fields, 1993), 231.

70. Officers were not supposed to occupy houses without express permission from brigade command (U.S. War Department, *Revised Regulations for the Army of the United States, 1861* [Philadelphia: J. G. L. Brown, Printer, 1861], 76).

71. Maj. Jones, diary, March 15, and April 18, 1862, MOC.

72. John O. Casler, *Four Years in the Stonewall Brigade*, 2nd ed. (1906; repr., Columbia: University of South Carolina Press, 2005), 101.

73. Sgt. William H. West, 6th Maine Infantry, diary, January–June 1862, William H. West Papers, MHS.

74. Rebecca Barbour Calcutt, *Richmond's Wartime Hospitals* (Gretna, La.: Pelican Publishing, 2005), 25.

75. Sgt. David C. Ashley, 6th New York Calvary, letter to parents, May 31, 1862, Ashley Family – CWMiscColl, USAMHI.

76. Pvt. Ephraim A. Wood, 13th Massachusetts Infantry, diary, July 5, 1862, Journal of Private Ephraim A. Wood, UVA. Temperatures soared into the nineties in July; see Robert K. Krick, *Civil War Weather in Virginia* (Tuscaloosa: University of Alabama Press, 2007), 65.

77. William R. Stilwell, *The Stilwell Letters: A Georgian in Longstreet's Corps, Army of Northern Virginia*, ed. Ronald H. Moseley (Macon, GA: Mercer University Press, 2002), 10; Robert Goldthwaite Carter, *Four Brothers in Blue: Or Sunshine and Shadows of the War of the Rebellion a Story of the Great Civil War from Bull Run to Appomattox*, ed. John M. Carroll (Austin: University of Texas Press, 1978), 231.

78. For evidence of Union scurvy, see OR, ser. 1, vol. 11, 3:228–29; and OR,

ser. 1, vol. 11, 3:350; for evidence of Confederate scurvy, see changes in ration ledgers (J. S. Melvin, Capt. and Adjutant Commissary of Subsistence, "The Subsistence Ledger 1862 Sept. 1–1863 July 31," Confederate States of America, 2nd Virginia, Stonewall Brigade, Boston Athenaeum, Boston, Mass.).

79. J. Franklin Dyer, *The Journal of a Civil War Surgeon*, ed. Michael B. Chesson (Lincoln: University of Nebraska Press, 2003), 17, 24–25.

80. Private Blackington to sister, June 24, 1862, Blackington, Lyman and Jacob–BlackingtonColl, USAMHI; Sergeant Ashley to parents, May 31, 1862, Ashley Family–CWMiscColl, USAMHI.

81. See Private Wood diary, July and August 1862, Journal of Private Ephraim A. Wood, UVA.

82. William Andrew Fletcher, *Rebel Private: Front and Rear*, ed. Bell Irvin Wiley (Austin: University of Texas Press, 1954), 13.

83. John C. Gunn, *Gunn's Domestic Medicine*, new rev. ed. (1830; repr., New York: C. M. Saxton, Barber, and Co., 1860).

84. Pvt. Lorenzo N. Pratt, 1st New York Light Artillery, to father, April 10, 1862, Pratt, Lorenzo N.–CWMiscColl (Enlisted man's letters, November 1861–December 26, 1864; Discharge & news article), USAMHI.

85. George M. Taylor to Charles Elisha Taylor, March 13, 1862, Papers of Charles Elisha Taylor, 1849–1874, UVA; Surgeon Boulware diary, June 11–13, 1862, James Richmond Boulware Diary, 1862–1863, LVA.

86. Handerson, *Yankee in Gray*, 40.

FIVE
Stumps in the Wilderness

AARON SACHS

Stumps littered the American landscape in the decades before the Civil War. Americans were intimately familiar with them—although, as in the paintings of Thomas Cole, a given stump field might take on complex and seemingly contradictory meanings (see Fig. 5.1).[1]

Sometimes stumps signaled clearing, progress, development, expansiveness. Sometimes politicians climbed on top of them, filled their lungs, and speechified for hours. At the same time, stumps also suggested a certain kind of loss, and they were capable of breaking plows: they sometimes caused Americans to stumble.

Once war broke out, of course, the stumps multiplied unimaginably (see Fig. 5.2).

Many Americans noted the grim parallel, the analogy, the linguistic echo, the bond of kinship between wounded veterans and devastated trees, the limbs and trunks cut down in their prime. Amputees, formerly a tiny minority, now became the limping symbols of the entire nation: they lined city streets, begging, singing melancholy ballads, demanding attention, sympathy, prosthetics. They embodied the lingering of war's horror.[2] And out in the countryside, rough patches of woodland from Maine to Georgia, from Virginia to California, ravaged by rapid expansion and military necessity, cast thin shadows on the blood-soaked fields (see Fig. 5.3).

Herman Melville, imagining postwar Virginia in his 1866 poem, "The Armies of the Wilderness," saw "stumps of forests for dreary leagues / Like a massacre."[3]

Wilderness: Before the war, there was a full spectrum of meanings. It could be a dark, howling place, full of wild beasts and "savage" Indians. It could be a place of sublime refreshment, dominated by natural ele-

Figure 5.1. Thomas Cole, *A View of the Mountain Pass Called the Notch of the White Mountains (Crawford Notch)*, 1839, oil on canvas. 102 × 155.8 cm. Andrew W. Mellon Fund, National Gallery of Art, Washington, D.C., 1967.8.1. Courtesy of National Gallery of Art, Washington, D.C.

ments, perhaps a waterfall, far from the madding crowd, offering a small minority a reprieve from the majority. It could be a wasteland, a desert not suitable for human dwelling, or a place already ruined by human misuse. It could be a rural region, a swath of middle landscapes, deriving its meaning from its lack of urbanity—a frontier, a margin, the forested edge of settlement, where human art blended with the forces of nature.[4] After May 1864, though, "the wilderness" meant a bloody, ragged patch of central Virginia, meant the hellish stench of scorched wood and flesh (see Fig. 5.4).

The Battle of the Wilderness. For many years, not yet having dug into the documentary history of the Civil War, and not having found any photographs of the landscape, I assumed that this particular "wilderness" was largely symbolic. All battles are chaotic (and all named retrospectively), but this one was particularly gruesome and confused.

It was at the Wilderness, perhaps, that Grant truly earned his reputation as an indomitable commander—and a butcher. It was an election year; northern civilians were tiring of the carnage and the stalemates; Lincoln felt sure he would be unseated by the Democrats, who had started to preach

Figure 5.2. Unidentified photographer, *Unidentified Soldier with Amputated Arm in Union Uniform in Front of Painted Backdrop Showing Cannon and Cannonballs*, Library of Congress. Courtesy of Library of Congress, Prints and Photographs Division, Washington, D.C.

Figure 5.3. Unidentified photographer, *Ft. Sanders, Knoxville, Tenn., 1863*, stereoscopic photograph, Library of Congress. Courtesy of Library of Congress, Prints and Photographs Division, Washington, D.C.

Figure 5.4. Alfred Waud, *Wounded Escaping from the Burning Woods of the Wilderness,* Library of Congress, pencil and "Chinese white" on brown paper. Courtesy of Library of Congress, Prints and Photographs Division, Washington, D.C.

peace, who seemed willing to offer independence to the Confederacy. The new leader of the U.S. military had only a few months in which to march on Richmond. And so it was on the night of May 5, after sustaining devastating losses, that he revealed the North's new strategy, the strategy that would lead to Appomattox one year later: absorb the casualties, bring in reinforcements, and press on. To reach the Promised Land, Grant decided, he had to go through the Wilderness.

Yet Virginia's Wilderness was also an actual piece of physical and cultural geography, whose name had been in use for decades before it saw the ruination of war, before it became Grant's desert. And while my superficial reading of Civil War history at first made me think of the Battle of the Wilderness mostly in metaphorical and biblical terms, its reputation in postbellum America, I now realize, hinged not just on its casualty rate and its strategic importance but also on its notorious terrain. This was a phantom struggle, for it was waged not in open fields but in a dense, tangled wood.[5]

One soldier called it "a battle of invisibles with invisibles,"[6] and almost every commentator mentioned the seeming impenetrability of the understory, the briary maze, thick with dead leaves, that led sometimes to dark groves of oak and pine, sometimes to bright swaths of pink lady's slippers, sometimes to crackling conflagrations, sometimes to smoking muskets. The Battle of the Wilderness brought out the significance of land, made Americans consider the collision of humanity, technology, and nature. Henry Elson, an early historian of the war, discovered an uncredited photograph showing the battle's impact on the region, which he published under the title, "Trees in the Track of the Iron Storm": "Over ground like this," he wrote, "where men had seldom trod before, ebbed and flowed the tide of trampling thousands on May 5 and 6, 1864. Artillery, of which Grant had a superabundance, was well-nigh useless, wreaking its impotent fury upon the defenseless trees."[7]

What Elson seems to have gotten wrong was the frequency with which the ground had been trodden. This was a human-made Wilderness. As early as the 1720s, the region's old-growth forest had started to fall, under the orders of Lieutenant Governor Alexander Spotswood, who had secured permission from England to mine and smelt the local iron ore and so needed a vast supply of wood (and labor) to fuel his blast furnaces. Depending on how densely packed the trees were on a given patch of ground, a single furnace could consume more than two acres of woodland in a day. Six smelters were in operation by 1750. With his slaves and a supply of indentured servants from Germany, Spotswood could be said to have launched the industrial revolution in the colonies, sending cheap pots, kettles, andirons, firebacks, and possibly even cannon over to the mother country, and leaving much of Orange and Spotsylvania Counties covered with stumps. The sylvan character of the region started coming back later in the century, though, as iron supplies dwindled, because Virginians found the local soil to be too acidic and too poorly drained for extensive farming. Gradually, in the age of American independence, a second-growth "Wilderness" developed, dominated by tangles of scrub and brush amid stunted trees that struggled to soak up enough nutrients from the ground.[8] By the 1850s, when Frederick Law Olmsted took a trip through the area, the Wilderness came across as somewhat ominous, "sadly worn and misused..., all-shadowing, all-embracing," though Olmsted also noted occasional small farms with a mixture of black and white tenants, who used the thickets and brakes as a commons for running their hogs—those "long, lank, bony, snake-headed, hairy, wild beasts," so foreign to an urbane northerner.[9]

In May of 1864 both northerners and southerners tended to feel threatened and puzzled by the nature of the Wilderness. Many tripped on the region's name: "I have been much in the North Woods," wrote Cpl. Norton C. Shepard, from upstate New York, "and find a great contrast in the meaning of 'wilderness' there and in the South. In the North a wilderness is a wood in a state of nature with great trees that have stood for ages.... In the South, however, most especially in Virginia, [much] of the land has been cleared off... and abandoned as useless. Then it grows up to pine and scrub oak to become a wilderness."[10] Of course, even within New York, "wilderness" could refer to different kinds of landscapes. Corporal Shepard had grown up near the Adirondacks; further south, Andrew Jackson Downing explored a part of the Hudson Valley called "The Wilderness" in 1847 and insisted that it was far from pristine, and "by no means savage in the aspect of its beauty.... The whole of this richly wooded valley is threaded with walks, ingeniously and naturally conducted so as to penetrate to all the most interesting points; while a great variety of rustic seats, formed beneath the trees, in deep secluded thickets, by the side of the swift rushing stream, or on some inviting eminence, enables one fully to enjoy them."[11] What Corporal Shepard effectively highlighted, though, was that when Americans tried to come to grips with the Battle of the Wilderness, they were struggling not just with the sickening brutality of the Civil War but also with their evolving relationship to nature—with

Figure 5.5. Albert Bierstadt, *Valley of the Yosemite*, 1864, oil on paperboard, 30.16 × 48.89 cm. Museum of Fine Arts, Boston, gift of Martha C. Karolik and M. Karolik Collection of American Paintings, 1815–1865, 47.1236. Photograph used by permission of Museum of Fine Arts, Boston.

the creeping anxiety that they might no longer be able to look to certain landscapes for solace, renewal, confirmation, kinship.

After the war, wilderness became something that had to be transfigured. But the process started even before the war had ended (see Fig. 5.5).

If Thomas Cole was the dominant American painter in the 1820s, 1830s, and 1840s, and if his disciple Frederic Church captured the most attention in the 1850s, then Albert Bierstadt's raging popularity in the 1860s and 1870s marked a shift toward American triumphalism and the grandiosity of western wilderness.[12]

This particular painting made such a splash, in part, because at the end of June – less than two months after the Battle of the Wilderness – Congress had granted the Yosemite Valley to the state of California as a new kind of park, "for public use, resort, and recreation."[13]

"The occasional contemplation of natural scenes of an impressive character," Olmsted wrote in the August 1865 report of the Yosemite Commission, "particularly if this contemplation occurs in connection with relief from ordinary cares, change of air and change of habits, is favorable to the health and vigor of men. . . . The want of such occasional recreation where men and women are habitually pressed by their business or household cares often results in a class of disorders the characteristic quality of which is mental disability . . . , incapacitating the subject for the proper exercise of the intellectual and moral forces."[14] The nation would re-create itself through recreation in the wilderness. Of course, Olmsted was writing at a time when a new class of people had been created who would always be incapacitated by their cares, who were haunted by phantoms of pain and grief that were impossible to leave behind, and in a sense his new conception of a pure separation between awe-inspiring, escapist wilderness areas and the spaces of everyday life just mirrored the growing divide in America between veterans and all the other citizens, who mostly wanted to forget about the war and move on.[15]

Whatever the flaws in America's wilderness preservation movement, it does seem possible to make the argument that the war helped spur its rise, and I also think the war helped move Americans toward conservation — the more efficient and careful use of natural resources, especially trees.

Toward the end of the war, the Reverend Frederick Starr Jr. wrote a report for the Department of Agriculture called *American Forests; Their Destruction and Preservation*, in which he emphasized that "the destruction of forests and timber during the war of rebellion has been immense." Soldiers on both sides, Starr explained, had cleared trees for fuel (for cooking, heating, and especially trains); for construction of camps, railroads, and bridges; and for various strategic purposes, such as improving sight lines, or facilitating (or hindering) the movement of troops, or erecting elaborate defensive fortifications like abatis, arrangements of felled trunks and branches with sharpened points sticking out toward the enemy. Starr emphasized that the fate of the American forests and soils ought to matter keenly to everyone, and if the politicians in Washington truly cared about Union, they would think about attending to wounded trees in the same terms as wounded veterans: "Let us then inquire, why government should aid such efforts? *The work is national.* Every part of the land suffers together."[16]

At the same time, though, it's worth pondering the various ways in which preservation and conservation may have differed from antebellum environmental traditions. Before the war, ideas about the environment were entangled with ideas about death, thanks in large part to the so-called rural cemetery movement (see Fig. 5.6).[17]

Nature began in the human body, and the frank cultural discourse surrounding mortality served to attach people to the cycles of nature. People

Figure 5.6. W. H. Bartlett, *Cemetery of Mount Auburn*, 1839, hand-colored engraving. Author's collection.

went to the new cemeteries in cities to slow down, to feel integrated with nature, to achieve a kind of repose; they buried their kin in the land and asserted a new sense of kinship *with* the land. Consider Walt Whitman: he had always looked to nature for his narratives of death and regeneration and had always been comforted by the intermingling of animals and plants: "And as to you corpse I think you are good manure, but that does not offend me, / I smell the white roses sweetscented and growing." After the war, though, the new growth would be different, for the earth had absorbed not just the decaying flesh of beloved elders, but "the red life-blood oozing out from heads or trunks or limbs" of anonymous young soldiers, "soaking roots, grass, and soil," leaving "the land entire saturated."[18] And in the new national cemeteries immediately after the war, burial took an entirely different form. The landscape of death was now, in some ways, industrial (see Fig. 5.7).[19]

Consider how stumps tended to look shortly before the war and then after (see Figs. 5.8 and 5.9).

We've traveled from a fertile valley, bathed in early sunlight, to a denuded mountain and its darkening, red meadows. It also seems that

Figure 5.7. Dayton National Cemetery, 2011. Photograph by the author.

we've traded neat, clean, industrial development for a rough-and-tumble rural homestead. Inness's gently curving train seems to blend smoothly with its environment; its smoke, like the smoke of the village factories, echoes the morning mist, becoming a natural feature of the scene. As the critic Leo Marx would later write, the painting seems to be "a striking representation of the idea that machine technology is a proper part of the landscape." The classic pastoral observer seems perfectly calm, at peace, accepting all the changes surrounding him, proud of American Progress. Inness must have pleased his sponsor — the president of the Delaware, Lackawanna, and Western Railroad.[20] But then twilight came to America. A stump field, one year after the end of the Civil War, could not represent progress and development: the destiny manifest here was tragic. The war had costs, just as frontier settlement did. Chastened, haunted, Americans finally began to realize, in the 1860s, that they had to confront limits, that logging caused ugly, long-lasting scars, that the renewal of timber resources would take a mighty effort. Perhaps Gifford's ravaged scene directly inspired a movement to protect trees in the United States: the artist sold his painting to a dear friend, James Pinchot, who one year earlier had named his first son Gifford; the canvas hung on the wall throughout

Figure 5.8. George Inness, *The Lackawanna Valley*, c. 1856, oil on canvas, 86 × 127.5 cm. Gift of Mrs. Huttleston Rogers, National Gallery of Art, Washington, D.C., 1945.4.1. Courtesy of National Gallery of Art, Washington, D.C.

Figure 5.9. Sanford Robinson Gifford, *Hunter Mountain, Twilight*, 1866, oil on canvas, 77.8 × 137.5 cm. Terra Foundation for American Art, Chicago, Ill., Daniel J. Terra Collection, 1999.57. Photograph used by permission of Terra Foundation for American Art, Chicago / Art Resource, New York.

the boy's childhood; Gifford Pinchot went on to become Theodore Roosevelt's chief forester and the author of *The Fight for Conservation*.[21]

But of course historical transitions are never quite so neat. Americans did see stumps differently after the war; they did become more broadly aware of forest destruction than ever before.[22] But they had already been worrying about the killing of trees, to some extent, for decades, and both settlement and industrial development, rather than getting reined in, entered a period of massive, devastating expansion as soon as the war ended.

If the president of the Delaware, Lackawanna, and Western approved of Inness's landscape, he missed the work's clear debt to the ambivalence embodied by the paintings of Thomas Cole and several other artists of the Hudson River School. Does the classical pose of the observer imply that he is truly satisfied with his view, that his repose will be undisturbed by the crash and clank of the straining locomotive? Has he willingly traded the curve of a river for the curve of track and fence, the shelter of a wood for a field of dead stumps? We can't be sure: we see only his hat, worn for shade, and his back, whose bright orange tint causes him to stick out of the foreground like another amputated tree. And then there are the layers of haze hovering over the valley, seeming to throw the town's future into doubt: the mountain mist, at least, will burn off as the day progresses, but the seemingly naturalized smoke of the train and factories will cause a permanent veil of pollution. This is Scranton we're looking at, during the iron and coal boom in eastern Pennsylvania, which had already left deep scars on the landscape; anyone who was paying attention had already noticed how double-edged the axe of Progress could be.[23]

Eleven years later, Gifford chose to confront industrial development in a much less direct way, despite the massive technological changes that had been occurring. His painting hints at the power of American capitalism: Hunter Mountain is at the heart of the Catskills—at the heart of tanning country. But the local tanning industry had already peaked: Gifford's grandfather was the last one in his family to be engaged in the trade. The story here was a romantic, nostalgic, rose-colored one, focused on a classic American family attempting to carve out a life in a beautiful bit of wilderness. But these settlers found themselves worrying that maybe the wilderness was not what it once had been. Just like *The Lackawanna Valley*, this scene pays clear homage to Thomas Cole, celebrating the mythic beauty of America's gently sloping valleys, but also asking whether we could ever dwell in such places without obliterating all of their sheltering qualities, without carving up the land and starving the cattle: the thinness of the animals in this pasture perhaps echoes the thinning of the surrounding forest. There is a desperate yearning here for the possibilities of the past. Immediately after the Civil War, Americans were convinced that they had to go back to the land, in order to heal themselves—but they were also convinced that the land had been tainted.[24]

In 1855 a foreground littered with tree stumps would have forced Americans to confront the killing of trees and the onset of industrialism, would have pointed to the sacrifices required by Progress, would have reminded everyone of the distinction between a good, necessary death and a potentially unnatural death. In 1866 Americans desperately wanted to understand every death as good and necessary, but suspected that almost all the killing of the war years had been utterly unnatural. In 1866, then, a foreground littered with tree stumps could no longer stand for itself. In a way, *Hunter Mountain, Twilight*, captures a full awareness of mortality and a heightened sense of kinship between people and trees—this is not the escapism of a typical Bierstadt canvas. But there's still a strange slippage here, a kind of denial, a failure to acknowledge that Civil War mortality had to be understood on an industrial rather than a pastoral scale. Rather than marking the beginning of the conservation movement in America, I think this painting may have marked an ending of sorts, may have ushered in the twilight of America's landscape tradition: after the Civil War, the American relationship to the environment could never be the same.[25]

Notes

This chapter is adapted from chapter 4, "Stumps," of my book, *Arcadian America: The Death and Life of an Environmental Tradition* (New Haven: Yale University Press, 2013), 137–209.

1. On Cole, see especially the nuanced discussion in Angela Miller, *The Empire of the Eye: Landscape Representation and American Cultural Politics, 1825–1875* (Ithaca: Cornell University Press, 1993), esp. 21–75.

2. See for instance Oliver Wendell Holmes, "The Human Wheel, Its Spokes and Felloes," *Atlantic Monthly* 11 (May 1863), 567–80. To Emily Dickinson, amputees perhaps embodied the nation's crisis of faith in the aftermath of war: "Those—dying then, / Knew where they went—/ They went to God's Right Hand—/ That Hand is amputated now/And God cannot be found—" (Poem 1551, in *Final Harvest: Emily Dickinson's Poems*, ed. Thomas H. Johnson (Boston: Little, Brown, 1961), 298). Also note the song sheets that have survived from this period, usually with titles like "The One-Legged Soldier"; the lyrics are almost all exactly the same (though the author of the original song is unknown, as far as I can tell), and individual veterans would have the sheets printed up with their names at the top, to personalize them. The soldiers would stand at street corners, singing and ask-

ing passersby to buy one of the sheets. A typical example, held today by the American Antiquarian Society, bears the heading, "George M. Reed, The One Arm and One Leg Soldier, Wounded at the Battle of Shiloh, Sunday Morning, April 6th, 1862."

3. Herman Melville, *Battle-Pieces and Aspects of the War* (New York: Harper and Brothers, 1866), 97.

4. The classic study tracking the intellectual history of wilderness is Roderick Frazier Nash, *Wilderness and the American Mind*, now in its 4th edition (New Haven: Yale University Press, 2001). My own work is especially influenced by the group of scholars who in the last fifteen years have increasingly questioned Nash and the somewhat simplified legacy his book celebrates. The keynote of this critique was sounded by William Cronon in his crucial essay, "The Trouble with Wilderness; or, Getting Back to the Wrong Nature," in *Uncommon Ground: Rethinking the Human Place in Nature*, ed. William Cronon, 69-90 (New York: Norton, 1996). Also see J. Baird Callicott and Michael P. Nelson, eds., *The Great New Wilderness Debate* (Athens: University of Georgia Press, 1998); Michael P. Nelson, ed., *The Wilderness Debate Rages On: Continuing the Great New Wilderness Debate* (Athens: University of Georgia Press, 2008); and Michael Lewis, ed., *American Wilderness: A New History* (New York: Oxford University Press, 2007). And, on the complex landscape tradition dominant in antebellum America, see my article, "American Arcadia: Mount Auburn Cemetery and the Nineteenth-Century Landscape Tradition," *Environmental History* 15 (April 2010): 206-35.

5. Sources I've depended on for my understanding of the Wilderness campaign include Gary W. Gallagher, ed., *The Wilderness Campaign* (Chapel Hill: University of North Carolina Press, 1997); Gordon C. Rhea, *The Battle of the Wilderness, May 5-6, 1864* (Baton Rouge: Louisiana State University Press, 1994); *The Wilderness Campaign, May-June 1864*, Papers of the Military Historical Society of Massachusetts, vol. 4 (Boston: Military Historical Society of Massachusetts, 1905); James M. McPherson, *Battle Cry of Freedom: The Civil War Era* (New York: Ballantine, 1989), 718-43; and Shelby Foote, *The Civil War: A Narrative*, vol. 3, *Red River to Appomattox* (New York: Random House, 1974), 146-91.

6. Quoted in the indispensable and wonderfully eclectic book by Stephen Cushman, *Bloody Promenade: Reflections on a Civil War Battle* (Charlottesville: University Press of Virginia, 1999), 199.

7. Henry W. Elson, *The Civil War through the Camera* (Springfield, Mass.: Patriot Publishing Co., 1912), part 11 (unpaginated). There are numerous Civil War stories about trees damaged by artillery and musket fire. One of the most famous incidents occurred just a week after the Battle of the Wilderness, on May 12, 1864, at the "Bloody Angle," where an oak with a diameter of twenty-two inches was felled by a long barrage of bullets. Part of the stump left over from this lead-filled tree was preserved and can now be viewed at the Smithsonian Institution. See Robert F. Krick, "An Insurmountable Barrier between the Army and Ruin: The Confederate Experience at Spotsylvania's Bloody Angle," in *The Spotsylvania Campaign*, ed. Gary W. Gallagher (Chapel Hill: University of North Carolina Press, 1998), esp. 108-10 and 124.

8. Frank S. Walker Jr., *Remembering: A History of Orange County, Virginia* (Orange,

Va.: Orange County Historical Society, 2004), 44–47, 60–62, 71–95, 226–35; T. Lloyd Benson, "The Plain Folk of Orange: Land, Work, and Society on the Eve of the Civil War," in *The Edge of the South: Life in Nineteenth-Century Virginia*, ed. Edward L. Ayers and John C. Willis, 56–78 (Charlottesville: University Press of Virginia, 1991); Robert B. Gordon, *American Iron, 1607–1900* (Baltimore: Johns Hopkins University Press, 1996), esp. 1–6, 33–44, 57–86; and W. H. Adams, "The First Iron Blast Furnaces in America," *Transactions of the American Institute of Mining Engineers* 20 (1891): 196–215.

9. Frederick Law Olmsted, *Journey in the Seaboard Slave States, with Remarks on Their Economy* (1856; repr., New York: Negro Universities Press, 1968), 87, 65; and also see Dana F. White and Victor A. Kramer, eds., *Olmsted South: Old South Critic/New South Planner* (Westport, Conn.: Greenwood, 1979), esp. introduction and part 1. On the hog commons, see Jack Temple Kirby, *Mockingbird Song: Ecological Landscapes of the South* (Chapel Hill: University of North Carolina Press, 2006), 113–55.

10. Raymond W. Smith, ed., *Out of the Wilderness: The Civil War Memoir of Cpl. Norton C. Shepard, 146th New York Volunteer Infantry* (Hamilton, N.Y.: Edmonston Publishing, 1998), 2.

11. Downing, "A Visit to Montgomery Place," in A. J. Downing, *Rural Essays*, ed. George William Curtis (1853; repr. New York: Geo. A. Leavitt, 1869), 197–98.

12. On Bierstadt and the artistic trends he embodied, see Gordon Hendricks, *Albert Bierstadt: Painter of the American West* (New York: Harry N. Abrams, 1974); Diane P. Fischer, *Primal Visions: Albert Bierstadt "Discovers" America* (Montclair, N.J.: Montclair Art Museum, 2001); William H. Goetzmann and William N. Goetzmann, *The West of the Imagination* (New York: W. W. Norton, 1986), 145–69; and Lee Clark Mitchell, *Westerns: Making the Man in Fiction and Film* (Chicago: University of Chicago Press, 1996), 56–72, 83–93.

13. U.S. statute cited in Nash, *Wilderness and the American Mind*, 106; on the rise of the national parks see ibid. 106–40.

14. Frederick Law Olmsted, "Preliminary Report upon the Yosemite and Big Tree Grove (1865)," in Victoria Post Ranney, ed., *The Papers of Frederick Law Olmsted*, vol. 5, *The California Frontier, 1863–1865*, ed. Victoria Post Ranney (Baltimore: Johns Hopkins University Press, 1990), 500, 502.

15. Olmsted was not insensitive to the needs of veterans; indeed, through his work as chief of the U.S. Sanitary Commission, from 1861 to 1863, he gained first-hand experience of the traumas of war, and he himself was clearly traumatized. Perhaps he genuinely hoped that even veterans would be able to find solace in places like the new park at Yosemite. But of course very few veterans would have had access to Yosemite, and it seems clear that the park was intended mostly for the leisured classes, and that its symbolism was meant to emphasize a kind of exclusive beauty. I suspect that Olmsted wished to erase what for many veterans could never be erased.

16. Rev. Frederick Starr Jr., *American Forests; Their Destruction and Preservation*, report published by the United States Department of Agriculture in 1865 and bound into a volume titled *Memorials*, with pieces by and about Starr, donated to the Cornell University Library (call # b 9178 S79) in 1867 by Miss Lucy Starr (pagination is that of the original USDA report), 220. It is also worth noting that

George Perkins Marsh published his landmark work (often referred to as conservation's founding text) in 1864: see Marsh, *Man and Nature*, ed. David Lowenthal (1864; repr., Cambridge, Mass.: Harvard University Press, 1965).

17. See Sachs, "American Arcadia."

18. Whitman, "Song of Myself," in *The Portable Walt Whitman*, ed. Mark Van Doren (New York: Penguin, 1977), 94; Whitman, *Memoranda during the War* (Camden, N.J.: author's publication, 1875–76), 14 and 57; and Whitman, *Specimen Days*, in *Portable*, 482.

19. David Charles Sloane has argued that the Civil War did not have a major impact on Americans' thinking about cemeteries; I respectfully disagree. The new national cemeteries were laid out in massive, democratic grids, with their simple white identical markers lined up in rows and columns that covered sprawling expanses of land—lined up in rigid military formation, with little topographical relief, to create an overwhelming effect of flatness and infinite extension, representing common, collective sacrifice, emphasizing unity over diversity, the group over the individual, statistics over human singularity. I find them deeply moving, humbling—yet also impersonal and abstract. To postbellum Americans, who had so recently embraced the rural cemetery movement, such places must have seemed strange and sobering. See Sloane, *The Last Great Necessity: Cemeteries in American History* (Baltimore: Johns Hopkins University Press, 1991), 112–13. Also note Munro MacCloskey, *Hallowed Ground: Our National Cemeteries* (New York: Richard Rosen, 1968), 11–45; and Robert M. Poole, *On Hallowed Ground: The Story of Arlington National Cemetery* (New York: Walker and Co., 2009), 1–101.

20. Leo Marx, *The Machine in the Garden: Technology and the Pastoral Ideal in America* (New York: Oxford University Press, 1964), 220–22 (quotation on 220). On Inness, also see Nicolai Cikovsky Jr. and Michael Quick, *George Inness* (New York: Harper and Row, 1985), esp. 74–77; Rachael Ziady DeLue, *George Inness and the Science of Landscape* (Chicago: University of Chicago Press, 2004), esp. 106–21; and Michael Quick, *George Inness: A Catalogue Raisonné* (New Brunswick, N.J.: Rutgers University Press, 2007), esp. 1:112–15.

21. Char Miller, *Gifford Pinchot and the Making of Modern Environmentalism* (Washington, D.C.: Island Press, 2001), esp. 108–10.

22. See David E. Nye, *America as Second Creation: Technology and Narratives of New Beginnings* (Cambridge, Mass.: MIT Press, 2003), esp. 75–78; Michael Williams, *Americans and Their Forests: A Historical Geography* (New York: Cambridge University Press, 1989), 393–96; and Thomas R. Cox, Robert S. Maxwell, Phillip Drennon Thomas, and Joseph J. Malone, *This Well-Wooded Land: Americans and Their Forests from Colonial Times to the Present* (Lincoln: University of Nebraska Press, 1985), 127–53.

23. Inness owed a huge debt to Thomas Cole; even a casual perusal of his opus suggests a powerfully direct influence and a deep investment in the pastoral mode. Besides the previously cited works on Inness, also see Adrienne Baxter Bell, *George Inness and the Visionary Landscape* (New York: George Braziller, 2003). For the Scranton connection, see Cikovsky and Quick, *George Inness*, 74, and on the iron and coal boom, see Martin V. Melosi, *Coping with Abundance: Energy and Environment in Industrial America* (New York: Alfred A. Knopf, 1985), 22–34.

24. On Gifford, see Kevin J. Avery and Franklin Kelly, eds., *Hudson River School Visions: The Landscapes of Sanford Gifford* (New York: Metropolitan Museum of Art, 2003); Ila Weiss, *Poetic Landscape: The Art and Experience of Sanford R. Gifford* (Newark: University of Delaware Press, 1987); and Andrew Wilton and Timothy Barringer, *American Sublime: Landscape Painting in the United States, 1820–1880* (London: Tate, 2002), esp. 120–21.

25. Note John Brinckerhoff Jackson, *American Space: The Centennial Years: 1865–1876* (New York: W. W. Norton, 1972), 35–36: "We sometimes call the postwar generation the one which discovered conservation, but it would be more accurate to call it the one which abandoned ancient attitudes toward the environment and began to transform it and redesign it to suit the needs and conveniences of men."

SIX

"The Strength of the Hills"
Representations of Appalachian Wilderness as Civil War Refuge

JOHN C. INSCOE

In a meeting with Frederick Douglass in 1847, the abolitionist John Brown pointed on a map to the "far-reaching Alleghenies" (a label applied to the Appalachians in general through much of the nineteenth century) and declared that "these mountains are the basis of my plan," both as an escape route out of the South and as a base of operations from which attacks on the plantation South could be launched. Douglass quoted Brown as saying, "God has given the strength of the hills to freedom; they were placed here for the emancipation of the negro race; they are full of natural forts . . . [and] good hiding places, where large numbers of brave men could be concealed, baffle and elude pursuit for a long time."[1]

When Brown finally enacted his attack on Harpers Ferry twelve years later, the highlands were still crucial to his aims. He hoped to move south through Virginia and the Carolinas, liberating the slaves of the plantation piedmont and sending them to a chain of fortresses established in the mountains to their west, from which they would hold their opponents at bay while reinforcements, black and white, gathered to form an army of liberation. "The mountains and swamps of the South," Brown reiterated to a fellow conspirator a year before his 1859 raid on that northern Virginia arsenal, "were intended by the Almighty as a refuge for the slave and a defense against the oppressor." Among his final words, while gazing upon the distant Blue Ridge Mountains as he moved across the Charleston jail yard toward the gallows, were simply, "This is a beautiful country."[2]

Brown was not alone in attributing such redeeming qualities to this particular part of the South. In *The Invention of Appalachia*, cultural anthropologist Allen Batteau detected a trend beginning in the 1850s in which "wild nature began to acquire a positive value as the heritage of the new nation," and noted that Appalachia specifically first took on its image as "other" in contrast to modernizing and civilizing forces that were beginning to redefine the landscape and society of America's eastern seaboard. For many urbanites, the idea of sustainable, even permanent wilderness was an appealing one, as were those perpetual "primitives" who inhabited such a region.[3] At the same time, the ever intensifying sectional crisis offered yet another, more politically charged image of Appalachia – that of the sole area of the South not burdened, or cursed, with the sin of slavery. For many, it represented a bastion of liberty where, according to a later chronicler, "the hills, in their exquisite isolation became havens for the disenchanted black and white . . . who needed to escape burdensome drudgery and slavery."[4]

In the early months of the Civil War, a Minnesota journalist picked up on these sentiments and suggested that the federal government embrace and utilize the support it enjoyed among those southerners residing in Appalachia. The reason, he maintained, was that "within this Switzerland of the South, Nature is at war with slavery." Bondage, he implied, was incompatible with high altitudes: "Freedom has always loved the air of mountains. Slavery, like malaria, desolates the low alluvials of the globe."[5] Others imposed these attributes upon the region in hindsight, as northerners after the war acknowledged the Union loyalty of many, if not most, southern highlanders. In an 1872 sermon, Ohio minister William Goodrich was among those who continued to extol the virtues of the highland South. "Explain it as we may," he preached, "there belongs to mountain regions a moral elevation of their own. They give birth to strong, free, pure and noble races. They lift the men who dwell among them, in thought and resolve. Slavery, falsehood, base compliance, luxury, belong to the plains. Freedom, truth, hardy sacrifice, simple honor, to the highlands."[6]

During the war, the southern highlands came to serve as a safe haven for far more than escaped slaves. Yael Sternhell devotes much of her splendid new book, *Routes of War: The World of Movement in the Confederate South*, to the premise that "the Civil War transformed the South into a land of runaways," as she explores "the social, political, and cultural consequences of the vast surges of mobility created by war."[7] While she covers the full range of such movement throughout the region as a whole, it is my contention that, for no other part of the Confederate (or border) South, and certainly none so extensive, did topography, terrain, and environment play as functional a role in shaping that "surge of mobility" as did the Appalachian wilderness, which attracted, embraced, and at times repelled a host of refugees and fugitives over the course of the war. In contrast to much of the rest of the wartime South where, as Lisa Brady has argued so effectively, the perception of wilderness continued to serve as "a terrifying symbol of chaos" with "dark and sinister" connotations, the highlands evoked far more positive sentiments both during and long after the war by a series of writers who made its physical distinctions integral as both setting and context for a wide range of narratives about the war as fought on that troubled terrain.[8]

The first such writer to apply these lofty ideas regarding the wartime moral geography of the Appalachian South was John Townsend Trowbridge. In the spring of 1864, his novel *Cudjo's Cave* was published in Boston, and it quickly became one of the most popular works of fiction published during the Civil War.[9] Set in 1861 in the Cumberland Mountains along the Tennessee and Kentucky borders, Trowbridge's narrative focuses on the dilemma faced by southern whites who remained loyal to the Union, and the unlikely alliances forged with slaves who had already taken refuge in the title locale. A New York native then living in Boston, Trowbridge moved in abolitionist circles that included Harriet Beecher Stowe; he came to model his writings after hers and shaped his literary efforts to advance the cause. He published three novels over the course of the war years; none was as well received as *Cudjo's Cave*, a work inspired by the passage of the Emancipation Proclamation the year before. In it, he sought to remind readers of the true purpose of the war. "The war of secession was a war of emancipation from the start," he later wrote in his memoir. "I was eager to bear my own humble part in the momentous conflict, and took up the only weapon I had any skill to use.... I was impatient to hurl my firebrand into the breach."[10]

While his effort to dramatize for northern readers the plight of both southern Unionists and slaves proved effective, the significance of Trowbridge's novel lies as much in the fact that he made his setting so integral to both his plot and his theme. That he chose to situate his saga of these heroic refugees in the Cumberlands suggests that he was familiar with how, by the war's midpoint, the Southern Appalachians had come to be perceived by many Americans, both North and South. As such, his became the first in what would become a long line of fictional and nonfictional chronicles in which the region was depicted as a rugged and remote region that offered safe haven for those seeking escape, protection, or respite from the dogs of war elsewhere.

While the roots of Trowbridge's abolitionist agenda are readily evident, it is not as clear what led him to foreground so readily the natural world in which he set *Cudjo's Cave*. There is no indication that he was ever a part of or even aware of the nascent environmental movement in the Northeast during the late antebellum era.[11] Rather, it was personal experiences through which he cultivated his appreciation of nature untamed. In his memoir, he recounted lengthy excursions he made as a young adult through the wilds of Minnesota and Maine. Of the latter, he wrote that he found "among the woods and waters of that wilderness, congenial subjects for my pen."[12]

As for making the southern mountains so integral to his agenda, Trowbridge seems to have taken to heart the declarations of John Brown and others as to "the strength of the hills" as "bastions of liberty and sanctuaries from oppression." Though he never met Brown, he was a protégé of Theodore Parker, one of Brown's most ardent supporters. On a later visit to Harpers Ferry and nearby Charles Town, where Brown was hanged, Trowbridge wrote: "I stood a long time on the spot . . . and looked at the same sky old John Brown looked his last on, the same groves, the same distant Blue Ridge, the sight of whose summits, clad in softest heavenly light, must have conveyed a sweet assurance to his soul," thus suggesting that he was well aware of the martyr's own attachment to those mountains, both in literal and figurative terms.[13] Trowbridge had not yet visited the South when he wrote his novel, and he knew the Cumberland Gap only through newspaper reports of military forays there, along with travel narratives and other secondhand descriptions. He may well have been familiar with President Lincoln's interest in the region as a Unionist stronghold, thus making it an especially effective and timely locale in which to place his drama.[14] Though it remained for Trowbridge a site unseen, he recreated it with remarkable accuracy, including the cave situated at the base of the gap on the Tennessee side (so much so that it now bears the name Cudjo's Cave).[15]

Cudjo's Cave opens as Penn Hapgood, a young schoolmaster and Pennsylvania native, is dragged out of the schoolhouse by an angry crowd of local ruffians and brutally beaten because of his Unionist proclivities and abolitionist convictions. Hapgood manages to escape the mob's clutches but eventually collapses in nearby woods, where he is rescued by two local slaves, who carry him up a mountainside and lay him on the floor of "an apartment of prodigious and uncouth architecture, dimly lighted from one by some opening invisible to him . . . a cavernous room with an irregular rocky roof that stretched away into vague and obscure distance." So is introduced the extensive maze of underground chambers within which much of the novel will play out, and its two equally remarkable residents – Pomp and Cudjo, fugitive slaves who are hiding out there (much as John Brown envisioned for those slaves he expected to liberate in his post–Harpers Ferry operation). With the outbreak of war, the two African Americans make their underground haven a base of operations from which they offer assistance and sanctuary to a range of colorful characters, all either "downtrodden fellows" or "deserving union men," of whom Hapgood was the first and most stalwart.[16]

The novel consists of a series of set pieces in which this threesome and those who come under their protection must confront and fend off a host of villainous antagonists. These include former owners and overseers seeking to retake their self-stolen property; Confederates, both individually and en masse, committed to putting down what has become a subterranean hotbed of subversion against the southern cause; and some simply waging personal vendettas against Hapgood or members of his ever-expanding cohort.

Over the course of the novel, the cave serves as fortress, battleground, hiding place, trap, and prison, as this band of refugees seeks to elude, defeat, or punish their numerous persecutors. As such, it becomes an integral, even proactive force to be reckoned with by friend and foe alike. As Pomp and Cudjo guide Hapgood through its subterranean wonders, the latter's astonishment is profound, for "he had formed no conception of the extent and sublimity of the various galleries, chambers, glittery vaults, and falling waters, embosomed there in the mountain."[17]

Each of the three major fugitives expresses his appreciation for the physical surroundings that offer safe haven and new meaning for their lives. Cudjo discovered the cave after escaping from a sadistic overseer a year before the war began; soon thereafter he took in Pomp, who had fled his own abusive master. In response to an inquiry as to how they could endure so dank and depressing a refuge, Pomp responds: "Dreadful? There are worse places, my friend, than this. Is it gloomy? The house of bondage is gloomier. Is it damp? It is not with the cruel sweat and blood of the slave's brow and back. Is it cold? The hearts of our tyrants are colder." And when Hapgood asks why he never escaped to the North, given the independence of movement he currently enjoyed, Pomp replies:

> Would I be any better off there? Does not the color of a negro's skin, even in your free states, render him an object of suspicion and hatred? . . . These crags

do not look scornfully upon me because of the color of my skin. The watercourses sing for me their gladdest songs, black as I am. And the serious trees seem to love me, even as I love them. It is a savage, lonely, but not unhappy life I lead—far better for a man like me than servitude here, or degradation at the north.[18]

The Quaker schoolmaster expresses similar sentiments when first exposed to the vista just outside the cave's entrance. "The scene filled him with rapture; the loveliness of earth and sky intoxicated him." Hapgood's realization that he is perched atop "the rugged ranges of the Cumberland Mountains, in the heart of Tennessee" serves as a sensory catharsis for him, as his gaze sweeps across the "tremendous billows of forest-crowned rocks, and "the ravines that opened into little valleys, and these spread out into a broad and magnificent interval, checkered with farms, streaked with roads, and dotted with dwellings." Yet such beauty carries moral meaning as well, with echoes of John Brown's rhetoric of a mere five years earlier. "O! And to think that all this divine loveliness is marred by the passions of men," Hapgood thinks. "Up here, what glory, what peace! Down yonder, what hatred, violence, and sin! No wonder, Pomp, you love the mountains so."[19]

Perhaps Trowbridge's most striking utilization of the cave is the racial role reversal it imposes on its occupants. He made much of the fact that, as the cave's original inhabitants, Pomp and Cudjo are, as Hapgood points out to a fellow beneficiary of their largess, "in a condition to do infinitely more for us than we can do for them."[20] This scenario of black initiative and ingenuity to protect a predominantly white cohort is easily the most radical theme Trowbridge imposed on northern readers; their status and authority hinge as much on their familiarity and adeptness in navigating this vast and treacherous cavern they call home as on their squatter rights to the place. As Hapgood extolls the cave's geological wonders during his first tour of it, "Cudjo kept repeating with fantastic grimaces of satisfaction: 'Dis yer all is my own house! Me found him all my own self. Nobody war eber hyar after me; Pomp am de next; and you's de on'y white man eber seen dis yer cave.'"[21] That fact alone will imbue the two hosts—the intelligent, educated Pomp as well as the more simple-minded Cudjo—with considerable clout and sense of self-worth throughout the ordeals ahead.

Trowbridge made clear to his readers that this cave is not the only means by which the southern mountains could and did serve as refuge for those seeking to escape Confederate persecution. As Southern troops appear to be closing in on the cave dwellers late in the novel, one occupant offers his companions another option: "It seems your retreat cannot remain long concealed," he warns them. "Make your preparations to disperse at any moment. You may be compelled to hide for months in the mountains and woods, hunted continually, and never permitted to sleep in safety twice in the same place."[22] The novel ends with a fierce clash between the cave-dwelling forces of good and those of treason, intolerance, and repression. Most of the former, and only a few of the latter survive; all soon disperse. Hapgood has evolved from mere fugitive to full-fledged combatant for the Union cause, and Pomp offers his services as secret agent and scout for Union forces in Kentucky.

In later recounting the origins of *Cudjo's Cave*, Trowbridge noted: "I had a title for my novel before a page of it was written." He thought of a cave as "a central fact to give unity to the action, and form at the same time a picturesque feature of the narrative." The whole thing, he wrote, "flashed upon me like a vision, as I lay awake one night, with my imagination aflame.... The cave, the burning forest, and the fire-lit waterfall, all came to me, as I recall, in two or three hours of intensely concentrated thought."[23] In other words, it was neither plot nor characters, and only partially ideology that shaped his initial conception of the project; his first sources of inspiration, and those he chose to remember nearly four decades later, were the physical settings in which it would all play out. Trowbridge never shied from the fact that the rugged and remote highland terrain could be treacherous, as was true of any wilderness area, and his literary successors also made much of its challenges and perils. And yet, he stressed those life-affirming qualities as even more defining traits of his highland setting. Higher altitudes went hand in hand with higher moral ground, as the physical environment became a crucial agent in restoring the morale of those—whether residents or outsiders—who sought protection or relief in its rugged wilderness. They drew both sustenance and meaning from the natural world that abetted their efforts.

But Trowbridge, and those who followed in his wake, also acknowledged that darker reality—the fact that not all of those seeking refuge in the southern highlands were worthy of the sympathy or admiration accorded his virtuous protagonists, both white and black. The region also attracted a variety of wartime dissidents, outcasts, and fugitives who became destructive forces in waging the brutal inner war that plagued southern Appalachia in the latter years of the larger conflict. Recent historians have established a strong correlation between wilderness areas and concentrations of fugitives, deserters, or outliers who often banded together to wreak havoc on more settled areas nearby or on troops who sought them out in their mountain lairs.

Kenneth Noe has shown how Webster County, "one of the most rugged places in all of western Virginia," became the "base, headquarters, and refuge for many of the bushwhackers operating out in southern West Virginia," and a hotbed of guerrilla activity early in the war. Union colonel George Crook applied his experience as an Indian fighter on the western frontier as he led the 36th Ohio in counterinsurgency missions, tracking down these bushwhackers and flushing them out of their "haunts."[24] The fact that these outliers used the wilderness to their advantage, remaining all but invisible and playing by rules of combat all their own, led these Ohioans to despise and demonize their tormentors. One vented: "Men on pickets had been shot by rebels in the brush until our men became almost furious at this sneaking cowardly fighting." Capt. Rutherford B. Hayes dismissed these mountaineers as "cowardly, cunning, and lazy," and claimed that "the height of their ambition is to shoot a Yankee from some place of safety."[25]

Madison County, North Carolina, became the scene of one of the more notorious incidents in the mountain war, the Shelton Laurel massacre in January 1863, in which Confederate forces captured and executed thirteen men and boys from this isolated community. This overreaction by the two regiments sent to track down Shelton Laurel's men—who had sought little more than to sit out the war as neutrals—lay in their frustration, like that of the Ohioans in western Virginia, in being able to combat or even confront a hidden enemy, which also included deserters returning home to hide in the woods. One leader of the 64th North Carolina later complained, "They never gave us a fair fight, square up, face to face, man to man, horse to horse." Yet another soldier vented in a letter home, telling his parents that he had captured a "moccasin ranger" who had "run into the woods 'til he did not know whether he was a wild beast or a human being! Sometime I think we are almost out of the world . . . and I expect if we stay here much longer we will all get wild."[26] The mood of the soldiers was brutal, Phillip Paludan wrote in his book *Victims*, "for they were in an environment guaranteed to terrorize both soldier and victim and to obscure the distinction between them. Surrounded by hostile people, moving in terrain know intimately by the invisible enemy, it was easy to surrender to brutality. In guerrilla warfare men can feel that the environment is itself hostile to them. . . . In regular battle death terrorizes, but not to the same extent."²⁷

Jonathan Sarris documented a similar situation in the mountains of north Georgia, as residents of Lumpkin County, largely Confederate, faced increasing harassment from its more remote neighbors in Fannin County, which eventually led to some of the more intense guerrilla conflict in the southern Appalachians. Sarris characterized Fannin as a "definitive frontier region," among the last areas of the state to be settled, with a populace far sparser and poorer than those in Lumpkin, which had boomed as the epicenter of the state's 1830s gold rush. One resident of the latter reported to Governor Joe Brown in 1862 that "a line of robbers extends from Rabun County to west of the Cohutta mountains," and pleaded for state troops to provide some protection from them. Another complained that Fannin's refugee population made for an intolerable situation: "These blue mountains are filled with tories and deserters and thieves and runaway negroes, and they are robbing soldiers' families." His own community was left increasingly defenseless, as "the tories ran wild, shamelessly abusing soldiers' wives and even ministers of the gospel."²⁸

Each of these scenarios demonstrates not only a strong correlation between wilderness areas and the types of people attracted to them, but also the combative advantages held by those entrenched in remote and rugged settings when faced by regular troops ill suited to such venues or such foes. Often it was their mere ability to evade detection in such settings that so frustrated their pursuers. In April 1863 Confederate camp guard John Robert Lowrey led a company into the North Carolina highlands "hunting up deserters and conscripts." With no success after three weeks of pursuit, he was forced to admit: "I think we are doing nothing and we never will catch them, for there are too many good hiding places in the mountains."²⁹ While the soldiers, whether Union or Confederate, making such appraisals had good reason to view these elusive refugee communities as hostile, destructive, or at least tremendously frustrating, we also have the voices of many of those refugees themselves, who as beneficiaries of secluded highland havens, offered far more generous assessments of the Appalachian environments that proved so crucial to their survival.

Many such testimonials come from fugitive prisoners of war, whose narratives of their escapes from Confederate prisons make up a significant subgenre of postwar memoirs and reminiscences. Several of those who had to cross the southern highlands lent credence to Trowbridge's plot, by testifying to the aid and shelter they received from local slaves, who served as guides or, in some cases, as fellow travelers as they too sought to free themselves by making their way into Union-occupied East Tennessee.[30] Others were struck by the sheer numbers of Unionists hiding out in the mountains, and wrote with great admiration of the sacrifices they made and the conditions they endured for the cause to which they were so firmly committed.[31] In September 1863 *Harper's Weekly* brought national attention to the phenomenon with a dramatic, if somewhat romanticized two-page illustration of forlorn-looking refugees – men and women, black and white, old and young – huddled at the entrance to a mountainside cave in East Tennessee. The accompanying text described them as Unionists "flying northward . . . in a scene that may be witnessed almost daily on any highway in Tennessee, Kentucky, or Missouri."[32]

J. Madison Drake, a Union officer from New Jersey, wrote in his memoir, *Fast and Loose in Dixie* (1880), that in crossing through the Carolina highlands, he had "little trouble finding 'friends,' for they are everywhere." In Caldwell County, he wrote of locals he encountered: "I associated with hundreds of this class," who were "boon companions with another class, called 'lyers-out,' [more often referred to as outliers], who, living in caves and other retreats in the mountains, had resisted the conscriptions of the rebel authorities through two years or more of vicissitudes and suffering." He found them a noble people embedded in an equally noble setting. "In all my wanderings, I had never seen a more intelligent or determined people. Mingling with them, as I did for weeks, I thought of the brave defenders of the Tyrol, of the hearty Waldenses, fighting and dying among the hills for dear Liberty's sake."[33]

Few others waxed as poetically as did Drake, but many confirmed the extent to which the mountains were overrun with a host of those seeking refuge from a variety of forces, some only a few miles from their homes, others far from homes in New England or the Midwest. A sketch by a New Yorker in an 1890 issue of *The Century* focuses on the resident highlanders, and describes staying with them in cabins or "sometimes at a cavern in rocks such as abound throughout the mountains, and which are called by the natives 'rock houses.' . . . Many were deserters, some of whom had coolly set at defiance the terms of their furloughs, while others had abandoned the camps in Virginia, and, versed in mountain craft, had made their way along the Blue Ridge and put in a heroic appearance in their native valleys."[34]

Nearly all of these fugitive chroniclers made the wilderness environs central elements of their dramatic ordeals. William Burson's account typ-

Figure 6.1. *Union Refugees in East Tennessee, Harper's Weekly*, September 19, 1863.

ifies the genre in terms of both the pitfalls these men faced and the ultimate rewards to be gained from enduring them. In his memoir, *A Race for Liberty* (1867), Burson, an Ohio captain fleeing west toward Tennessee after escaping from the Confederate prison camp in Salisbury, North Carolina, wrote that he left the main road and "entered the forests and crags of the mountains. Onward I went as noiselessly almost as a cat, yet making very good time. The owls hooted, the wild-cat screamed, and occasionally the growl of a bear was heard in some lonely hollow, making my way anything but pleasant." He concludes with a more uplifting sentiment, stating: "But Sweet Liberty would crown my efforts at the end of my race." Thinking of his wife and children eager to hear from a missing husband and father, a mother wondering about her lost son, and brothers and sisters "impatient for the return of this wanderer," Burson declared that he "was nerved with renewed exertions to make my way through these mountain wilds" and counted on God to be both his "guardian and guide." Upon stumbling upon an orchard laden with apples, he extolled his and his companions' good fortune: "Surely a kind Providence has not forgotten us. As the children of Israel were guided through the wilderness, we felt the same kind hand was guiding us."[35]

Like so many such fugitive narratives, Burson made specific land features—caves, coves, hollows, and ravines—integral components of the stories he told. In assessing the local color writings of Tennessean Mary Noialles Murfree in the 1870s and 1880s, Allen Batteau noted that "the mountains were not a neutral backdrop, but significant participants in the action, at times reflecting human moods, at times offered a carefully constructed stage setting, usually providing physical barriers to signify social distinctions, and at times even coming alive to participate in, or otherwise overshadow, human action."[36] Though Murfree rarely focused on the war years, this description is equally apt for those who did. Just as Cudjo's Cave and the surrounding wilderness "came alive to participate in human action" in Trowbridge's saga, other natural sites and environmental factors served similar functions in a number of works produced in the postwar decades. The war and its moral imperatives often served to elevate nature's functionality, making it an even more intrinsic component of both narrative and message.

If the idea of wilderness as synonymous with sanctuary was prevalent for many of those chroniclers of Appalachia's Civil War, the more literary among them stressed the paradox that so sublime a setting often spawned especially brutal violence. No one played on that contradiction between natural beauty and human atrocity as blatantly as did Will Wallace Harney in one of the earliest and more influential postwar descriptions of the mountain South. While traveling through the Cumberland Mountains in 1869 with his new bride, the Louisville, Kentucky, native recorded his impressions of the region and its people, and later shaped them into an essay he titled "A Strange Land and Peculiar People," which was published in *Lippincott's Magazine* in 1873. In addition to florid descriptions of the area's "geological and botanical curiosities," Harney devoted equal attention to its inhabitants, and particularly to what they told him of their Civil War experiences, still fresh in their memories four years after the war's end.[37]

Harney prefaced the most striking of those incidents by stating, "War is a bad thing always, but when it gets into a simple neighborhood, and teaches the right and duty of killing one's friends and relatives, it becomes demoniac.... We were shown the scene of one of these neighborhood vengeances... a low house at the side of a ravine, down whose steep slope the beech forest steps are persistently erect, as if distrusting gravitation." In the fall of 1863 a group of thirty Confederates gathered at this isolated cabin for a "country-side frolic" with fiddle music and pretty mountain girls. Harney was as taken with the outside setting as what transpired inside. "The moon went down," he wrote, "and the music of the dance, the shuffle of feet on the puncheon floor, died away into that deep murmurous change, the hymn of Nature in the forest." Accompanied by "these solemn dirges of the great dark woods," the soldiers soon fell into "a deep, healthful sleep, lulled by the chant of the serene motherforest," the sounds, scents, and sights of which he described in rapturous and prolonged prose. "There are no sounds of Nature or art so true in harmony as this ceaseless murmur of the American woods," Harney concluded just before turning to the dastardly and unnatural deed that shattered this idyllic scene:

> A light step, like a blown leaf: the loose wooden latch rises at the touch of a familiar hand; familiar feet, that have trodden every inch of that poor log floor, lead the way; and then all at once, like a bundle of Chinese crackers, intermingled with shrieks and groans and deep, vehement curses, the rapid reports of pistols fill the chambers. The beds, the floors, the walls, the doors are splashed with blood, and the chambers are cumbered with dead and dying men in dreadful agony. Happy those who passed quietly from the sweet sleep of Nature to the deeper sleep of death!

Only at this point did Harney inform the reader that six Federal scouts had slipped through the woods "to do this horrible work" and that not one of the thirty young men had survived.[38] Their crime, he seemed to suggest, was all the more heinous because it so defied and defiled the sublimity of the natural setting in which it was committed.

Two prominent women writers, Rebecca Harding Davis and Constance Fenimore Woolson, published short stories set in wartime Appalachia. Two such tales appeared in national magazines within months of each other in the mid-1870s; in both, the wilderness as refuge is a central theme and closely tied to the moral agendas each author sought to promote. Likewise, both stories center on mountain families, not outsiders, who see their homes as their refuge from the outside world, though they ultimately find themselves sucked into a war against which even the most secluded of locales could not protect them.

Davis was born and raised in Wheeling when it was still Virginia's northernmost city; that, along with college years in nearby Washington, Pennsylvania, attuned her to the particular challenges faced by those living on either side of the border when the Civil War broke out. She became a prolific writer of both short stories and novels about homefront tensions and conflicts faced by families in the border states, several of which were set in the highland areas of Ohio, Pennsylvania, and newly created West Virginia. One of the few stories Davis set in southern (versus central) Appalachia is "The Yares of Black Mountain," which appeared in *Lippincott's* in 1875.[39] Like Trowbridge, Davis chronicled the heroic stance taken by southern Unionists and the risks they took in doing so. As such, the story is considered seminal in drawing national attention to Appalachia as a wartime bastion of Union support.[40]

Davis's protagonist, or narrator, is a young New England widow, identified only as Mrs. Denby, who along with her small son, Charley, is traveling with a group of northern tourists through western North Carolina shortly after the war; as they move into the higher elevations of the Black Mountains near Asheville, she finds herself mesmerized by the mountains, and hires a driver, Jonathan Yare, to take her and her sickly child to explore the wilds of the rugged Black range.[41] Her companions worry about her escort, having heard from Asheville residents that he is a brutish hunter and part of a family "with a terrible history – they live like wild beasts." Yet determined to venture out, she was invigorated by the scenic beauty, by the pure air, and with the highlands' spiritual and aesthetic powers well beyond its health benefits. "She had penetrated to the highest summits of the Appalachian Range, the nursery or breeding-place from which descend the Blue Ridge, the Alleghenies, the Nantahala – all the great mountain-bulwarks that wall the continent on the eastern coast. . . . She looked up at the fixed, awful heights, forgetting even the child on her knee. It was if God had taken her into one of the secret places where He dwelt apart."[42]

To take shelter from a storm and obtain fresh milk for her baby, Yare takes Mrs. Denby to his home – "a low log house built into the ledge of the mountain." Her first impression is that "human nature could reach no lower depths of squalor and ignorance than these," and she is quick to note what she sees as a contradiction between such a primitive existence and so magnificent a setting: "Nature," she concludes, "does not always ennoble her familiars." She is soon proved wrong, as the hospitable Yares put her at her ease and tend to her and her baby's needs. "The Yares were, in fact, a family born with exceptionally strong intellects and clean, fine instincts: they had been left to develop both in utter solitude and without education, and the result . . . was the grave self-control of Indians and a truthful directness and simplicity of thought and speech which seem to grow out of and express the great calm Nature about them as did the trees or the flowing water."[43]

The Yares all but adopt Denby and her son, and over the course of their extended stay, they reveal the reason Asheville residents shun them. It was their wartime loyalties that earned them such animosity from that nearby hub of Confederate commitment and activity. Jonathan's eighty-year-old father explains: "It was not their fights with wolves and bears that turned the people of Asheville agen the name of my boys and their father. They were the only men anigh hyear that stood out fur the Union from the first to the last. They couldn't turn agin the old flag, you see." When his sons, "known as extraordinar' strong men and powerful bearfighters," were much sought after by Union forces from Tennessee urging them to join their ranks, "they couldn't shed the blood of their old neighbors," and thus avoided military enlistment with either side. With the pressures of Confederate conscription in 1862, the elderly Yare told his guest, "they was driv out—four of them, Jonathan first—from under this roof, an' for five years they lay out on the mounting." They were hunted down "just as if they war wolves," their father stated. "But the boys knowed the mountings. Thars hundreds of caves and gullies thar whar no man ever ventured but them."[44]

The Yare boys found a means of supporting the Union cause from those caves and gullies by piloting "rebel deserters home through the mountings" and escorting fugitive Union prisoners safely to Federal lines in Tennessee. "Hundreds of them hev slep' in this very room, sayin' it was as ef they'd come back to their homes out of hell. They looked as ef they'd been thar, rally," the old man declared. Such activity led to repeated harassment by Confederate forces and Home Guardsmen, and in one shoot-out with the latter, Jonathan was badly injured, and his brother reports that "he war dyin' in a cave two mile up." Their sister Nancy took it on herself to sneak up and nurse him, which meant avoiding guards who had been posted to shoot any of the Yares on sight. While Jonathan survives, the family is plagued by further harassment that culminated in the Confederate arrest of not only Nancy, who was held in an Asheville jail for a month, but also their father, who is taken to Libby Prison in Richmond and held until all four boys give themselves up to authorities there. This they do, and come within a week of being hanged, saved only by Lee's surrender.[45]

Mrs. Denby, enamored of the family and their tale of continuing woe, urges them to move north, where they could become the beneficiaries of some of the hundreds of men whose lives they'd saved and paid so high a cost in doing so. But the Yares refuse her invitation, with Nancy explaining: "The Yares hev lived on the Old Black for four generations, Mistress Denby. It wouldn't do to kerry us down into towns. It must be powerful lonesome in them flat countries, with nothing but people about you. The mountings is always company, you see."[46] Thus, Rebecca Harding Davis suggested that, contrary to the conclusion to which her protagonist jumps when first confronted with the Yares and their habitation, nature could indeed ennoble its familiars, and in their case, it certainly had.

Constance Woolson's tale, "Crowder's Cove: A Story of the War" appeared in *Appleton's Journal* in March 1876, nine months after Davis's story was published in *Lippincott's*. A Midwesterner who wrote a number of stories and novels during the 1870s and 1880s, many of them based in the Great Lakes region, Woolson is probably remembered most for her romantic attachment to Henry James when they were both in Europe in the early 1880s, and for leaping to her death from a villa in Venice in 1894. She traveled through the South with her mother and sister for several months during Reconstruction, and at one point ventured into North Carolina's Blue Ridge Mountains. That trip inspired a series of southern-based sketches, including "Crowder's Cove," probably the best known of them.[47]

Woolson established in her first paragraph just how isolated and inaccessible her title locale is, and soon went on to convey just how welcome that isolation is to its sole residents, John Crowder and his family. "Crowder's Cove was far up in the mountains; the peaks seldom suffer level spaces so near their great chins," she wrote. "But this was a chance corner formed by the closely pressed meeting sides where the great cones are crowded together near the end of their chain," (by which she presumably meant Tennessee's Smoky Mountains). With only one point of access, a narrow gorge opening to the west, the cove "was like a little triangular shelf fitted into the corner of a room – as though some cyclop long ago had placed it there, high up under the sky, where he could keep his odds and ends conveniently."[48] Long after the cyclops had abandoned it, John Crowder found it and made it his own.

A nameless narrator who had made her way up to the cove soon after the war (a framing device suspiciously like that of Davis) asks Crowder if he is lonesome, which leads him to launch into a lengthy wartime narrative that serves as the centerpiece of the story. His wife, Miss Minerva, had been an Illinois schoolteacher who came south before the war to summer in the healthful mountain air. Upon marrying her, their household came to include his Yankee sister-in-law, Elinor, and an adolescent orphan, Sally, whom Minerva took under wing. The news of the attack on Fort Sumter drifted only slowly up to the cove; when it reached them, John simply went on with his planting, and he and his wife "were not easily turned from their comforts by anxieties for Charleston Harbor." More than most, Woolson stressed the linkage between geographical isolation and indifference to the war. While "from many a highland farm adventurous spirits rode off down the glens at night, and in the mornings they and the best horses were gone, gone to join Zollicoffer or John Morgan," she wrote, most made more practical choices:

> It took all their daylight to wrest a living from their stony fields, and they had no lounging-places where they could hear the news and be inspired. Each man lived with his family high up among the peaks or buried in some wild gorge, and was always at home by nightfall; for the rest he solaced himself cannily now and then with a moderate drop or two of the "moonlight whiskey," for which the mountains were famous, and bothered not about "the flag."[49]

By late 1861 the war could no longer be held at bay, and "even the remote mountain settlements began to wake." Both Union and Confederate forces eventually wend their way into Crowder's Cove, where its sole male occupant insists on identifying himself as neutral, which both sets of troops find far more offensive than if he'd merely claimed allegiance to the opposing side. As a result, Crowder finds himself harassed regularly by all comers, and the story consists of a series of travails that lead him and his family to the brink of ruin. It is the two girls who are ultimately drawn into the fray, as Elinor, a Unionist, and Sally, a Confederate, compete in a dramatic race by horseback down the mountain in attempts to warn the commands of rival forces gathering in the valley below. Each sought to relay to one army or the other plans they had overheard from a young misguided scout the girls had nursed when he'd wandered, badly wounded into the cove. Woolson concocted a rather implausible climax – Sally arrives first and saves the day for the Confederates – yet what remains most striking about her story, like Davis's "The Yares," is that she makes the physical environment a central determinant in the neutrality – or attempt at neutrality – claimed by her protagonist, as it was by many southern highlanders.

It was well over a century later that perhaps the most fully realized treatment of Appalachia as Civil War refuge appeared. Certainly, no fictional account of the war so consciously or so profoundly embraces the moral geography of the region as does Charles Frazier's *Cold Mountain* (1997). This intimate epic follows Inman, a western North Carolina native, and his struggle to escape a brutal and increasingly senseless war by returning home to an idealized natural world – one might even say a fully realized ecosystem – that for him will serve as both physical and spiritual refuge. Frazier clearly drew on much of the work discussed here, especially those postwar "escape" narratives by fugitives from Confederate prisons. In particular, he based his story on the experience of his own great-great uncle, Confederate enlistee W. P. Inman, who in late 1864 escaped from an Illinois prison camp and made the trek home – on foot no less – to his North Carolina home near Cold Mountain, a high but nondescript peak some twenty miles southwest of Asheville, where the Blue Ridge Mountains merge with the Great Smokies. He was within three miles of home when he met his death in a skirmish with an especially ruthless Home Guard unit that had plagued local residents for much of the war.[50]

Frazier wrote in a far different era of environmental consciousness, and yet he, like Trowbridge, seems to have drawn less on any affiliation with either preservation, ecological, agrarian, or back-to-the-land movements (though the influence of all of those are evident in his text) and more on personal experiences. A native of western North Carolina, he was raised in the Smoky Mountain communities of Andrews and Franklin, and his grandparents had a farm at the foot of the actual Cold Mountain, which he spent childhood summers exploring on foot. Yet his first writings were on very different mountain locales. His doctoral dissertation at the University of South Carolina was titled "The Geography of Possibility: Man in the Landscape of Recent Western Fiction," (1986); the year before, he produced a travel narrative based on an extensive trip he made through South America, called *Adventuring in the Andes* (1985), published by the Sierra Club.[51]

Perhaps the most intriguing influence on Frazier's environmental thinking was the work of an ancient Chinese poet who was associated with a remote mountain retreat named Han-shan, which by sheer coincidence, happens to mean "Cold Mountain" in Chinese. According to legend, this farmer, a Zen Buddhist (and called Han-Shan as well), left a home plagued by poverty and family discord. After several years of wandering, he found himself at Cold Mountain and spent the rest of his life pursuing enlightenment through communing with the natural world, a quest he expressed through his poetry. Frazier seems to have come to Han-shan's poetry through translations by 1960s environmentalist and poet Gary

Snyder, who wrote that "Chinese poetry, at its finest, seems to have found a center within the tripod of humanity, spirit, and nature. With strategies of apparent simplicity and understatement, it moves from awe before history to a deep breath before nature." The appeal of that approach to Frazier is abundantly clear in the fictional Inman's turning from war – or the forces of history, and retreating to his own Cold Mountain where he can fully "take a deep breath before nature." Frazier uses a passage from Han-Shan's poetry as the novel's epigraph, and often conveys Inman's musings over the link between spiritual peace and place through mere paraphrases of his poems.[52]

Frazier places his protagonist in a Confederate hospital in Raleigh, where he was treated for a neck wound received during the siege of Petersburg. Fearful that he will be sent back into the hellish fray that the Virginia theater had become, Inman deserts and begins a long cross-state trek, moving westward toward home and a mountain, "a healing realm that soared in his mind as a place where all his scattered forces might gather." From the beginning, Inman imbues his highland homeland with unique qualities that alone could serve as the balm for the psychic wounds from which he suffers so deeply. While the war had "burned away" whatever religious faith he had once had, he "could not abide by a universe composed of only what he could see, especially when it was frequently foul. So he had held to the idea of another world, a better place, and he figured he might was well consider Cold Mountain to be the location of it as anywhere."[53]

Most scholarly assessments of *Cold Mountain* have acknowledged the strong sense of place it evokes and its emphasis on the natural world, but none has done so more fully or effectively than Albert Way. In an insightful essay on the environmental knowledge demonstrated by the novel's leading characters, Way notes that like other Appalachian writers, Frazier treats the environment as a character, with the human players distinguished by how they read nature, and by their familiarity (or lack thereof) with folkways related to flora, fauna, agricultural practices, and seasonal change as understood in the mid-nineteenth century. As such, Way sees the novel as a product of that romanticized vision of people's relation to the land and sense of order so closely associated with the southern agrarian tradition.[54] I would argue that it fits fully within this other tradition as well – that in which the war drove perceptions of the mountain South as moral high ground, and made of it both a literal, psychological, and emotional refuge from a world gone terribly wrong.

Inman's displacement from the mountains and his utter disillusionment with the war lead him to judge his lowland surroundings as both aesthetically and functionally inferior to his native habitat and to newly appreciate the comparative merits of high altitudes over low. Moving through the eastern Carolina sandhills early in his journey, he comments on his surroundings: "Nothing but trash trees. Jack pine, slash pine, red cedar. Inman hated these planed-off, tangled pinebrakes. All this flat land. Red dirt. Mean towns. He had fought over ground like this from the piedmont to the sea, and it seemed like nothing but the place where all that was foul and sorry had flowed downhill and pooled in low spots." As he approaches the wide and uncrossable Cape Fear River, Inman's frustration at the obstacle it poses spurs his animosity; he describes it as "a shit-brown clog to his passage" and a "broad ditch [that] was a smear on the landscape," with waters as "foul as the contents of an outhouse pit." All of this is a far cry from what he thought running waters should and could be: "Where he was from, the word *river* meant rocks and moss and the sound of white water moving fast under the spell of a great deal of collected gravity. Not a river in his whole territory was wider than you could pitch a stick across, and in every one of them you could see the bottom where you looked."[55]

The idea of mountains as refuge from the forces of war play out in more specific ways as Inman eventually moves into the western part of the state and closer to home. One of his most memorable encounters is that with a "pinched-off little scrag of a person" he meets as she is setting traps in a forest of hemlocks; "there was not much but its head and shoulders showing above a bed of talk bracken burnt by frost, each brown fern tip adangle with the bright drop of collected fog." (As the story shifts into the mountains, Frazier works harder at forefronting nature's many layers and intricacies; more than most of his nineteenth-century predecessors, the flora and fauna are as integral to his Appalachia as is its topographical distinctiveness.) When Inman appears faint, the strange little woman invites him to her nearby camp. She leads him up and over craggy cliffs and great slabs of rock, and as the fog clears, he realizes they're on "a great knobby mountain," on whose north flank "was a figuration of rocks, the profile of an immense bearded man reclining across the horizon." In short, she lives on Grandfather Mountain, the most pronounced – and allegedly the oldest – peak among the Blue Ridge Mountains.[56]

Frazier lingers over the physical setting that Inman's benefactor calls home, and on the sheer materialism of her existence. Her camp consists of a "narrow and heavily treed cut in the mountain, a dark pocket of cove, odorous with plant rot and soggy earth." He sees a decrepit old wheeled caravan—"a construction that had evidently begun life nomadic but had taken root." Three large ravens strut around on the roof, and two dozen goats wander the grounds. Upon entering the dim cramped quarters, he finds pinned to the walls "spidery pen-and-ink sketches of plants and animals ... with a great deal of tiny writing around the margins. Bundles of dried herbs and roots hung on strings from the ceiling, and various brown peltry of small animals lay in stacks among the books and on the floor. The wings of a nighthawk ... rested upon the highest book pile." This goat woman, for all of her hermitic eccentricities, knows well and fully appreciates the natural world into which she has cast her lot—and as such, she emerges as the most indelible of Frazier's many supporting characters. She describes to Inman the life she has shaped for herself at this site:

> What I soon learned was that a body can mainly live off goats, their milk and cheese. And their meat in times of year when they start increasing to more than I need. I pull whatever wild greens is in season. Trap birds. There's a world of food growing volunteer if you know where to look. And there's a little town about a half day's walk north. I go barter off cheese for taters, meal, lard, and the like. Brew simples from plants and sell them. Medicine, Tinctures, Salve. Conjure warts.[57]

She then asks Inman about the war, why it was waged and why men felt compelled to fight it. She forces him to ponder for the first time why indeed he had been drawn to a conflict in which he felt very little vested interest; he ultimately concludes that while "men talked of war as if they committed it to preserve what they had and what they believed," he guessed that "it was boredom with the repetition of the daily rounds that made them take up weapons. The endless arc of the sun, wheel of seasons. War took men out of that circle of regular life and made a season of its own, not much dependent on anything else." As irrational or superficial as that seemed, he was forced to conclude that "he had not been immune to its pull."[58] Through his deceptively spare and simple prose, Frazier captures the essence of issues with which historians have grappled for years, and make this realization all the more poignant by making his inquisitor this wise and wizened old hermit.

Inman's encounter with the goat woman proves transformative. Although not the first refuge he has sought or taken advantage of, it is certainly the most meaningful to him and to Frazier (who devotes a twenty-page chapter to this episode), in part because it is a refuge fully defined by its Appalachian setting. As he is nursed back to full strength, Inman finds himself becoming once more attuned to the natural bounties offered by mountain life, if only because it offers such contrast to the unnatural existence he has endured over the past three years. "Sooner or later, you get awful tired and just plain sick of watching people kill one another for every kind of reason at all, using whatever implements fall to hand," he tells himself. "So that morning he had looked at the berries and the birds and had felt cheered by them, happy they had waited for him to come to his senses, even though he feared himself deeply at variance with such elements of the harmonious." From his encounter with this woman who has chosen for herself a life of refuge that has nothing to do with the war, Inman again toys with the idea that he himself could restore his spiritual or psychic equilibrium by emulating her model of living off the land. He "tried to picture himself living similarly hermetic in just such a stark and lonely refuge on Cold Mountain. Build a cabin on a misty frag of rock and go for months without seeing another of his kind. A life just as pure and apart as the goat woman's seemed to be."[59]

When Inman eventually makes his departure from the goat woman and resumes his journey home, she tells him simply "Watch yourself" and then offers him a gift. It's a "square of paper on which was drawn in great detail a globular blue-purple berry cluster of the carrion flower plant in autumn."[60] So ends the chapter and so Frazier signals once again what infuses this particular encounter with such significance, by offering a consummate depiction of the qualitative sense of this particular natural world that bound it so closely to the larger issues of war and its senselessness.

Meanwhile, back on the home front toward which Inman slowly moved, the war has devolved into the vicious irregular warfare that infested so much of the southern highlands. A band of outliers have become cave dwellers, which allows Frazier to provide that venue with a very different set of residents with very different agendas than the noble uses to which Trowbridge's characters put Cudjo's Cave well over a century earlier. Pangle, one of Cold Mountain's ne'er-do-wells, had taken up residence in its cave before the war. "Raised somewhat casually," Frazier tells us, the general feeling was that Pangle held no value, for he could not think right nor could be pressed into labor, so "he had therefore been set loose in early manhood and had spent the time since wandering Cold Mountain." Like the goat woman on Grandfather Mountain, Pangle came to know Cold Mountain's "every slit and chink"; but unlike her, he has practically morphed into one of its wild creatures:

Ate what presented itself, with little discrimination between grubs and venison. Paid little heed to time of day, and during the brighter moon phases went largely nocturnal. In summer he slept on the beds of fragrant duff between hemlock and balsam except in rains of some duration, when he sheltered under rock ledges; In winter, he took instruction from toad and groundhog and bear: he denned up in a cave, scarcely moving during the cold months.[61]

When, late in the war, outliers took up residence in his cave, Pangle merely joins their band and welcomes their company. Stobrod, the father of Ruby, Ada's mountain mentor, takes Pangle under his wing and teaches him to play a fiddle, and then a banjo the band had confiscated during a raid on a well-to-do farmer nearby. This man Walker, "a leading slaveholder [who] fell afoul of the cave society," becomes their target in what seems to be their only partisan-driven action during the war. The plunder from that raid makes for a transformed subterranean refuge, and for some of Frazier's most striking imagery. The outliers use their loot to create a finely decorated, if incongruous, cavern décor: "Washington propped in a niche of the wall, candles in silver holders. Table set with Wedgwood and silver, though many of [the outliers] had eaten all their lives from table service made entirely of gourd and horn." It also leads to a new level of decadence and degeneracy among the cave dwellers, who do very little after the raid but make music. (Walker's banjo was the prize possession claimed by Pangle and Stobrod.) Other than that, they drink his good liquor and ate nothing but stolen jellies. "They slept only when they were too drunk to play, and they have not traveled to the cave mouth frequently enough even to keep track of when day and night occurred."[62]

Such capitulation to newfound wealth by these corruptible and purposeless outliers stands in great contrast to the behavior of the threesome inhabiting Cudjo's Cave, each of whom has a far higher calling in the utilization of their rocky refuge. They are also the creation of a far more ideologically driven novelist with a far more political agenda that one would expect to see in 1864 more than one would in a novelist writing of the same war and the same dilemmas in 1997. But the contrast is nonetheless revealing, for just as caves served multiple agendas and functions based on the character of those they harbored, so too did the Appalachian wilderness at large. For Trowbridge and Frazier, and those multiple writers in between, aspects of nature, topography, and flora and fauna serve as active agents in shaping both the morals and morale, for better or worse, of those who sought refuge in the Confederacy's southern highlands.

Frazier articulated his intent far more fully than did anyone but Trowbridge. Just as the latter insisted he was first inspired by visions of caves, burning forests, and waterfalls, so Frazier later wrote of his research agenda: "I wanted to know what that world's processes—human and nonhuman—were, how things looked and how they worked. Subsistence farming, vernacular architecture, herbal medicine, and the mysterious ways of wild turkeys, for instance." His priorities seem not so far removed from those of Inman himself. "Walking a few miles of remnant dirt road that once linked two now-vanished villages," Frazier wrote, "or sitting awhile in a small tract of Appalachian forest often proved far more useful than a stack of Matthew Brady photographs in shaping my sense of the past, or at least the particular slice of the past that held my interest."[63] Both novelists saw the physical environment of southern Appalachia as central to the stories they sought to tell and how they chose to tell them. To varying degrees, so too did every other writer discussed here, whether recounting their own experiences or building on the accounts of others to create more imaginary versions of the strength of those hills.

Frazier used as a second epigraph to *Cold Mountain* an odd statement made by Charles Darwin in an 1839 journal entry: "It is difficult to believe in the dreadful but quiet war of organic beings going on in the peaceful woods & smiling fields."[64] If Darwin was referring to those creatures, from insects to rodents, who live their lives relatively unseen by human beings, Frazier obviously had something more in mind. War, he seemed to suggest, is antithetical to wilderness. And yet, the Civil War, like most wars, was waged as fully in peaceful woods and smiling fields as in any other setting. Indeed its battlegrounds usually consisted of those very settings, and its most destructive clashes took place in one or the other. But it played out as well in that most extensive and formidable of southern wildernesses—Appalachia—in very different ways determined by both the region's demographic and environmental peculiarities. During the war, sparse settlement, vast uninhabited forests, and rugged terrain drew different sorts of people to the region—bushwhackers, fugitives, escaped prisoners, deserters, and civilian refugees. It was also home to residents who merely thought they could simply sit the war out because they had chosen to carve lives for themselves in so remote and inaccessible a region.

Yet sitting out the war or hiding from it rarely proved realistic options for any of these people, as the conflict came to permeate nearly every part of the southern highlands to one degree or another. Indeed, it was often the very presence of those seeking refuge in mountain hollows, caves, and coves that spurred the guerrilla warfare that so plagued local inhabitants. For nearly all of the individuals dealt with here, whether imaginary or real, such respite proved at best, temporary, at worst, nonexistent.

Penn Hapgood thought he could distance himself from the world below by moving into the Cumberlands, and yet the very act of Cudjo and Pomp in taking him into their cavernous hideaway drew unrelenting harassment and combat to their door. Hapgood's distinction between highland and lowland – "Up here, what glory, what peace! Down yonder, what hatred, violence, and sin!" – proved all too fleeting a reality, and all too flawed an assumption, as it did for so many others as well. Both the Yares and the Crowders demonstrated their naiveté in believing that the sheer seclusion of their homes would ensure that they could remain neutral and aloof from a conflict waged elsewhere. And Inman's belief that merely by returning home he would find peace and order proved a tragic miscalculation when he was brutally gunned down just before he reached his beloved Cold Mountain. Of all the characters considered here, only the goat woman on Grandfather Mountain manages to distance herself from the war, at least until she chooses to bring a wounded deserter into her lair. Other than engaging Inman in a discussion of the conflict and its meaning, of which she has only secondhand knowledge, the war has no impact on her daily existence, thus making her the sole success story cited here in terms of situating herself in a wilderness that fully shields her from the brutal upheavals beyond.

Just as these writers portrayed southern highlanders in both positive and negative terms – treating them with either admiration and affection or contempt and condescension, their depictions of the distinctive environment that so shaped their characters' identities, experiences, and fates are just as varied, as they conjured settings that were sometimes sublime and ennobling, but just as often sinister and treacherous. Will Harney's title "A Strange Land and Peculiar People" quickly became a catchphrase applied to southern Appalachia for many decades thereafter; as pejorative as it was, or came to be, it does suggest that the people and the land on which they lived were inextricably linked to a greater extent than was true elsewhere. The Civil War made that linkage even more inextricable, as it imposed upon the highlands a sense of moral geography that few other parts of the South could claim. For this war and these people, the wilderness was very much an active player. As for so many highlanders themselves, any claims to its neutrality proved futile.

Notes

1. Frederick Douglass, *The Life and Times of Frederick Douglass* (1892; repr., New York: Macmillan, 1962), 273–74.

2. Richard Hinton interview with John Brown and John Kagi in August 1858, in Richard Warch and Jonathan F. Fanton, eds., *John Brown* (Englewood Cliffs, N.J.: Prentice-Hall, 1973), 54 (second quote). For other treatments of the southern highlands as central to Brown's insurrection plan, see Wilbur H. Siebert, *The Underground Railroad from Slavery to Freedom* (New York: Macmillan, 1898), 118; and Jules Abel, *Man on Fire: John Brown and the Cause of Liberty* (New York: Macmillan, 1971), 245–48. For his final words, see David S. Reynolds, *John Brown, Abolitionist: The Man Who Killed Slavery, Sparked the Civil War, and Seeded Civil Rights* (New York: Vintage Press, 2005), 395.

3. Allen W. Batteau, *The Invention of Appalachia* (Tucson: University of Arizona Press, 1990), 53. The correlation between the region's human inhabitants and moral geography was not always positive, of course. Ellsworth Huntington, a Yale geographer, reflected the views of many early twentieth-century observers in linking the low character of southern highlanders to the perpetual wilderness in which they settled, noting that "better land gets the better people" ("A Geographer's Views of Mountaineers," unpub. manuscript, ca. 1920, Ellsworth Huntington Papers, Yale University Library, quoted in Jill Fraley, "Missionaries to the Wilderness: A History of Land, Identity, and Moral Geography in Appalachia," *Journal of Appalachian Studies* 17 [Spring/Fall 2011]: 35).

4. First quote in Leon F. Williams, "The Vanishing Appalachian: How to 'Whiten' the Problem," in *Blacks in Appalachia*, ed. William H. Turner and Edward Cabbell (Lexington: University Press of Kentucky, 1985), 201; the second from Maryville College president Samuel Tyndale Wilson in 1906, quoted in John C. Inscoe, "Race and Racism in Nineteenth-Century Appalachia: Myths, Realities, and Ambiguities," in *Appalachia in the Making: The Mountain South in the Nineteenth Century*, ed. Mary Beth Pudup, Dwight B. Billings, and Altina Waller, 103–31 (Chapel Hill: University of North Carolina Press, 1996).

5. James W. Taylor, *Alleghania: A Geographical and Statistical Memoir* (St., Paul, Minn.: James Davenport, 1862), 1–2, 15–16.

6. William Goodrich, *God's Handiwork in the Sea and the Mountains: Sermons Preached after a Summer Vacation* (Cleveland: Privately published, n.d.), quoted in Jan Davidson's introduction to Frances Louisa Goodrich, *Mountain Homespun* (Knoxville: University of Tennessee Press, 1989), 13.

7. Yael Sternhell, *Routes of War: The World of Movement in the Confederate South* (Cambridge, Mass.: Harvard University Press, 2012), 7, 4.

8. Lisa M. Brady, *War upon the Land: Military Strategy and the Transformation of Southern Landscapes during the Civil War* (Athens: University of Georgia Press, 2012), 14. In her introduction, Brady offers an astute analysis of the distinctions between "nature," "landscape" and "wilderness" (12–14) in nineteenth-century usage, terms with which I play a little more fast and loose here. See also Brady, "The Wilderness of War: Nature and Strategy in the American Civil War," *Environmental History* 10 (June 2005): 421–47.

9. According to Robert A. Lively, sixty-nine novels about the Civil War were published between 1862 and 1869; by Albert Menendez's count, seventy-six such novels appeared between 1860 and 1868; see Lively, *Fiction Fights the Civil War: An Unfinished Chapter in the Literary History of the American People* (Chapel Hill: University of North Carolina Press, 1957), 22; Menendez, *Civil War Novels: An Annotated Bibliography* (New York: Garland, 1986), x–xi. For a thorough discussion of the reception of *Cudjo's Cave*, see Dean Rehberger's introduction to a recent edition of John Townshend Trowbridge, *Cudjo's Cave* (Tuscaloosa: University of Alabama Press, 2001), v–vi, xiv. All references to the novel are to this edition.

10. John Townshend Trowbridge, *My Own Story, With Recollections of Noted Persons* (Boston: Houghton, Mifflin, 1903), 260–62. For another treatment of Trowbridge's wartime and postwar writings, see Edmond Wilson, *Patriotic Gore: Studies in the Literature of the American Civil War* (New York: McGraw Hill, 1962), chap. 6.

11. Coincidentally Trowbridge's novel appeared within a few weeks of the publication of George Perkins Marsh's seminal *Man and Nature*, though Trowbridge never acknowledged the latter as an influence. See David Lowenthal, introduction to George Perkins Marsh, *Man and Nature* (Cambridge, Mass.: Harvard University Press, 1965), xxi.

12. Trowbridge, *My Own Story*, 137.

13. Ibid., 272. Trowbridge may also have been influenced by Harriet Beecher Stowe's second novel, *Dred: A Tale of the Great Dismal Swamp* (1856), in which, as her subtitle suggests, she made the physical setting of a fugitive slave hideout integral to her plot; Trowbridge made several references to *Dred* in his memoir (*My Own Story*, 228, 243). See Ian F. Finseth, *Shades of Green: Visions of Nature in the Literature of American Slavery, 1770–1860* (Athens: University of Georgia Press, 2009), 251–71.

14. Tourism in southern Appalachia increased considerably during the 1850s, as did accounts of the region in literary monthlies like *Atlantic* and *Harper's*, periodicals in which Trowbridge himself published. See Kevin O'Donnell and Helen Hollingsworth, eds., *Seekers of Scenery: Travel Writing from Southern Appalachia, 1840–1900* (Knoxville: University of Tennessee Press, 2004), 18–20. On Lincoln's interest in the area, see Earl J. Hess, *Lincoln Memorial University and the Shaping of Appalachia* (Knoxville: University of Tennessee Press, 2011), chap. 1.

15. After the war, Trowbridge visited East Tennessee as part of the tour that would result in what is now his best-known work, *The South*, and congratulated himself on how well he had described the physical setting of his sole Appalachian-based novel. Rehberger, introduction, viii–xi, xvii. For his impressions of the region more broadly, see J. T. Trowbridge, *The South: A Tour of Its Battlefields and Ruined Cities; A Journey through the Desolated States, and Talks with the People, 1867*, ed. J. H. Segars (repr. Macon, Ga.: Mercer University Press, 2006), chaps. 31 and 32.

16. Lively, *Fiction Fights the Civil War*, 49–51. Lively points out that *Cudjo's Cave* is one of the few fictional treatments of the war in which slaves play a prominent role.

17. Trowbridge, *Cudjo's Cave*, 142–43. Trowbridge devotes a full chapter to "The Wonders of the Cave," in which later refugees are presented with even more of its features, several of which would turn deadly for those unwanted intruders soon

to follow. In an "author's note" at the novel's end, he explained that two separate and distinct caves have been combined into one for his story, "which is for the most part imaginary, but which, I trust, will not be considered as too improbable fiction in a region where caves and 'sinks' abound" (503). For an insightful treatment of another, far more prominent cave with a very different association with slaves through the antebellum and war years, see Peter West, "Trying the Dark: Mammoth Cave and the Racial Imagination, 1839–1869," *Southern Spaces*, February 2010, http://www.southernspaces.org/2010.

18. Trowbridge, *Cudjo's Cave*, 225–26, 132–33.
19. Ibid., 145.
20. Ibid., 219.
21. Ibid., 143.
22. Ibid., 400.
23. Trowbridge, *My Own Story*, 261. The moral geography of the Cumberland Gap was further accentuated by the fact that Union general O. O. Howard chose it as the site of Lincoln Memorial College in 1897 as a means of rewarding the descendants of wartime Unionists in the region. See Hess, *Lincoln Memorial University*.
24. Kenneth W. Noe, "Exterminating Savages: The Union Army and Mountain Guerrillas in Southern West Virginia, 1861–1862," in *The Civil War in Appalachia: Collected Essays*, ed. Kenneth W. Noe and Shannon H. Wilson (Knoxville: University of Tennessee Press, 1997), 114–16, 119. On how guerrillas used the environment to their advantage in the Arkansas and Missouri Ozarks, see Matthew M. Stith, "'The Deplorable Condition of the Country': Nature, Society, and War on the Trans-Mississippi Frontier," *Civil War History* 58 (September 2012): 322–47.
25. Ibid., 110. For similar examples, see Brian D. McKnight, *Contested Borderland: The Civil War in Appalachian Kentucky and Virginia* (Lexington: University Press of Kentucky, 2006.)
26. Both quotes from Philip Shaw Paludan, *Victims: A True Story of the Civil War* (Knoxville: University of Tennessee Press, 1981), 92. Paludan's book remains the most thorough account of the Shelton Laurel massacre.
27. Ibid., 92, 94–95.
28. Jonathan D. Sarris, *A Separate Civil War: Southern Mountain Communities at War, 1861–1865* (Charlottesville: University Press of Virginia, 2006), 86–87.
29. Quoted in Sternhell, *Routes of War*, 127. In a chapter entitled "Southerners on the Run," Sternhell reminds us that "the geography of flight" was a phenomenon evident throughout the wartime South, and involved disparate groups of fugitives, often interracial, who were thrown together through their joint efforts to evade Confederate authorities.
30. See William B. Hesseltine, "The Underground Railroad from Confederate Prisons to East Tennessee," *East Tennessee Historical Society's Publications* 2 (1930), 55–69; Arnold Ritt, "The Escape of Federal Prisoners through East Tennessee, 1861–1865" (MA thesis, University of Tennessee, 1945); and John C. Inscoe, "'Moving through Deserter Country': Fugitive Accounts of the Inner Civil War in Southern Appalachia," in Noe and Wilson, *Civil War in Appalachia*, 158–86 (on slaves as collaborators, see pp. 165–71).

31. Several noted that they took refuge in caves and caverns, and often encountered Unionists, deserters, or other outliers there. See, for example, J. Madison Drake, *Fast and Loose in Dixie* (New York: Authors Publishing Co., 1880), section entitled "In the Earth's Bowels," 157–59; W. H. Shelton, "A Hard Road Out of Dixie," *Century Magazine* 40 (October 1890): 940; and John W. Ennis, *Adventures in Rebeldom* (New York: "Business Print," 1863), 34.

32. *Harper's Weekly*, September 19, 1863, 600–601, text on 603.

33. Drake, *Fast and Loose in Dixie*, 178–79.

34. Shelton, "A Hard Road Out of Dixie," 938–39.

35. William Burson, *A Race for Liberty; or My Capture, My Imprisonment, and My Escape* (Wellsville, Ohio: W. G. Foster, 1867), 98, 114.

36. Batteau, *Invention of Appalachia*, 40. See also the introduction to O'Donnell and Hollingsworth, eds., *Seekers of Scenery*, esp. 1–14.

37. On Harney and his journey through the Cumberlands, see Henry D. Shapiro, *Appalachia on Our Mind: The Southern Mountains and Mountaineers in the American Consciousness, 1870–1920* (Chapel Hill: University of North Carolina Press, 1978), 3–5. Shapiro opened his book with a description of Harney's travels, and claimed that "in a real sense it was Harnett and the editors of *Lippincott's* who 'discovered' Appalachia, for they were the first to assert [its] 'otherness'" (4). The essay, "A Strange Land and a Peculiar People," is reproduced in W. K. McNeil, ed., *Appalachian Images in Folk and Popular Culture* 2nd ed. (Knoxville: University of Tennessee Press, 1995), 45–58 (quote on 47).

38. Harney, "Strange Land and Peculiar People," 55–56.

39. O'Donnell and Hollingsworth, eds., *Seekers of Scenery*, 173. O'Donnell also notes that this story likely served as the impetus for Mary Noialles Murfree to set her stories in the region. "The Yares of the Black Mountains" appears in full in this volume (173–92), and is the version cited here. Curiously, a recent anthology of Davis's Civil War short stories does not include this story; nevertheless, it offers valuable context for her wartime experiences and how she translated them into fiction. See Sharon H. Harris and Robin L. Cadwallader, eds., *Rebecca Harding Davis's Stories of the Civil War Era: Selected Writings from the Borderlands* (Athens: University of Georgia Press, 2010); see also Jane A. Rose, "The Fiction of Rebecca Harding Davis: A Palimpsest of Domestic Ideology beneath a Surface of Realism" (PhD diss., University of Georgia, 1988).

40. Kenneth W. Noe provides the fullest treatment of this story and its significance in "'Deadened Color and Colder Horror': Rebecca Harding Davis and the Myth of Unionist Appalachia," in *Back Talk from Appalachia: Confronting Stereotypes*, ed. Dwight B. Billings, Gurney Norman, and Katherine Ledford, 85–97 (Lexington: University Press of Kentucky, 1999). For later manifestations of this Unionist myth, see John C. Inscoe, "'A Northern Wedge Thrust into the Heart of the Confederacy': Explaining Civil War Loyalties in the Age of Appalachian Discovery, 1900–1921," in Andrew L. Slap, ed., *Reconstructing Appalachia: The Civil War's Aftermath* (Lexington: University Press of Kentucky, 2010), 323–49.

41. North Carolina's Black Mountains are a small range wedged among the Blue Ridge a few miles northeast of Asheville. They form the tallest peaks in the southern Appalachians, and include Mount Mitchell, the highest point east of the

Rockies. See Timothy Silver, *Mount Mitchell and the Black Mountains: An Environmental History of the Highest Peaks in Eastern North America* (Chapel Hill: University of North Carolina Press, 2007).

42. Davis, "Yares of the Black Mountains," 183, 185.

43. Ibid., 185–86.

44. Ibid., 187–88.

45. Ibid., 188–91.

46. Ibid., 192.

47. Woolson's southern-based fiction, including "Crowder's Cove," was compiled into book form as *Rodman's Keeper: Southern Sketches* (1880), though citations here are to the original version that appeared in *Appleton's Journal*, March 18, 1876, 357–62. See Kathleen Diffley, ed., *Witness to Reconstruction: Constance Fenimore Woolson and the Postbellum South, 1873–1894* (Jackson: University Press of Mississippi, 2011).

48. Ibid., 357.

49. Ibid., 358.

50. Charles Frazier has given several versions of this story. See "Cold Mountain Diary: How the Author Found the Inspiration for His Novel among the Secrets Buried in the Backwoods of the Smoky Mountains," Salon.com, July 9, 2007; and Frazier, "Some Remarks on History and Fiction," in *Novel History: Historians and Novelists Confront America's Past (and Each Other)*, ed. Mark C. Carnes (New York: Simon & Shuster, 2001), 311–15.

51. M. Thomas Inge, "Charles Frazier: Cold Mountain," in *Still in Print: The Southern Novel Today*, ed. Jan Nordby Gretlund (Columbia: University of South Carolina Press, 2010), 19–20, 24.

52. Ibid., 24–27 (poem quoted on 27). Inge is the first scholar to advance the influence of Han-shan and Zen Buddhism on Frazier's thinking, and does so quite convincingly.

53. Charles Frazier, *Cold Mountain* (New York: Atlantic Monthly Press, 1997), 17.

54. Albert Way, "'A World Properly Put Together': Environmental Knowledge in Charles Frazier's *Cold Mountain*," *Southern Cultures* 10 (Winter 2004): 33–54. Another insightful essay that puts the novel in a more theoretical environmental context is Terry Gifford, "Terrain, Character, and Text: Is *Cold Mountain* by Charles Frazier a Post-Pastoral Novel?" *Mississippi Quarterly* 55 (Winter 2001–2), 87–96.

55. Frazier, *Cold Mountain*, 53, 65.

56. Ibid., 207–09. Drew A. Swanson provides an invaluable environmental treatment of this locale in "Marketing a Mountain: Changing Views of Environment and Landscape on Grandfather Mountain, North Carolina," *Appalachian Journal* 36 (Fall 2008/Winter 2009): 30–63. For a more contemporary description, see Jehu Lewis, "The Grandfather of North Carolina," *Lakeside Monthly*, September 1873, reprinted in O'Donnell and Hollingsworth, *Seekers of Scenery*, 307–17.

57. Frazier, *Cold Mountain*, 214–15.

58. Ibid., 216.

59. Ibid., 218. It is passages like this that most reflect the influence of the Chinese poet Han-Shan on Frazier. Note the striking parallels in this poem to Inman's sentiments: "If I hide out at Cold Mountain / Living off mountain plants and

berries – / All my lifetime, why worry? / One follows his karma through. / Days and months slip by like water, / Time is like sparks knocked off flint. / Go ahead and let the world change – / I'm happy to sit among these cliffs." Quoted in Inge, "Charles Frazier," 27.

    60. Frazier, *Cold Mountain*, 223.
    61. Ibid., 263.
    62. Ibid., 264–65.
    63. Frazier, "Some Remarks on History and Fiction," 315.
    64. Frazier, *Cold Mountain*, front matter.

SEVEN

Nature as Friction

Integrating Clausewitz into Environmental Histories of the Civil War

LISA M. BRADY

In late December 1862 Union general Ambrose Burnside developed plans to march across the Rappahannock and execute a massive turning movement against Confederate general Robert E. Lee's troops entrenched along the southern banks of the river. Burnside hoped to ring in the new year by trapping Lee and his Confederates against the river, capturing his army, and redeeming the recent Union defeat at Fredericksburg. In so doing, he would also establish a strong position for marching against Richmond, the ultimate Union goal. Under ideal conditions, Burnside's plan was viable, if risky. However, as often happens in war, conditions were nowhere near perfect.

On January 20, 1863, the day before Burnside planned to initiate the campaign, a winter wave cyclone passed into the area, bringing with it significant amounts of precipitation. "As soon as the general got his army in motion," historian James McPherson wrote, "the heavens opened, rain fell in torrents, and the Virginia roads turned to swamps."[1] As geographer Harold Winters has pointed out, the soils of the region are primarily ultisols—fine-grained, massive, heavily weathered soils that tend to form underlying clay layers that impede percolation of water once saturated. Excess moisture must then run off into streams or pool on the surface.[2] Despite worsening conditions, Burnside chose to push forward. Winters noted that the "churning action from moving men, horses, and equipment" turned the roads into "deep muddy tracks," and the end of the day on January 21 saw Burnside's nearly 75,000 men "bogged down and their equipment immobilized."[3] The next day the humiliated Union troops, still on the northern banks of the Rappahannock, retreated to their original base at Falmouth, haunted by jeers and taunts from their Confederate enemies. After Burnside's disaster, no Union general commenced a winter campaign in Virginia again.[4]

In analyzing why Burnside's so-called Mud March became such a colossal failure, several factors require attention. One element centers on Burnside's strategy and whether or not it was inherently flawed. By the standards of the day, his plan was neither brilliant nor incompetent, but it only had reluctant support from Burnside's fellow officers — a clear mark against it. However, had the rains not come and the roads stayed passable, the operation had a reasonable chance of success despite its critics. In the planning stages, Burnside had enjoyed fair weather and based his operations on the assumption that similar conditions would prevail. Another matter concerns whether or not the plan was effectively executed. The soldiers and the officers conducted themselves largely according to plan — as far as it was in their power to do so. A third issue is a question of leadership. Though the change in weather brought conditions that merited caution, Burnside's decision to press on was not unwarranted. Harold Winters noted, "As is common in military operations, the mission was paramount to all other factors. On that basis, and regardless of the weather," Burnside made his decision.[5] In addition to strategic imperatives, there were political influences that impinged on Burnside's deliberations. The Union troops had suffered a demoralizing defeat only a month before. The northern populace was losing faith in the army and Lincoln was pressing for a clear and decisive victory. All of these external pressures weighed on Burnside when he resolved to proceed.

In the end, the problem lay not with planning or execution but in leadership. It was Burnside's decision, and his alone, that resulted in failure. He erred in thinking his troops and his plan could overcome the obstacles nature presented. Burnside's lapse in judgment was a classic example of leadership failure in the face of what the nineteenth-century Prussian military theorist Carl von Clausewitz called "friction" (Ger.: *Friktion*).

In his now-classic treatise, *On War*, first published in 1832, Clausewitz outlined a universal paradox of warfare. He noted, "Everything [in war] looks simple; the knowledge required does not look remarkable, the strategic options are so obvious that by comparison the simplest problem of higher mathematics has an impressive scientific dignity. Once war has actually been seen the difficulties become clear; but it is still extremely hard to describe the unseen, all-pervading element that brings about this change of perspective." Clausewitz identified the source for this perceptual shift as friction, which he described as "the only concept that more or less corresponds to the factors that distinguish real war from war on paper." He explained, "The military machine – the army and everything related to it – is basically very simple and therefore seems easy to manage. But we should bear in mind that none of its components is of one piece: each part is composed of individuals, every one of whom retains his potential of friction." To illustrate, Clausewitz described the ideal workings of a battalion in which experience, leadership, and discipline seamlessly guide the actions of all involved. Practice, however, is "very different" from theory, Clausewitz noted, because "every fault and exaggeration of the theory is instantly exposed in war. A battalion is made up of individuals, the least important of whom may chance to delay things or somehow make them go wrong."[6] As a point of friction (or, in other words, as an agent of historical change) the individual, no matter how insignificant his role, becomes the fulcrum upon which war pivots.

Clausewitz argued that overcoming friction is a primary task of any good commanding officer. "An understanding of friction is a large part of that much-admired sense of warfare which a good general is supposed to possess. To be sure, the best general is not the one who is most familiar with the idea of friction, and who takes it most to heart," he explained. Instead "the good general must know friction in order to overcome it whenever possible, and in order not to expect a standard of achievement in his operations which this very friction makes impossible."[7] Here was where Burnside failed – he pressed forward without deviating from his original plan despite clear indicators that conditions were against him. Burnside's decision, an obvious example of Clausewitzian friction, cost him the campaign and his career.

If Burnside's choice demonstrates the element of human friction in war, the change in weather and resulting degradation of marching conditions illustrates another aspect of Clausewitz's theory. Clausewitz argued that the friction of human agency – that is, the problem of individuals making decisions or acting independently – is compounded by additional elements of chance. The most visible example of this, perhaps, is weather, which Clausewitz singled out for explanatory purpose: "Fog can prevent the enemy from being seen in time, a gun from firing when it should, a report from reaching the commanding officer. Rain can prevent a battalion from arriving, make another late by keeping it not three but eight hours on the march, ruin a cavalry charge by bogging down the horses in mud, etc." While he acknowledged that "it would take volumes to cover all difficulties" and that he would "exhaust the reader" if he "really tried to deal with the whole range of minor troubles that must be faced in war," Clausewitz's choice of natural forces as the most illustrative case of chance is revealing and extremely useful.[8]

As Clausewitz pointed out, wars may be planned on paper but they are fought in nature, and environmental forces and conditions are therefore fundamental players in military engagements. This was not a revelation when *On War* was published, nor will it astonish anyone who has ever thought about war. It was certainly no surprise to Civil War combatants, regardless of rank, who contended with mud, disease, heat, and insects, among other environmental challenges, on a daily basis. However, we can draw deeper insight from the platitude if we recast nature away from existing only as an element of chance, as Clausewitz suggested it was, toward possessing agency, as environmental historians have argued it does. In doing so, Clausewitz's notion of friction can provide a linguistic and conceptual bridge between military and environmental history, making mutually intelligible two fields that have a history of talking around each other.

What follows is not a new analysis of specific Civil War battles or strategies but rather an attempt to reveal confluences of analytical approaches between military and environmental history through the lens of a specific natural phenomenon – acoustic shadows. The outcome of several Civil War battles, and the careers of their commanding officers, hinged in part on this acoustical anomaly. Where they occurred, acoustic shadows created uncertainty, thereby causing the battle to diverge from plans and testing the leadership skills of the officers in charge. This uncertainty fits the definition of friction as well as the concept of nature's agency, revealing that military and environmental historians share common ground after all.

Defining Nature as Friction

Carl von Clausewitz (1780–1831) wrote *On War* between about 1816 and 1831, after the end of the Napoleonic Wars and during the initial stages of the Industrial Revolution. Although his treatise occasionally compares armies to machines, it is unlikely that Clausewitz was adopting the language of industrialization to elucidate his ideas.[9] Instead, he developed his theory of warfare based on his observations of human nature, the commonalities he saw in the history of warfare, and on his direct experiences with combat prior to 1815. His goal in writing *On War* was not to establish principles for conducting warfare – he was well aware that every war, indeed every battle, was unique—but instead to present methods for learning how to respond to the exigencies of war.[10] Among his most durable propositions is that war universally entails an element of uncertainty—that is, friction—that cannot be avoided. Great leaders might be able to overcome its challenges, but they cannot prepare for every chance occurrence.

Clausewitz scholars long have debated the meaning of friction as well as the continued applicability of his treatise as a whole to military affairs.[11] In recent years, some have turned to the social, behavioral, and natural sciences for models and insight. In 1993 Alan Beyerchen published "Clausewitz, Nonlinearity, and the Unpredictability of War," in which he suggested that nonlinear science and chaos theory better approximate Clausewitz's notions of friction and chance than any other interpretive framework. He argued that Clausewitz saw war as a "nonlinear phenomenon" that "is inherently unpredictable by analytical means."[12] He further asserted that Clausewitz "perceived and articulated the nature of war as an energy-consuming phenomenon involving competing and interactive factors, attention to which reveals a messy mix of order and unpredictability."[13] Beyerchen noted that, for Clausewitz, friction encompassed "two different but related notions": one was "the physical sense of resistance embodied in the word itself, which in Clausewitz's time was being related to heat in ways that would lead ultimately to the Second Law of Thermodynamics and the concept of entropy"; the other is more analogous to information theory's definition of "noise," which describes the difficulty of extracting important information from a constant communication stream.[14]

Like Beyerchen, Barry D. Watts looked to science to make sense of Clausewitz's notion of friction. Where Beyerchen hoped to elucidate the concept in light of Clausewitz's general theory, Watts intended to analyze friction as it applied to modern and future war. He, too, concluded that nonlinear dynamics was the best model for understanding friction, but his chapter on evolutionary biology adds particular insight into the friction phenomenon. There, Watts examined the ways that human physiological and psychological capabilities limit soldiers' abilities to perform during battle. "There are," he argued, "finite limits, grounded in biology and evolution, to the capabilities of humans to receive sensory data, orient themselves by integrating that input with prior experience and information, reach plausible decisions about what to do next, and act upon those decisions."[15] Although his conclusions appear somewhat deterministic with regard to human evolution, he acknowledged that technology might serve to reduce friction in war. However, Watts noted, "friction will probably manifest itself in other ways or in areas that we may not even be able to predict."[16] This led him to examine what nonlinear dynamics might reveal about friction. "Nonlinear dynamics arise from repeated iteration or feedback. A system, whether physical or mathematical, starts in some initial state. That initial state provides the input to a feedback mechanism which determines the new state of the system" and so on, creating a system that "can be more complex and less predictable than one might suppose."[17]

Nonlinear dynamics and chaos theory are familiar to environmental historians, who often turn to the science of ecology for insight into the dynamic relationships human societies have developed with the nonhuman world.[18] Current ecological models recognize that, like human organizations, natural forces and systems are not monolithic and do not tend toward stasis or order. They, too, have constituent parts that may act independently of one another in ways that may not be anticipated. That is, nature's complexity is not always obvious, and elements of it may act in unexpected ways. For example, in a 2008 study, ecologists Becks and Arndt concluded, "In nature, environmental conditions may change on various time scales. Thus, transitions between different types of dynamic behavior may occur frequently. . . . This makes it likely that short bursts of chaos occur commonly but are often overlooked in the real world."[19] Nature's mutable and potentially unpredictable character approximates the role of the individual in Clausewitz's theory, demanding that humans adapt their actions and their decisions on changing environmental conditions. Thus, applying Clausewitz's definition of friction to nature, as well as to the human individual, allows us to understand the history of war in promising new ways.

Nature as Friction: Acoustic Shadows

One particularly instructive example of nature as friction is the phenomenon of acoustic shadows, which are created by a variety of natural conditions that affect the transmission of sound, leading to problems with communication and, in at least three instances during the Civil War, challenges in leadership. Acoustic shadow is a phenomenon characterized by sound traveling in unexpected ways. Often generated by anomalous weather events or topographical conditions, acoustic shadows cause sound to either be stifled or amplified, depending on the peculiarities of the situation. In an acoustic shadow, sounds such as cannon fire might be carried more than fifteen, perhaps as far as fifty, miles away, giving the impression that a battle is raging in a place it is not; or the same sound might fail to travel even two miles, thus preventing reinforcements from knowing an engagement is taking place. Physicist Charles Ross, who has written articles and a book about acoustic shadows during the Civil War, identified four potential causes for the occurrence of the phenomenon. The first two, wind direction and sound absorption, Ross suggested, are the "simplest and most common." Individuals downwind from the source of sound hear it better than those upwind. "In the second instance – sound absorption – material [such as vegetation, dense fog, or terrain] between the sound source and the listener absorbs most of the original energy, rendering the sound inaudible." A third reason for an acoustic shadow is air temperature change due to increases in altitude. Sound waves travel faster in warmer air, thus "the part of the sound wave nearer the ground travels faster than the upper part," bending the entire wave upward and "making audibility at a distance worse than it would be if the air were all the same temperature." Sometimes, however, temperature inversions, in which warmer air lays atop cooler air, cause sound to bend back toward earth, thus improving audibility. The fourth possibility is due to changing wind speed, also affected by altitude. "Winds generally move faster the farther they get from ground and its friction. As in a temperature inversion, this condition causes the upper part of a sound wave to travel faster, bending the wave back toward earth. This effect, known as wind shear, competes with the normal upward-bending effects of air cooling as altitude increases." In such instances, the sound bounces back and forth, "causing alternating rings of sound and silence rippling away from the original sound." Thus, a sound might jump over listeners normally within range, and reach those who would otherwise be out of earshot.[20]

Ross pointed to numerous examples of acoustic shadow affecting Civil War battles, including engagements at Chancellorsville, Five Forks, and Seven Pines (Fair Oaks), and on several separate occasions during the battle of Gettysburg.[21] Three other battles, however, are particularly instructive because acoustic shadows played decisive roles in their outcomes and, in two cases, in the futures of their commanding officers. Heavy precipitation, high winds, and irregular terrain created acoustic shadows during the battles of Fort Donelson, Iuka, and Perryville, respectively, and constituted points of friction that threatened Union success in each case. In the first example, excellence in leadership helped to overcome the

Clausewitzian friction caused by the acoustic shadow and helped to establish the reputation of the commanding officer, Ulysses S. Grant, as an able commander. Circumstances in the second instance revealed how nature can be a primary cause in the breakdown in communication, with potentially disastrous results; at Iuka, acoustic shadow paired with difficult terrain to nearly derail Union success in Mississippi. The third occasion of acoustic shadow resulted in a Military Commission inquiry investigating alleged misconduct by the ranking officer, Don Carlos Buell, and caused his professional downfall.

FORT DONELSON, TENNESSEE

On February 6, 1862, General Grant cooperated with Flag Officer Andrew Foote of the U.S. Navy to capture the Confederate position on the Tennessee River at Fort Henry. The joint army–navy operation took mere hours, partly because the fort's commander, Brig. Gen. Lloyd Tilghman, recognized his untenable position early in the battle and moved most of his 2,500-man garrison twelve miles east to the much better situated Fort Donelson, located on the banks of the Cumberland River. Grant intended to move against Donelson on the 8th, but reported to the chief of staff, Brig. Gen. G. W. Cullum, that he was "perfectly locked in by high water and bad roads, and prevented from acting offensively, as I should like to do."[22] Despite continued muddy roads and high waters, Grant finally moved his forces on February 12 from Fort Henry to outside Fort Donelson, where he invested the Confederate defenses. His position was somewhat tenuous, as he was unable to transport his siege artillery because "half the country [was] under water."[23] Nevertheless, Grant had to take Donelson; Grant's commanding officer Henry Wager Halleck had predicted that Fort Donelson would be "the turning point of the war," stating that it "must be taken at whatever sacrifice."[24]

To capture Fort Donelson, Grant once again required assistance from Foote's ironclads. "Hoping to repeat the Fort Henry experience," James McPherson wrote, "Grant ordered the navy to shell the fort while his troops closed the ring to prevent the garrison's escape."[25] Fort Donelson sat atop a hundred-foot bluff, and its guns enjoyed a decided advantage against Foote's already damaged fleet. Early on the first day of battle, February 14, the Confederate artillery picked off Foote's ironclads, leaving Grant to continue the attack alone. The same bluffs that enabled the Confederates to neutralize the naval threat left them little means for escape, however, if Grant's superior numbers succeeded in fully encircling the fort. To prevent the capture of nearly twenty thousand Confederate troops, the fort's commander, John Floyd ordered an attack against Grant's southern flank on the morning of February 15.

The Confederates benefited in their efforts from a major change in the weather. Early February brought unseasonably warm temperatures, but on the 13th, a storm front had moved in, bringing with it sleet, snow, and a strident north wind, plus temperatures in the low teens.[26] Brig. Gen. John A. McClernand reported that "the weather turned intensely cold, a driving north wind bringing a storm of snow and sleet upon the unprotected men of my division. The night set in gloomily, and the mingled rain and snow congealed as they fell, thus painfully adding to the discomfort of a destitution of tents and camp equipage, all of which had been left behind."[27] Gen. Lew Wallace noted that his Union soldiers "laid down as best they could on beds of ice and snow, a strong cold wind making the condition still more disagreeable."[28] Most of the Union soldiers had discarded their overcoats and blankets, seeing them as unnecessary during the recent warm spell. This left them vulnerable to exposure and physically weakened.

When the Confederate attack commenced on the morning of the 15th, with the storm still raging, Grant was five miles away conferring with Foote and was unaware of any of the developments along his line. He had expected no action unless he himself initiated it, so he ordered "his division commanders to hold their positions until further notice."[29] Despite being only a few miles from the action, he did not hear the sounds of battle and could not issue updated orders. According to Charles Ross, "The sounds of the engagement did not make it to his location for two reasons: a howling wind blew from north to south, carrying the sound in the opposite direction from him, and a fresh blanket of snow absorbed sound in all directions."[30] McClernand's command bore the entirety of the offensive and fell back from their positions for nearly a mile. "Demoralized and out of ammunition, they were in no condition to stop the rebels from escaping through the breach."[31] The Confederates, too, suffered heavy losses and did not take advantage of the break in Grant's line. During the night, Confederate officers John Floyd, Gideon Pillow, and Nathan Bedford Forrest escaped with only a few thousand troops, leaving Grant's former West Point classmate Simon Bolivar Buckner to face the consequences as the ranking Confederate officer. On February 16 Grant reported to Halleck, "We have taken Fort Donelson and from 12,000 to 15,000 prisoners, including Generals Buckner and Bushrod Johnson."[32]

Grant's congratulatory orders to his troops included acknowledgment of the natural forces they had had to overcome: "For four successive nights, without shelter, during the most inclement weather known in this latitude, they faced an enemy in large force in a position chosen by himself. Though strongly fortified by nature, all the safeguards suggested by science were added. Without a murmur this was borne, prepared at all times to receive an attack, and with continuous skirmishing by day, resulting ultimately in forcing the enemy to surrender without conditions."[33]

Grant's capture of Fort Donelson provides an opportunity to understand how the forces of nature constitute an element of Clausewitzian friction, as well as how more traditional understandings of friction were also at play. In this particular case the acoustic shadow shaped the outcome of the battle, and Grant's career, not just through its chance occurrence, but because Grant acted quickly and effectively in response to it when he became aware of the obstacle. He was able to staunch the flow of the Confederate retreat through redirecting his own army's energy in a timely manner. He recognized the friction, understood its direction, and took measures, as any good Clausewitzian commander would, to remediate the damage. Unlike Burnside, who allowed the change in weather to defeat him, Grant took decisive action and turned a potential failure into a stunning, and personally important, victory. Grant succeeded, and earned the admiration of the Lincoln administration, because he adapted most effectively to the friction that nature, as an agent of historical change, presented.

IUKA, MISSISSIPPI

Iuka, a small settlement located along the Memphis and Charleston railroad near the Tennessee River in northeastern Mississippi, became a flashpoint in mid-September 1862. Gen. Braxton Bragg, commander of Confederate forces in the West, intended to launch a two-pronged invasion into Tennessee and Kentucky and needed his subordinates in Mississippi to keep Grant, newly promoted to commanding officer in the West, occupied in that state. Bragg ordered Maj. Gens. Sterling Price and Earl Van Dorn to engage Grant at Corinth, Mississippi, an important junction that served as a main Confederate rail connection in the Mississippi Valley. Price enjoyed early success in these efforts when he forced Col. Robert Murphy's federal troops from their positions protecting a large stockpile of supplies in Iuka, twenty miles southeast of Corinth, on September 14, 1862. In response, Grant ordered a pincer maneuver to commence on September 18, intending not just to stop Price from advancing to Corinth but also to capture his entire army. According to Union plans, Maj. Gen. William S. Rosecrans was to conduct a flanking movement, approaching Price's army from the southwest, and turning the Confederate front toward that direction. Grant instructed Maj. Gen. Edward O. C. Ord to take two divisions east along the railroad to attack what ideally would then be Price's rear. Success depended on tight coordination and clear communication. However, in a classic case of friction, unexpected natural forces hamstrung Grant's plan.

The landscape between Corinth and Iuka, and south to Jacinto (the town from which Rosecrans was to initiate his part of the operation) was not ideal for cooperative campaigning. Though the roads were generally good, except during times of heavy precipitation, they were separated by thick forests and swampy ground. On the surface, this seemed to favor the Union plan to establish strongholds on each transportation route leading out of Iuka toward the south and west. If the Union troops could maintain control over each of these roads, Price would be cut off from Van Dorn's divisions in western Mississippi. Furthermore, if Ord successfully enveloped the Confederates from the rear, Price would be surrounded and unable to support Bragg's invasion of Tennessee and Kentucky. However, according to historian Michael Ballard, "the campaign that unfolded fell victim to many problems, including fatal problems with communications, most attributable to rugged, swampy, and hilly terrain that had not been well scouted by Union cavalry."[34]

Ord's two divisions moved out by rail along the Memphis and Charleston railroad to his position six miles west of Iuka, where he awaited sounds of battle before joining the fight. Ord, in fact, had specific orders not to engage Price's troops "unless he should hear firing."[35] In contrast, a number of factors hampered Rosecrans's march. First, his troops moved out toward Jacinto during a major storm, which resulted in some of his troops getting lost as they tried to maneuver in the wet darkness through the thickly forested terrain.[36] These troops had to countermarch for more than four hours to get to their prescribed positions, which put Rosecrans and the entire Union operation behind a full day. Furthermore, Rosecrans found as he neared Iuka that his plan to cover both roads into town made for an untenable situation in terms of communication. The Fulton Road to the east and the Jacinto Road to the west were separated by "thickly brushed, swampy land," making "mutual support impossible."[37] Instead, he had to concentrate his strength along the western road, leaving Price a potential route for escape along the eastern route.

The troublesome landscape and poor weather created for Rosecrans what historian Russell Weigley called "yet another onset of the perennial friction of war."[38] Rosecrans's troops began skirmishing with Price's early on the morning of September 19 and became fully engaged with them until around 4:30 that afternoon. When news reached Price of Rosecrans's movement to Iuka, he did what Grant had expected him to: he moved two brigades to face the imminent threat, leaving a smaller, vulnerable force in front of Ord. Ord failed to take advantage of the situation, however, because he never heard the cue to attack – the sound of cannon fire. He later reported that on the afternoon of the battle Gen. L. F. Ross saw "dense smoke" around 4 p.m. "arising from the direction of Iuka." At the time, Ord concluded "that the enemy [were] evacuating and destroying the stores."[39] The next morning, Ord heard guns and "moved rapidly into Iuka and found it had been evacuated during the night." He was surprised because those guns "were the first heard by us, although on the afternoon of the 19th the head of General Rosecrans' column had engaged the enemy 2 miles south of Iuka about the time that General Ross reported a smoke in the direction of Iuka. The wind, freshly blowing from us in the direction of Iuka during the whole of the 19th, prevented our hearing the guns and co-operating with General Rosecrans."[40] He defended his actions in his official report to Grant by reiterating Grant's own orders: "You expressed the opinion that General Rosecrans was from last accounts from him too far from Iuka for us to attack on our front until further information was received as to his whereabouts, which was manifestly true. At the same time you directed me to move my whole force forward to within 4 miles of Iuka, and there await the sounds of an engagement between Rosecrans and the enemy before engaging the latter."[41] In the end, Price escaped on the road Rosecrans failed to block, and when the "Union pincers finally closed," James McPherson wrote, "they grasped an empty town."[42]

Historians of the battle note many elements of friction in the contest for Iuka, but all point to natural phenomena as the reason for Ord's failure to engage when needed. Charles Ross attributed it to an acoustic shadow caused by wind direction.[43] Russell Weigley's assessment is the same: "A strong north wind kept Ord from hearing the fight."[44] Without stating the cause, James McPherson noted that "an acoustic shadow masked all sound of the fighting from Ord, whose troops remained in blissful ignorance of Rosecrans's battle a few miles away."[45] Peter Cozzens provided the most extensive analysis, pointing to numerous reports among Ord's command that no cannon fire had been heard and, coincidentally, that a strong wind was present. Cozzens also noted that such testimony "does not square with the recollections of those on the battlefield." There, "soldiers in both armies spoke of a heavy, still air that kept the smoke of the battle close to the ground. Assuming everyone's recollections of weather conditions were accurate," Cozzens argued, "the most reasonable conclusion is that the rolling ground close to the fighting dissipated the breeze Ord's men felt, and that the damp air on the battlefield deadened sounds beyond a mile or two."[46] In other words, September 19 brought together a combination of at least two of the main factors leading to acoustic shadow.

Once again, nature constituted a point of friction in the outcome of the battle. The Union strategy at Iuka hinged on two factors: first, the readiness of all divisions to strike on September 18; second, Ord's ability to hear Rosecrans's guns as the signal for his troops to move against Price's front. Both miscarried. Stormy weather and rough terrain impeded the timely progress of Rosecrans's troops against Price. Poor communication between Grant and his subordinate officers, due in part to bad weather and difficult terrain but also to simple bad management, was made worse by the larger phenomenon of acoustic shadow and prevented Ord from completing his orders. In the battle of Iuka, the Union officers charged with making on-the-ground decisions failed to adapt their plans to changing environmental conditions and allowed the enemy to escape. Their one consolation, perhaps, was that even though they did not capture Price, they did prevent him from invading Tennessee, a primary objective of Union strategy in the region.

PERRYVILLE, KENTUCKY

In 1862 Kentucky was still up for grabs and both sides were determined to take control. Maj. Gen. Braxton Bragg, supported by Edmund Kirby Smith and Leonidas Polk, led the Confederate Army of the Mississippi. In July Bragg conducted the largest Confederate railroad operation of the war, moving more than forty thousand troops into Tennessee. In early September Kirby Smith entered Kentucky via Knoxville with approximately 21,000 troops; Bragg marched north from Chattanooga, bringing with him 22,500 Confederates, hoping to gain men, materiel, and support from the locals. Maj. Gen. Don Carlos Buell commanded the 60,000 troops opposing Bragg. Federal strategy required that Kentucky remain in Union hands, so a fight was sure to ensue.

The battle of Perryville on October 7 and 8, 1862, began over access to water. "The particular battle that developed," Russell Weigley observed, "was not the one intended by either side. Federal troops were trying to ease a water shortage – the weather was still warm and uncommonly dry – from pools along Doctor's Creek," a small stream that ran north and west of the town.⁴⁷ On October 7 Polk took up defensive positions with his sixteen thousand troops just west of Perryville's main stream, the Chaplin River. That evening Maj. Gen. Thomas Crittenden's 2nd Corps "arrived and attacked unsuccessfully to gain control of the few stagnant pools in a tributary of the river."⁴⁸ The following morning, Philip Sheridan's 11th Division launched an offensive that captured Doctor's Creek and the surrounding hills. "Sheridan might have set the stage for a decisive Union victory," Weigley suggested, but none of his fellow Union commanders knew anything about his fight. In particular, Sheridan's commanding officer, Buell, was completely ignorant of the unfolding events.

A westerly breeze blew through the area, creating an acoustic shadow over Buell's headquarters just three miles from the battlefield. As historian Kenneth Noe remarked, "Nature as well as habitual overmanagement, overconfidence, and the consequences of his bruising fall the previous evening now combined to play a cruel joke on Buell." The wind and the rolling terrain of the Chaplin Hills "bent the sound waves produced by the musketry west of the field" so only a few of the cannon were audible at Buell's headquarters. Furthermore, "no smoke rose along the horizon either, as the wind drove it north or east." Finally, "unable to fathom that the Confederates might not wait for him to perfect his lines and attack on the morrow as planned, Buell immediately concluded that either another artillery duel or at worst a skirmish had flared up." He perceived the sounds as indicators of a waste of ammunition and powder and ordered it stopped. However, two hours later Buell "finally learned that both his army and his career were in for the fight of their lives."⁴⁹

Ultimately, Buell's failure to support Sheridan's effort resulted in a court of inquiry regarding the commanding officer's conduct during operations in Kentucky and Tennessee. The following report by J. Holt to the Secretary of War briefly explains the reasons for the investigation:

> There are circumstances attending this brief but bloody engagement which baffle comprehension. General Buell, who had approached Perryville conscious of the presence there of the enemy in force, retired to headquarters, 2 ½ miles in the rear of his left wing, and, surrounded by a large and well-organized staff, was ignorant of the struggle until too late to render aid, although he heard the furious cannonade that gave token of a combat about

2 o'clock, pronouncing it a waste of ammunition and demanding that it should stop, took no steps, either through the signal corps then in operation or by his staff, to investigate the cause, or, if necessary, to apply a remedy.[50]

In his defense, Buell noted, "It has been a matter of surprise that so severe an engagement could have taken place within 2 ½ miles of my headquarters without my knowledge. The commander of an army covering a line 6 or 7 miles long, interspersed with woods and hills, must of necessity depend on the reports of his generals for information of what is transpiring on different parts of the field." He stated that because his army did not get into position when he expected, he did not anticipate a major engagement on the 8th. Furthermore, "a good deal of artillery firing had been going on between the advance guards of the two armies since our arrival the evening before, excepting at night. The cause of this was well understood, and the greater or less rapidity of the firing at intervals was not a matter to attract particular attention, especially as it was to be expected that information of anything of serious import would be promptly conveyed to me. For that reason," Buell continued, "I received with astonishment the intelligence of the severe fighting that commenced at 2 o'clock. Not a musket-shot had been heard nor did the sound of artillery indicate anything like a battle." Buell explained that his failure to hear the sounds of battle "was probably caused by the configuration of the ground, which broke the sound, and by the heavy wind, which it appears blew from the right to the left during the day." He claimed that hundreds could be brought before the commission to testify to that effect.[51]

In his history of the battle, Russell Weigley wrote, "Here was another example of acoustic shadow, similar to the one at Iuka: the failure sometimes of even the sound of a large-scale battle to carry to nearby troops." Weigley attributed the acoustic shadow to "the unevenness of the ground."[52] According to James McPherson, "Less than half of the Union army was engaged in this fighting, while a freak combination of wind and topography . . . prevented the right wing and Buell himself from hearing the battle a couple of miles away."[53] Charles Ross suggested that the "weather was clear and cool on the day of the battle at Perryville" and that "the refraction effect" was "extreme." He noted that the "terrain and bizarre acoustics contributed to making Perryville a very chaotic fight, with units on both sides unexpectedly finding themselves mixed in with the enemy."[54] If the acoustic shadow caused Buell to be "bathed in silence," in Ross's words, then it provided Bragg an advantage during his retreat. Weigley wrote that Bragg "contrived to break off the action and to slip away, no small tactical accomplishment even with the help of the quirky passage of sound."[55] In this instance of acoustic shadow, nature created a point of friction that Buell simply could not overcome.

The battle of Perryville is considered by many historians as one of the most savage of the war. Perryville was arguably a Confederate victory, albeit a pyrrhic one. Massive casualties and the belief that Buell was bringing his entire force to bear against his own tattered troops the following day (in reality, Buell's entire army had been there the whole time, just not engaged), Bragg chose to withdraw. Perryville was the last battle in the Confederacy's bid for Kentucky, but Buell's failure to participate in the fight meant that he earned no credit for that important development in the Union's war efforts. Buell lost his command later that month, and though his arrogance and frequent missteps contributed to his fate, the friction caused by acoustic shadow at Perryville proved to be the fatal blow to his military career.

Concluding Thoughts

The foregoing pages intended to demonstrate the ways in which the concepts common to military history, Clausewitz's notion of friction in particular, might be useful to environmental historians as they embark on analyses of nature's role in the Civil War. Clausewitz provided clear analysis of the major factors affecting military outcomes and, most importantly for our purposes here, he developed language that those who study the war can use to communicate effectively, regardless of their disciplinary background. Military historians and geographers have long seen the utility of Clausewitzian analysis and have integrated his theories and terminology into their work on the Civil War. In recent years environmental historians interested in the intersections of war and nature have discovered mutually beneficial overlap in their work and that of military scholars. However, they have also correctly pointed out that though they and their military counterparts share common ground in wanting to understand the reciprocal influences between environmental forces and conditions and military developments, they often fail to communicate. This breakdown in communication need not continue to impede the fruitful discussions environmental and military scholars are cultivating within the context of the Civil War, especially since Clausewitz's notion of friction, so familiar to historians of war, is closely analogous to environmental historians' use of the concept of agency with regard to nature. We need not continue to reside in academic acoustic shadows. Instead, like Clausewitz's "good general," we must "know friction in order to overcome it" and we must push our analyses of the Civil War beyond an exercise on paper and into the real world of nature.

Notes

I would like to acknowledge the participants of The Blue, the Gray, and the Green conference at the University of Georgia, especially Steven Berry, Brian Drake, and Bert Way, and the members of the Environment and Society Interdisciplinary Research Group at Boise State University for their insightful critiques and their encouragement and support. Special thanks to the anonymous reviewers whose comments inspired me to improve my thinking and my writing.

1. James McPherson, *Battle Cry of Freedom: The Civil War Era* (New York: Oxford University Press, 1988), 584.

2. Harold A. Winters et al., "Too Much and Too Wet: The Civil War Mud March and Flanders' Fields," in *Battling the Elements: Weather and Terrain in the Conduct of War* (Baltimore: Johns Hopkins University Press, 1998), 36.

3. Ibid., 38.

4. Ted Steinberg, "The Great Food Fight," *Down to Earth: Nature's Role in American History* (New York: Oxford University Press, 2002), 91.

5. Winters et al., "Too Much and Too Wet," 38.

6. Carl von Clausewitz, *On War*, ed. and trans. Michael Howard and Peter Paret (Princeton: Princeton University Press, 1976), 119. See also Clausewitz, "Friktion im Krieg," *Vom Kriege* (Darmstadt: Weltbild Verlag, 1990), 77–79.

7. Clausewitz, *On War*, 120.

8. Ibid.

9. Stephen J. Cimbala, *Clausewitz and Chaos: Friction in War and Military Policy* (Westport, Conn.: Praeger, 2001), 2.

10. Jon Tetsuro Sumida, *Decoding Clausewitz: A New Approach to "On War"* (Lawrence: University Press of Kansas, 2008), 2.

11. See, for example, Raymond Aron, *Clausewitz: Philosopher of War*, trans. Christine Booker and Norman Stone (London: Routledge and Kegan Paul, 1983); Cimbala, *Clausewitz and Chaos*; Peter Paret, *Clausewitz and the State: The Man, His Theories and His Times* (Princeton: Princeton University Press, 1985); and Sumida, *Decoding Clausewitz.*

12. Alan Beyerchen, "Clausewitz, Nonlinearity, and the Unpredictability of War," *International Security* 17, no. 3 (1992–1993): 90.

13. Ibid., 70.

14. Ibid., 76–77. Beyerchen explained, "From this perspective, [Clausewitz's] famous metaphor of the 'fog' of war is not so much about a dearth of information as how distortion and overload of information produce uncertainty as to the actual state of affairs" (77). Here Beyerchen refers to Clausewitz's statement, "Finally, the general unreliability of all information presents a special problem in war: all

action takes place, so to speak, in a kind of twilight, which, like fog or moonlight, often tends to make things seem grotesque and larger than they really are" (*On War*, 140). Eugenia C. Kiesling questions whether Clausewitz saw fog as an apt metaphor for the chaos of war. See Kiesling, "*On War* without the Fog," *Military Review*, September–October, 2001, 85–87.

15. Barry D. Watts, *Clausewitzian Friction and Future War*, McNair Paper 52 (Washington, D.C: Institute for National Strategic Studies, National Defense University, October 1996), 84.

16. Ibid., 104.

17. Ibid., 106.

18. Donald Worster, "The Ecology of Order and Chaos," *Environmental History Review* 14, no. 1/2 (1990): 1–18.

19. Lutz Becks and Hartmut Arndt, "Transitions from Stable Equilibria to Chaos, and Back, in an Experimental Food Web," *Ecology* 89, no. 11 (2008): 3225–26.

20. Charles Ross, "Shh! Battle in Progress!," *Civil War Times Illustrated* 35, no. 6 (1996): 56–58. See also, Ross, *Civil War Acoustic Shadows* (Shippensburg, Pa.: White Mane Books, 2001).

21. Ross, "Shh! Battle in Progress!," *passim*.

22. Ulysses S. Grant to G. W. Cullum, February 8, 1862, *Official Records of the War of the Rebellion* (hereafter OR) ser. 1, vol. 7, 596.

23. Henry Wager Halleck to Don Carlos Buell, February 12, 1862, OR, ser. 1, vol. 7, 609.

24. Halleck to George B. McClellan, February 16, 1862, OR, ser. 1, vol. 7, 626.

25. McPherson, *Battle Cry of Freedom*, 398.

26. Grant to Halleck, February 14, 1862, OR, ser. 1, vol. 7, 613.

27. John A. McClernand to Grant, February 28, 1862, OR, ser. 1, vol. 7, 174.

28. Lew Wallace to John A. Rawlins, February 20, 1862, OR, ser. 1, vol. 7, 237.

29. McPherson, *Battle Cry of Freedom*, 400.

30. Ross, "Shh! Battle in Progress!," 59. Interestingly, Grant attributed no cause to this failure, other than that he did not expect a Confederate attack. See Grant to Cullum, February 16, 1862, OR, ser. 1, vol. 7, 159–60.

31. McPherson, *Battle Cry of Freedom*, 400.

32. Grant to Halleck, February 16, 1862, OR, ser. 1, vol. 7, 625.

33. Grant, "General Orders No. 2," OR, ser. 1, vol. 7, 629.

34. Michael B. Ballard, *The Civil War in Mississippi: Major Campaigns and Battles* (Jackson: University Press of Mississippi, 2011), 60.

35. Ulysses S. Grant to Henry Halleck, October 22, 1862, OR, ser. 1, vol. 24, 67.

36. Robert Collins Suhr, "Small but Savage Battle of Iuka," *America's Civil War* 12, no. 2 (1999), 45.

37. Ballard, *The Civil War in Mississippi*, 64.

38. Russell F. Weigley, *A Great Civil War: A Military and Political History, 1861–1865* (Bloomington: Indiana University Press, 2000), 156.

39. E. O. C. Ord to Grant, September 19, 1862, OR, ser. 1, vol. 24, 119.

40. E. O. C. Ord to Grant, September 20, 1862, OR, ser. 1, vol. 24, 110.

41. Ibid.

42. McPherson, *Battle Cry of Freedom*, 523.

43. Ross, "Shh! Battle in Progress!," 58.
44. Weigley, *A Great Civil War*, 156.
45. McPherson, *Battle Cry of Freedom*, 522–23.
46. Peter Cozzens, *The Darkest Days of the War: The Battles of Iuka and Corinth* (Chapel Hill: University of North Carolina Press, 1997), 129–30.
47. Weigley, *A Great Civil War*, 158–59.
48. McPherson, *Battle Cry of Freedom*, 519.
49. Kenneth W. Noe, *Perryville: This Grand Havoc of Battle* (Lexington: University Press of Kentucky, 2001), 215.
50. J. Holt by request of Lt. Col. Platt, to Secretary of War, May 23, 1863, OR, ser. 1, vol. 22, 20–21.
51. Don Carlos Buell, "Statement of Major-General Buell in review of the evidence before the Military Commission," sub-inclosure no. 2, May 5, 1863, OR, ser. 1, vol. 22, p. 50–51.
52. Weigley, *A Great Civil War*, 159.
53. McPherson, *Battle Cry of Freedom*, 520.
54. Ross, "Shh! Battle in Progress!," 61.
55. Weigley, *A Great Civil War*, 159.

EIGHT

War Is Hell, So Have a Chew
The Persistence of Agroenvironmental Ideas in the Civil War Piedmont

DREW A. SWANSON

> "Their life is yellow tobacco."
> —John Ott (1885)

Alanson Haines of the 15th Regiment of New Jersey Volunteers found himself a Union occupier in the southern Piedmont in the late spring of 1865. Haines's unit was part of the Federal force that garrisoned the market center of Danville, Virginia, after the Confederate surrender at Appomattox Courthouse; he and his fellow soldiers camped a few miles south of the city in northern Caswell County, North Carolina. Haines was glad to see the end of fighting, but he was less enthused about his environs, revealing particular disgust with the agricultural practices of the rural Piedmont. He described the region's farmland as "miserably cultivated, and only with the view to get the most from it for the present crop, regardless of the future." Haines went on to connect locals' abuse of the landscape to their abuse of former slaves. He noted that desperate farmers and Confederate foragers had stripped clean all edible crops from an already slovenly farmscape, and as a result, "Colored men and boys crowded our camps, asking for employment, and saying nothing of wages if they were only fed."[1] Haines was not alone in his critique. Other occupying soldiers, as well as prisoners of war who had been incarcerated in Danville during the final stages of the conflict, were equally critical of the region's agriculture, landscapes, and labor force.[2] Haines equated poor stewardship of the land with the past dominion of masters over their slaves, a charge leveled at patterns of land use central to the production of the region's most lucrative crop: bright leaf tobacco.

Haines's and similar critiques seem typical of comments by northerners regarding an exhausted staple crop South, and would continue throughout Reconstruction and beyond.[3] These observations combined northern farmers' general aversion to the extensive methods of plantation agriculture—tied to a firm belief in free-soil ideology—with a sort of grim admiration of the destructive power wrought by the Union war effort. Danville's gullied and overgrown fields simultaneously symbolized the "right" and the "might" of the northern cause. But Haines and kindred observers had the story wrong. The war did have some harmful effects on regional agriculture, and southern Piedmont tobacco growers were hardly perfect land stewards, but the landscapes that drew critics' ire were the products of a thriving crop culture that survived the war intact. In fact the very war that observers credited with laying destruction on top of dereliction had actually promoted the expansion and entrenchment of this Piedmont staple, forging a tobacco kingdom that would outlast both Civil War and Reconstruction.

To put the central issue concerning tobacco cultivation in the Virginia and North Carolina Piedmont during the Civil War in the form of a question: Why did the war do so little to upset or disrupt tobacco planting? A number of factors seemed to be at work against tobacco's continued success. The struggle between the Union and Confederacy temporarily eliminated two of the region's most important antebellum markets, the American Northeast and Europe. The war drew planters, overseers, and some slaves off local farms and into military endeavors. And Confederate and state governments consistently worked to limit tobacco cultivation in favor of food and fodder production.

The answer to this question lies not in greed, stupidity, habit, or stubbornness, though all of these essential human qualities were present in Piedmont tobacco fields and warehouses, but rather in the region's environmental particularities, the biology of bright tobacco plants, and the ways in which many farmers understood the best use of local landscapes. Environmental historians are beginning to find such intersections of nature and agriculture to be fertile ground (pardon the pun), belatedly taking Donald Worster's advice that the field should pay more attention to farms as environments—or agroecology.[4] While environmental historians as a group have been relatively slow to adopt agriculture as central to environmental history, historians interested in southern environments have taken Worster's call much more to heart. Indeed, southern environmental history has been an especially fruitful place to explore the intersections of agriculture, nature, and labor in new ways.[5]

Civil War environmental history, as the other articles in this collection repeatedly note, has lagged behind southern environmental history in general (which has itself been noticeably sparser than the environmental history of other American regions), and historians have been especially slow to explore the conflict as an agroenvironmental event. Lisa Brady and Megan Kate Nelson have recently argued that the Civil War altered ideas about landscapes, especially southern ones, in subtle but persuasive ways; the war symbolically (and sometimes literally) transformed farmland into wilderness or ruins.[6] While there is truth in these claims, vast swaths of southern rural land were little damaged by the direct hand of war. Like much of the tobacco district, these landscapes and the people living in them felt the economic and ideological pressures of the war more than the stresses of combat, forcing rural communities to tackle how they should use agricultural land in a rapidly changing national context. Farming in all its myriad forms persisted during the war, in a nation that remained predominantly rural. Spring, summer, fall, and winter meant more than campaign seasons between 1861 and 1865, they also continued to pace agricultural life, though often in ways influenced by war. In some places traditions transformed, in others they persisted. Tobacco is one place to begin revealing this story.

The region's agricultural staple was a newcomer. Bright leaf tobacco, known for its golden yellow color once cured and used first in chewing plugs and later cigarettes, originated in the sandy countryside surrounding Danville in the early 1840s. Myth and tradition trace the crop to Caswell County planter Abisha Slade and his slave, Stephen. According to the tale, Stephen accidentally perfected a curing system of hot charcoal fires that resulted in an attractive and flavorful tobacco. While tending a curing barn, Stephen fell asleep, letting the wood fires all but die, and upon awakening rushed hot coals from the plantation's blacksmith forge to the barn, creating unusually high temperatures. This hot fire led to yellow-colored, sweet-flavored tobacco. In reality, the development of bright leaf, which combined horticultural selection with the identification of soil types and experiments in curing technology, was a gradual process undertaken by a number of farmers and their workforces in the region surrounding Danville. By the mid-1840s, a recognizable and distinctive (if variable) form of bright leaf agriculture existed, with a number of planters and farmers experimenting with the new crop.[7]

The southern Piedmont environment was a crucial factor in the birth of bright tobacco. The region's first Euro-American settlers, trickling westward from Tidewater Virginia and south from the Great Valley, brought tobacco cultivation with them, but the crop was the fire-cured "dark" tobacco that dominated the greater Chesapeake Bay. This tobacco performed well on the Piedmont's richer bottomland soils, but grew poorly on the sandier uplands. Much of the area surrounding Danville was composed of rolling hills with a sandy topsoil from a few inches to a foot deep that overlay red or yellow clay subsoils, soils modern scientists classify as Appling, Cecil, Durham, or Granville sandy loam, depending on their exact composition. These acidic topsoils had little organic matter, and were thus relatively low in nitrogen.[8] What proved a liability for dark tobacco farmers turned out to be a blessing for growers interested in creating a lighter, yellower form of tobacco. Local farmers discovered that certain varieties of tobacco seed, when planted on these poor uplands, produced plants that were smooth tasting. (Chemists would later link this smooth flavor to lower levels of nicotine, which in turn came from soils relatively deficient in nitrogen.)[9] By bringing together seed and soil, and through experimentation with curing methods that could bring out an attractive color while converting the starches in the leaf to sugars before fixing taste and appearance, tobacco growers in the southern Piedmont drew on environment and technology to craft a distinctive commodity.

What seemed a subtle shift in agricultural practice — from dark tobacco to bright — had dramatic effects on regional economy, culture, and society. Of perhaps most evident importance, tobacco growers could potentially realize enormous profits. Bright tobacco cured well (never an easy task) was easily twice as profitable as the traditional crop. By the 1850s, planters who had mastered the culture of bright leaf consistently sold their tobacco for twenty to forty dollars per hundredweight, at a time when their dark-tobacco producing neighbors could expect less than ten dollars per hundredweight for their best crops.[10] Bright leaf's soil requirements also permitted growers to reorder their farmscapes in productive ways. As they moved their tobacco fields from bottomlands to hillsides and ridges, they often raised corn and wheat on lowlands freed by the transfer. This shift reinforced the notion among farmers that bright tobacco aided in the "best use" of the Piedmont landscape. Extremely profitable tobacco could be raised on land once considered waste, or at the very least unproductive, and grain crops improved by their relocation to the area's most fertile grounds. In essence, soil weakness had become a strength.[11]

Bright tobacco's economic success transformed the region in the years leading up to the Civil War. Slave populations in the three counties surrounding Danville increased both as a percentage of the population and in absolute terms from 1840 to 1860, contrary to statewide trends in Virginia and North Carolina. During the two decades the enslaved population in Caswell, Halifax, and Pittsylvania grew from 32,898 to 38,592, and slaves came to make up more than half of the regional population for the first time. Over the same years, the percentage of Virginia's population who were enslaved declined from 36.2 percent to 30.7 percent, and in North Carolina the percentage increased only slightly, from 32.6 percent to 33.4 percent.[12] Bright tobacco's strong profit potential and the resulting growth in slave population made the appeals of agricultural reformers – of whom there were a number in the region and who typically viewed a reliance on tobacco production unfavorably – weak at best. After all, the reformers' main goal in touting crop rotation, diversification, and intensive farming was to keep Piedmont farmers on their farms and off the roads leading to Mississippi and Texas. Bright tobacco achieved this goal, and subverted agricultural reform most effectively.[13]

Bright tobacco cultivation contributed to a booming regional manufacturing industry as well. Richmond and Lynchburg had long transformed tobacco from the Piedmont of southern Virginia and northern North Carolina into manufactured products, but Danville and smaller surrounding towns became manufacturing centers as well during the 1840s and 1850s, thanks in part to convenient access to high quality leaf and substantial numbers of slaves who had experience handling tobacco. At the outbreak of the Civil War, there were at least fifty-three tobacco factories of various sizes in Caswell, Halifax, and Pittsylvania counties, with the majority concentrated in or near Danville, Milton, and Yanceyville.[14] Within a few years of the founding of its first factory, Danville had grown to be the fifth largest tobacco-manufacturing center in the world, trailing only Richmond, New York, Petersburg, and Lynchburg.[15] By 1860 Danville tobacco factories purchased more than three and a half million pounds of local tobacco annually, employed almost five hundred hands, and produced finished goods worth $610,332.[16] In the first ten months of 1854, the company of Sutherlin & Ferrell alone purchased 389,574 pounds of tobacco for $37,574, and sold $52,950.45 worth of manufactured tobacco.[17] These factories specialized in high-grade chewing tobacco production, and the close proximity of so many tobacco growers and the quality of regional yellow tobacco made local factories unusually profitable on the whole. The rate of return among Danville factories was the highest in the state at 24 percent.[18]

As rumblings of war swept the South in 1861, bright tobacco was thoroughly entrenched as the economic engine of the countryside surrounding Danville. More than that, though, a bright tobacco culture existed that connected people to the environment in various ways. Tobacco cultivation rested on soil qualities, climate, wood resources, and modified seeds. The crop also shaped new understandings of the "best" use of local landscapes, ultimately turning on their heads conventional ideas of rich and poor lands. And these notions of farmers' places in the world in turn helped thwart the message of agricultural reformers and recommitted white landowners to the institution of slavery. The region existed within a bright tobacco paradigm. The war would openly challenge these agro-environmental relationships but was ultimately unable to vanquish them.

Growing Piedmont tobacco production was linked to rising national and regional consumption. Demand for tobacco in the southern states during the war reflected a continuing mid-nineteenth-century national obsession with tobacco. Whether as chewing plugs, snuff, pipe tobacco, or cigars (cigarettes would not become popular before the 1890s), Americans consumed the addictive plant in enormous quantities.[19] By 1859 United States manufacturers annually produced roughly two pounds of finished tobacco products for every man, woman, and child (including slaves) in the nation. Much of this manufactured tobacco remained in the country, where it was supplemented by foreign cigars and an undetermined quantity of home-manufactured products.[20] Foreign travelers often commented on the ubiquity of chewing, smoking, and spitting in the antebellum United States, from the rural South to the eastern cities. Charles Dickens, during an 1842 visit to the nation's capital, remarked with distaste on the omnipresence of tobacco in even the most formal settings. "In all the public places of America, this filthy custom is recognized. In the courts of law, the judge has his spittoon, the crier his, the witness his, and the prisoner his; while the jurymen and the spectators are provided for, as so many men who in the course of nature must desire to spit incessantly. In the hospitals, the students of medicine are requested by notices upon the wall, to eject their tobacco juice into the boxes provided for that purpose, and not to discolour the stairs."[21] This widespread usage continued during the Civil War. Union soldiers in particular commented on the ubiquity of tobacco in the South. As one Massachusetts soldier given to hyperbole wrote, "The little girls in these parts about seven or eight years old chew tobacco like veterans and babies smoke before they are weaned."[22] Tobacco was everywhere, used by almost everyone.

The outbreak of hostilities may have increased per capita consumption among the nation's men. Hundreds of thousands of soldiers from across the South (and the North as well) spent much of the war stationed in northern and eastern Virginia. These troops lived and fought near the Virginia and North Carolina tobacco belt, Confederate forces received many of their supply trains from Danville, and both sides sought distraction from the alternating terror and boredom of the front in activities as varied as cards, sports, drinking, and religious meetings. Perhaps the most common diversion was the consumption of tobacco. As historian Bell Irvin Wiley observed, "It is doubtful if any single item except food, water, and letters from home was so highly cherished by Johnny Reb as 'the delightful weed.'" He goes on to suggest that southern generals feared "an anticipated cut in tobacco" nearly as much as the enemy. Southside families also sent care packages that included tobacco to their relatives in service or in northern prisons, which they gratefully consumed, shared, or sold. Tobacco was a ubiquitous part of American life, and the Civil War only encouraged the habit.[23]

While national demand was high, the onset of war immediately barred Piedmont producers from two significant antebellum markets: northeastern manufacturers and the European trade. But the nation's changing political geography presented manufacturers with opportunities to capitalize on Piedmont tobacco's natural advantages. The blockade that accompanied the conflict cut off the Piedmont from markets in the North and overseas, but it also eliminated many competitors for southern sales. The back-and-forth campaigns in northern and eastern Virginia made tobacco cultivation in those districts uncertain, Maryland and New England tobacco no longer came South, and most significant, the substantial Kentucky tobacco trade was cut off from southern markets. The Piedmont of Virginia and North Carolina remained the most significant tobacco district left in the Confederacy, and the region suddenly enjoyed the advantage of near monopoly in addition to a reputation for high quality. Some tobacco was smuggled across enemy lines, perhaps most effectively in southeastern Virginia and eastern North Carolina where the front fluctuated with regularity, but this contraband trade was a tiny trickle compared to the antebellum torrent.[24] Unlike cotton growers, however, tobacco farmers benefited from the presence of native manufacturers, though those manufacturers had to decide early in the war whether there was an immediate future for manufactured tobacco in the South. Danville and regional manufacturers quickly determined that by emphasizing the high quality of their products they might seize control of the surviving market, and concentrated on more effectively marketing their goods in the Confederacy.

While native manufacturers were determined to continue tobacco production, they were joined by additional competition as the war progressed. The city filled up with refugees after the commencement of hostilities, looking for a safe haven away from the combat theaters of the war. Among them were tobacco businessmen looking to continue their livelihood in their new city. A number of Richmond tobacconists and warehousemen – among them James Thomas Jr., the capital's largest antebellum tobacco industrialist and maker of the famous "Lucky Strike" plugs (and later cigarette brand) – moved their operations to Danville during the war to avoid the risk of the front lines. Natives and newcomers competed for warehouse and manufacturing space.[25]

No regional manufacturer and planter benefited from the war's changing markets more than William Sutherlin, already on his way to industrial and political prominence when Virginia seceded. Sutherlin was born on a small tobacco farm in Pittsylvania but turned his energies to tobacco dealing and then manufacturing as a young man, and by the 1850s he operated one of the largest chewing tobacco facilities in the southern Piedmont, Sutherlin & Ferrell. His business interests also included stakes in two banks, insurance, real estate, mining, and textile production, and he engaged in politics, serving as the president of the board of aldermen for Danville, and then as the town's mayor in 1855. But above all William Sutherlin was a tobacconist.[26] Sutherlin's correspondence and business papers highlight the opportunities the war created for those involved in bright tobacco. Sutherlin's agents across the South noted that consumers demanded good bright leaf, a product already associated with soils along the Virginia/North Carolina border, and merchants from New Orleans to Columbus to Fredericksburg wrote the manufacturer requesting products that were as "bright as possible."[27] A fellow manufacturer from Leatherwood along the Henry/Pittsylvania line in Virginia wrote Sutherlin that it was the nature of a crowded market to select for the best product, and he advised Sutherlin to follow his lead and "get the fine wrappers if you can."[28] A Lynchburg correspondent offered similar advice, stating of dark tobacco products that "nobody seems to want these grades... bright tobacco... is the sort that is *wanted*."[29] Taking this advice to heart, Sutherlin concentrated on producing high quality tobacco in an effort to dominate the newly constricted market.

In consequence of this growing preference for yellow tobacco products,

Sutherlin's sales expanded throughout the Deep South as the war progressed. In addition to New Orleans and Columbus, he soon had agents in Atlanta, Memphis, Augusta, and Mobile, as well as smaller towns such as Eufala and Huntsville, Alabama, and Albany and Americus, Georgia. Sutherlin was not alone in his efforts; even in rural reaches of the Gulf South his agents encountered other Danville salesmen hawking manufactured bright leaf.[30] Danville warehouse owners T. D. Neal and T. J. Talcott were among Sutherlin's Piedmont competition marketing bright leaf in the Deep South, though unlike Sutherlin, their company specialized in selling unprocessed yellow tobacco to southern manufacturers. In the spring of 1864, Neal and Talcott forged a partnership with an Augusta merchant to sell their tobacco across the Georgia Piedmont.[31] Wartime marketing also increased an antebellum trend, as Danville manufacturers sent wagon trains of their twists and lumps across the region, touting the fine color and taste of tobacco produced along the Virginia/North Carolina border. These wagon trains allowed manufacturers to cut out the middleman fees of antebellum tobacco agents, all while emphasizing the quality and the provenance of their products.[32]

By late 1861 Sutherlin and his fellow bright leaf manufacturers faced a dilemma: demand for regional tobacco was so strong that they were having difficulty filling orders. Sutherlin's brand names—from Yellow Bar to Old Virginia Fancy Twist—touted his company's reliance on bright leaf, and his buyers scoured southern Pittsylvania, southwestern Halifax, and northern Caswell for quality crops.[33] As early as August of 1861, agent Johnson Owen warned Sutherlin that the business might have to cut corners to meet demand. He advised his employer that Atlanta consumers were less discerning than in other reaches of the South; the company might be able to use low-quality tobacco for plug and twist fillers "if the Wrapper is bright," but he cautioned that such a trick would not work everywhere, as buyers in cities such as Memphis demanded only "good stock."[34] Sutherlin seemed to take Owen's advice, as he bought two- and three-year-old crops and hail-damaged leaf, and he even tried to work with tobacco that had been cured poorly or was moldy. Even this poor tobacco brought higher prices than bright leaf had at the war's onset.[35] As the war progressed, area manufacturers faced additional problems as the Confederacy's rail system became increasingly tied up with military traffic, and licorice and other common tobacco flavorings became more difficult to procure.[36]

A public disagreement between Sutherlin and one of his business partners in 1863 provides a window into this intra-South trade and illustrates the tensions of the tight wartime market and importance of quality and provenance in tobacco marketing. James Millner, a small-scale tobacco reseller from Pittsylvania County, entered an agreement with Sutherlin to market Danville-manufactured twists and plugs in Georgia. With Millner acting as the partnership's Georgia agent and Sutherlin providing most of the upfront money, the two men purchased either 745 or 1300 (the number varies in the various accounts) boxes of low-grade finished tobacco, which they attempted to sell at a 100 percent profit on the Augusta market, relying on the reputation of Danville twists to make the sale. By all accounts, Sutherlin and Millner planned to parlay war shortages into speculative profits. The boxes failed to sell at the anticipated price, and each partner accused the other of dishonest dealing. Millner claimed that he was unable to sell some of the leaf, while Sutherlin asserted that Millner had sold the entire lot, lied about the quantity and price, and pocketed the difference. In March, after efforts at arbitration failed, Millner published a pamphlet in which he accused Sutherlin of besmirching his good name by blaming him for the poor sales. Millner charged that Sutherlin used the deal to dump poor quality tobacco out-of-state, while trying to gouge his partner in the process, thus threatening the name of both Millner and Piedmont bright leaf (if Owen's and Sutherlin's plan to adulterate Atlanta-area manufactured tobacco was any indication, Millner had cause to question Sutherlin's attention to quality). He degenerated to name calling, referring to Sutherlin as a "knight of tobacco trash," and an "ass in a lion's skin," and in a last bit of bluster, predicted that "buzzards will roost upon his tomb."[37] Millner's attack brought into question Sutherlin's personal character, but also challenged the manufacturer's dedication to making first-rate manufactured tobacco.

In a business where quality of product and quality of character went hand in hand, Sutherlin felt the need to respond in kind to Millner's accusations. In his own pamphlet, he described market conditions in Georgia, claiming that inflation and scarcity had pushed the prices of manufactured tobacco to between seventy-five and eighty cents per pound, and with an honest effort Millner should have been able to get equivalent prices. According to Sutherlin, Millner displayed an "utter disregard of truth." An experienced local businessman and politician, Sutherlin used calm insinuations rather than brash diatribe throughout his pamphlet, though near the end of the publication he did resort to race baiting, accusing Millner of using his stolen profits to purchase a *"fancy negro girl."*[38] (Sutherlin's use of the word "fancy" was a play on words that would have been quite apparent to white tobacco planters, who used the term to denote both slaves and tobacco light in color, or "high yellow.") Although Millner and Sutherlin's argument was in some ways a petty squabble, their case illustrates both the ability of regional manufactures to find markets for their products during the war, and the difficulties inherent in the process. This public disagreement also demonstrates the assumptions of connections between personal character and the quality of an agricultural product that underlay tobacco cultivation and manufacturing. Both Millner and Sutherlin believed that the proper type of land made good bright tobacco, and only quality merchants were suited to make and sell that tobacco.

Responding to demand from manufacturers such as Sutherlin, many Piedmont farmers and planters still believed tobacco their most profitable option, and they continued to plant the leaf despite Confederate appeals for increased food production.[39] Although total tobacco production trended down in 1861, the year's crop of bright leaf was exceptionally large. Anderson Willis of Caswell wrote Sutherlin that war rumblings had done little to limit planting in his neighborhood, where his farm alone cured around thirty thousand pounds of bright leaf. He declared it "the best fire-cured [flue-cured] crop I ever made . . . we cured more fine Yellow than I ever did."[40] Farmers with a long history of viewing tobacco as the only certain cash crop in the region clung to the crop as security in unsettling times. In 1863 farmer George Jones was serving in the army but still directing operations on his Pittsylvania farm through letters to his wife. He instructed her to continue selling tobacco despite requests from the Confederate government that farmers switch to foodstuffs, and stated, "I had rather had it [tobacco] than Confederate bonds," as good leaf was appreciating faster than bonds at the time.[41] Caswell County's William Hatchett gave his brother similar advice, declaring that the region's farmers should "make all the tobacco we can," as in the constricted wartime market "the article is bound to sell high."[42]

Speculative bright tobacco planting led to Confederate officials complaining that farmers spent too much time and energy on tobacco and paid too little attention to producing food.[43] Confederate quartermasters and local politicians urged Piedmont farmers to turn the soils of their farms into military resources by producing more wheat, corn, and meat.[44] Opponents of wartime tobacco production appealed to farmers' patriotism, and condemned growing the crop until after the Confederacy achieved independence. Charles N. B. Evans, the editor of the *Milton Chronicle* (Caswell County), was among the most outspoken tobacco opponents. In the fall of 1863, an editorial in the paper declared continued tobacco cultivation kept food prices artificially high, and laid blame on the tobacco manufacturer as well as the grower, noting that factory owners with wallets fattened by wartime profiteering were willing to pay inflated prices in order to feed their workers. According to Evans, "It would be a glorious deed for this Southern Confederacy if every Tobacco Factory in it were burnt to the ground and their very ashes scattered to the four winds of heaven.... Our idea is that the people can do better without tobacco than meat and bread."[45]

What Confederate quartermasters and politicians sought in the Piedmont was the creation of a southern breadbasket, a region sheltered behind the main lines of the war's eastern theater that could funnel grain to the Army of Northern Virginia. The expectation was somewhat reasonable; farmers along the Virginia/North Carolina border had experience growing grain crops. In 1859, the three counties surrounding Danville (Halifax, Pittsylvania, and Caswell) had produced more than 2.5 million bushels of corn, oats, wheat, and rye.[46] Increased production of these crops during wartime would have required little additional investment in farm equipment. Most farmers already owned scythes and cradles, and the same shovel plows, coulter cultivators, hoes, and drags used in tobacco culture worked for raising grain as well. And farm wagons, rail cars, and bateaux hauled barrels of flour and corn just as easily as hogsheads of tobacco. In short, the region had a prewar grain infrastructure — though a small-scale one — and replacing a portion of tobacco production with grain posed no real logistical difficulties as long as the price for the latter was high enough.

Environmental realities, however, posed more concrete challenges for expanded grain production. The region's poor hill soils produced low per-acre yields of corn and wheat. Just as particular soils and climates encouraged continued tobacco cultivation, they worked to discourage larger grain crops. While the South's richer lands could produce yields of sixty bushels of corn or twenty bushels of wheat per acre, the Piedmont's sandy ridge lands were much less productive. In the districts surrounding Danville, farmers often harvested only ten bushels of corn or seven bushels of wheat per acre. And though the richer bottomlands opened up by bright tobacco's movement to the hills produced healthy grain crops, these landscapes were of limited expanse. Much of the region's grain production had been consumed on the farm, either eaten by planters and slaves or fed to livestock, and these trends continued during the war. Farmers understood these soil limitations; they had dealt with them for years in many cases, and they continued to have their doubts about the "suitability" of widespread grain production in the southern Piedmont environment. In order to overcome these perceptions, bright tobacco markets needed to struggle while the price paid for grain skyrocketed, and this never entirely proved the case.[47]

On farms with soils productive enough to produce surplus grain, food crops and livestock faced an uncertainty that did not apply to tobacco. As the war progressed, state and national governments turned to taxes on farm produce to procure supplies for soldiers in the field. In June of 1863 the Confederate government circulated an order to the region's quartermasters that imposed a 10 percent "in kind" tax on certain agricultural commodities. The order authorized government commissaries to inspect local farms and take one tenth of the surplus grain, livestock, fodder, and fiber available on each property.[48] On Samuel Wilson's plantation in Pittsylvania, the quartermaster visited in 1863 and 1864, and confiscated bacon, corn, sorghum, oats, wheat, hay, and fodder, but did provide Wilson with a small quantity of salt (an increasing rarity in the Confederacy) in return.[49] A North Carolina agent's visit to Pleasant Womack's Caswell farm in 1864 garnered a similar variety of agricultural produce. The official took a portion of Womack's corn, fodder, oats, peas, wheat, cotton, and bacon.[50]

By the second half of the war, this tax-in-kind system failed to produce the quantity of foodstuffs necessary for the continued supply of the military, and the Confederate government resorted to more draconian measures. Quartermasters in the three counties were authorized to seize supplies from farms at below-market prices, or for IOUs, and in all cases to pay with Confederate paper money, which was depreciating at a rate that made the bills all but worthless. If farmers refused to yield the demanded crops or animals, officials could seize them without payment.[51] In a typical broadside advertising the new rules from November 13, 1863, quartermaster Jason Paxton, in charge of securing supplies from the southwestern Virginia Piedmont, laid claim to all surplus corn, rye, oats, hay, fodder, and straw in the district. Paxton instructed local farmers to deliver these goods to regional military stables, where they would receive rates ranging from $1.30 for one hundred pounds of wheat straw to $4.00 for a bushel of shelled corn.[52] Officials visited Samuel Wilson's plantation again under the new rules, and seized wheat, oats, rye, hay, fodder, and wool.[53] Army officials also impressed mules and horses for cavalry and artillery units, further undermining local farmers' ability to cultivate their fields.[54]

Quartermasters on occasion commandeered local fields more directly, as when they pastured horses and mules on plantations in northeastern Halifax County during the months before and after the Battle of the Staunton River Bridge in 1864. During the campaign, William Sims complained of the depredations of soldiers stationed on his property to guard the bridge. He lamented, "They take every thing on the plantation in the way of fruit & vegetables they can lay their hands on. I dont think by the fall I will have a potatoe."[55] Danville resident Robert Withers remembered the thoroughness of the quartermasters' agents in his memoir forty years after Appomattox. He described the "inspections of corn cribs and smokehouses all through the country by officers of the Quartermaster and Commissary Departments delegated for the purpose, and all surplus food [was] carried off."[56] These confiscations and taxes in kind certainly blunted the profitability of raising foodstuffs during the war, and must have added to tobacco's appeal.

As tobacco's economic prospects, the poor suitability of Piedmont soils for grain cultivation, and the uncertainties of food production encouraged farmers to resist Confederate calls for food and meat-oriented agriculture, tobacco farming along the states' border also presented obstacles to wartime manpower procurement. The Confederacy needed white men to serve in the army and slaves to work on military construction projects, but the tobacco boom contributed to local planters' resistance to all forms of conscription and impressment. Slave impressment was widespread in the three counties, as in the rest of the state, as southern officials demanded that planters loan their laborers to the cause. An October 3, 1862, act permitted Confederate officials to impress slaves for military work—though it exempted slaves on plantations producing only grain—and promised masters of impressed slaves sixteen dollars per month in exchange for their services. Virginia's Piedmont slaveholders faced a total of seven impressment orders during the remainder of the war; the commonwealth ordered the first three and the final four were direct orders of the Confederate government (affecting Caswell as well).[57] Among other tasks, impressed slaves built defensive works, laid and repaired railroad lines, worked in the Danville hospital and arsenal, and assembled rifles in Belhartz Hall's Pittsylvania firearms shop. Some of these work projects were quite large. The first commonwealth impressment in October of

1862 drew a total of 873 slaves from Halifax and Pittsylvania to labor on the earthworks surrounding Richmond.

Local slaves' opinions of impressment went unrecorded, and likely varied, but white slaveholders' thoughts on the orders were quite clear. The profitability of wartime bright leaf production caused many planters to balk at slave impressment. Pittsylvania and Halifax planters complained that the war's demands on white labor—from soldiering to raising food—made the work of every slave necessary, and tobacco planters seemed particularly reluctant to part with their workers. Under each impressment order, Virginia's individual counties were given target numbers of slaves, and the southern Piedmont proved the worst region of the state in meeting the Confederacy's call for military workers.[58] The head surgeon of the Danville hospital (which relied on slave labor to assist in the care of Union prisoners and injured Confederate soldiers), frustrated with his inability to hire or impress slaves from the surrounding countryside, sent the following complaint to the commonwealth's chief surgeon: "Having failed after diligent efforts to procure colored men and women in sufficient number to meet the demands of the hospital, I respectfully suggest the expediency of authorizing the Quartermaster of this Post to impress the hands of Planters engaged in cultivating tobacco. It would I presume be inexpedient to cripple the agricultural force of the farmers who are raising breadstuffs and other subsistence supplies, but there is a very considerable number of persons in this region . . . who have turned a deaf ear to every appeal to the patriotism and have appropriated their best hands to the production of tobacco during the present season. It would be fit and proper to make these men bear a share of the necessary burdens of the war."[59] Many farmers were reluctant to yield their slaves to the war effort, but tobacco producers were the most militant. This reluctance to lease their hands to the government was due in large part to the continued profitability of bright leaf cultivation.

While some slave laborers encountered the new disease environment of wartime hospitals, most impressed slaves worked in the regional environment in familiar ways; they toiled in the Piedmont sun and rain to move earth and build infrastructure for military projects much as they had cultivated regional landscapes. From 1862 to 1864, construction of an extension of the Richmond and Danville Railroad from the latter city to Greensboro, North Carolina, relied on as may as 2,500 slave laborers, at least 300 of whom came from a single Piedmont county: Pittsylvania.[60] Before the Battle of the Staunton River Bridge in 1864, rebel forces had a reported three hundred slaves digging earthworks along the river, and Confederate officials also impressed slaves from the surrounding countryside to work on the fortifications surrounding Danville in the last year of the conflict.[61] Rebel officials considered these projects instrumental to the war effort, but they were also the sort of demanding physical labor on the landscape that had long been associated with regional slavery.

Equally troubling to many planters was the difficulty finding overseers during the war. As adult males of fighting age who often lacked the resources to purchase a substitute, the region's overseers were particularly susceptible to both martial fever and conscription. Planter William Sims hired a replacement for himself at the start of the war, but complained that two of his overseers were mustering for the army. Noting similar instances in the Black Walnut community, he worried that the impending war "has broken up almost entirely this neighborhood."[62] The shortage of qualified overseers only worsened over the course of the war, causing white planters and their wives anxiety over the state of agricultural production and their safety surrounded by so many slaves. Sims's aunt, Phoebe Bailey, wrote him in the spring of 1864, requesting that Sims assist her in locating a new overseer to help her run the Baileys' substantial plantation; for the fourth time in three years, her overseer had been drafted.[63]

As Piedmont planters used environmental conditions to justify continued tobacco cultivation and fought Confederate efforts to conscript local labor, allied manufacturers turned to natural imagery and language to market their agricultural products. Regional tobacconists attempted to connect place of production with quality of product, building a reputation for bright tobacco rooted in soil and place, what today's viniculturists might term a notion of terroir. This process began during the 1850s and continued during the war. The highest quality bright leaf brands often bore names that emphasized their use of yellow or "fine" tobacco, their Piedmont origins, or that suggested their smooth taste. Among these illustrative brands were Golden Pomegranate, Peaches and Cream Twist, Old Virginia Fancy Twist, Fine Star, Wedding Cake, Yellow Bar, and Gold Leaf. (By the late 1850s the terms "fancy" and "fine" had become all but synonymous with yellow color.)[64] Other products bore the names of bright leaf growers or factories with a history of producing the best leaf.

Products named after local manufacturers and those touting the inclusion of bright leaf tobacco branded the border region along with a particular tobacco product. Like California fruit and vegetable growers in the latter part of the nineteenth century, who shipped their oranges and raisins in crates painted with scenes of the state's sunny valleys and idyllic vistas, Piedmont tobacco manufacturers attempted through branding to convince consumers that the best tobacco came only from their region.[65] Although these early tobacco brands did not include pictures of growers' fields (as far as can be determined), their wording, to borrow from historian Douglas Sackman, "turned the landscape ... into a brand."[66] Whether they chewed Yellow Bar or Old Virginia Fancy Twist, branding encouraged consumers in stores from Maysville, Kentucky, to Mobile, Alabama, to think about the qualities and origin of their tobacco.[67]

While branding associated certain tobacco products with regional manufacturers and the Piedmont landscape, bright tobacco's most powerful advertisement lay in another sort of "natural" advertisement: the leaf itself. Brands adorned the crates that manufacturers shipped to the merchants and served as a reference in transactions between store owner and customer, but the wrapper—an intact leaf wrapped around a finished lump or twist—on each individual plug of chewing tobacco acted as a visual representation of quality.[68] Manufacturers from Danville and other regional factories finished their products, from top-shelf plugs to middle-grade tobacco, with the yellowest wrappers available. These yellow wrappers survived the pressing process without losing their color or texture, and the resulting golden plugs stood out amid the traditional dark twists and lumps that crowded merchants' shelves.[69] Even if consumers chose to discard the wrapper rather than chewing it along with the rest of the plug—as some did, due to its tendency to dry out—it had served its purpose by attracting attention and promising interior quality. As a combination of environmental and cultural expressions, yellow wrappers made Caswell, Pittsylvania, and Halifax products unique. Like the shiny peel of an orange or apple, golden yellow tobacco wrappers promised a flavorful interior, yet, as was the case with fruit aesthetics, the bright leaf was perhaps more important for its appearance than its taste. Strong twist and lump sales in the late 1850s and continuing throughout the war indicated that consumers found these wrappers and the bright fillers that were often inside them appealing.

Protected from the front lines for most of the war, the conflict finally enveloped the southern Piedmont border in the spring of 1865, if only briefly. As Confederate forces retreated from Richmond down the Richmond and Danville Railroad, the city on the Dan served briefly as the Capital of the Confederacy. Then Southern officials fled, Union troops arrived, and the war was over. Tobacco manufacturing records for this period are scarce; factories and warehouses no doubt closed for a few weeks or longer, but this pause was temporary. Some local farmers, such as Pittsylvania's William Sours, found the situation grim:

> Imagine the country devastated by two ravenous and beligerant armies of greater numbers than in former wars every thing devoured from sucking Pigs to lean milch cows, all grain and vegitables destroyed, and trodden under foot and all avenues of trade shut out with thousands within to feed and then you will only have a faint idea of real Hard times. but we think the nigger song of hard times come again no more will in cours of a year or two will be realised. excepting with the freed Nigger if they are not colonized will remain a lasting monument of root Hog or die Their condition today is a thousand times worse of than when they were servants and thousands of them already say so.[70]

Regional manufacturers tended to be more sanguine. Following quickly on the heels of occupation, the southern Piedmont's golden tobacco once again flowed northward to New England and across the Atlantic. By the fall, William Sutherlin was celebrating the resumption of the international tobacco trade, had entertained Gen. George Meade of Gettysburg fame, and was placing orders for French champagne, claret, sherry, and Javanese coffee from merchants in New York City.[71]

Sutherlin's vision of the future proved more prophetic than that of Sours, at least over the short term. If Haines and his fellow observers misinterpreted contemporary agricultural practices in the bright tobacco belt, they were equally amiss in their calculations of bleak regional prospects following the war. Despite northern observers' (and Sours's) claims about a ravaged landscape, the bright tobacco economy boomed along the Virginia/North Carolina border following the war's end. Building on its relative wartime success, Danville remained a tobacco marketing and manufacturing center, and Durham, Wilson, Oxford, and Winston-Salem, North Carolina, became major tobacco hubs as well, with Durham and Winston-Salem eventually surpassing Danville as centers of bright leaf warehousing and manufacturing. Tobacco cultivation spread south and east as well, moving into the sandy eastern Piedmont and coastal plain of the Tar Heel state, although Pittsylvania, Halifax, and Caswell remained significant producers into the late twentieth century. The rise of the cigarette cemented bright tobacco's place in the southern Piedmont, expanding consumer markets across the globe, spawning the American Tobacco Company monopoly, and structuring grower and manufacturer relationships to the present day.[72]

Haines and Sours ultimately proved correct in their dark visions of the future, however. The long-term legacy of this culture for land and people (especially African Americans) proved grim. Profitable tobacco meant that white landowners were less likely to sell land to freedpeople than in many parts of the cash-strapped postwar South, and landowners often asserted their control over freedpeople's labor through violent means. In 1900, African Americans made up roughly half the population of Halifax and Pittsylvania, yet they owned only 4 percent of Halifax's acreage, and only 2 percent of the land in Pittsylvania.[73] The situation was similarly inequitable in Caswell. Despite the fact that almost 55 percent of the population was black, African Americans owned only 60 of the 1,745 farms in Caswell in 1899.[74] Postwar struggles over race and labor in the South often centered on perceptions of landscapes and crops, with tobacco a prime example. This was a battle "centered on the just landscape that the freed people desired and the racially repressive and exploitative landscape that reactionaries tried to impose," as Mark Fiege has noted of Reconstruction in general.[75]

Ecological changes presented grave problems as well. Continuous tobacco cultivation, encouraged by notions of "best use" fostered before and during the war and misconceptions about regional soils, eventually exhausted soil fertility below the levels necessary to produce bright leaf, and farmers turned to tobacco-specific commercial fertilizers that ultimately contributed to debt peonage. Soil erosion played havoc with the region's fragile hillsides, made worse by deforestation to fuel tobacco barns, and by the early twentieth century all of the topsoil was gone from broad swaths of the countryside surrounding Danville. The situation was so bad that New Dealers in the Soil Conservation Service declared the region one of the nation's most serious environmental problems, establishing a demonstration district in Pittsylvania County, and the Farm Security Administration launched numerous land use reform campaigns across the broader region in the hopes of encouraging farm and forest conservation.[76] Put in more human terms, as one observer noted in 1934, "where tobacco is grown almost exclusively, there is the most apparent poverty, not poverty of money alone, but poverty of culture, poverty of soil; poverty of good homes and social environment; poverty of health and of everything that goes to make rural life that ideal mode of living."[77] In its racial and environmental difficulties, the bright tobacco district had become the rural New South in all of its inglorious glory.

There is a temptation in this story to attribute to tobacco a sort of agency, to argue that the plant itself helped further its spread through its addictive qualities. Michael Pollan has cleverly used this inversion in his botanical history, *The Botany of Desire*, demonstrating that crop cultivation often benefits plants' genetic lines as much or more than their human cultivators (he makes the argument most relevant to tobacco in his chapter on marijuana).[78] While clever and rhetorically useful, in the case of bright tobacco in the Civil War Piedmont this reconceptualization is ultimately unsatisfying. Bright leaf did benefit from people's slavish attention to its cultivation in the face of obstacles, and addiction had real power to keep consumers invested in tobacco cultivation, but for all their biological foundations, both human interest in yellow forms of tobacco and the arguments against its cultivation were largely cultural constructs. After all, all forms of tobacco were addictive. In the end, ideas about nature and agriculture carried at least as much weight as material realities.[79]

Time and again during the war the demands of the Confederacy and local understandings of the best use of the land butted heads, and the beliefs of Piedmont planters and farmers in the essential nature of tobacco and landscape consistently carried the argument. It is tempting to view this as a simple case of greed, but the victory of tobacco over patriotism (or insurrection, depending on one's viewpoint) was similar to its victory over dark tobacco and then prewar agricultural reform, as locals had come to think of a particular form of tobacco as a key component in the "best" use of the land. And in these conceptions of agricultural landscapes lies tobacco's lesson for broader Civil War history. For all the war's cataclysmic effects, regional ideas about where people fit into agriculture and nature could prove more powerful; tobacco culture persisted during the war and emerged as the southern Piedmont's central concern following the surrender. The case of bright tobacco illustrates the durability of environmental conceptions, even in the face of threats of national and community destruction.

Notes

Epigraph. John Ott, quoted in Robert Ragland, *Major Ragland's Instructions How to Grow and Cure Tobacco, Especially Fine Yellow* (Richmond, Va.: Southern Fertilizing Company, 1885), 2.

1. Alanson A. Haines, *History of the Fifteenth Regiment New Jersey Volunteers* (New York: Jenkins and Thomas, 1883), 310–11 (quotes on 311).

2. For examples, see Charles M. Snyder, "A Teen-Age G.I. in the Civil War," *New York History* 35 (1954): 29; William Henry Newlin, *An Account of the Escape of Six Federal Soldiers from Prison at Danville, Va.: Their Travels by Night through the*

Enemy's Country to the Union Pickets at Gauley Bridge, West Virginia, in the Winter of 1863–64 (Cincinnati: Western Methodist, 1888), 22–24.

3. Some prominent northern travel narratives that included derogatory descriptions of Piedmont agriculture during the years immediately following the war include John Richard Dennett, *The South As It Is, 1865–1866*, Henry M. Christman, ed. (Athens: University of Georgia Press, 1986), 93–95, 103; Edward A. Pollard, *The Virginia Tourist: Sketches of the Springs and Mountains of Virginia* (Philadelphia: J. B. Lippincott & Co., 1871), 18; John Townsend Trowbridge, *The South: A Tour of Its Battlefields and Ruined Cities, A Journey through the Desolated States, and Talks with the People, 1867*, ed. J. H. Segars (Macon, GA: Mercer University Press, 2006), 225; George Bagby, cited in James Tice Moore, *Two Paths to the New South: The Virginia Debt Controversy* (Lexington: University Press of Kentucky, 1974), 9.

4. Donald Worster, "Transformations of the Earth: Toward an Agroecological Perspective in History," *Journal of American History* 76, no. 4 (1990): 1087–106. For a recent reappraisal of Worster's call for agroenvironmental history, see Paul Sutter, "The World with Us: The State of American Environmental History," *Journal of American History* 100, no. 1 (2013): 105–9.

5. Work that explicitly emphasizes the agricultural nature of southern environmental history includes Jack Temple Kirby, *Poquosin: A Study of Rural Landscape and Society* (Chapel Hill: University of North Carolina Press, 1995); Mart A. Stewart, *"What Nature Suffers to Groe": Life, Labor, and Landscape on the Georgia Coast, 1680–1920* (Athens: University of Georgia Press, 1996); Steven Stoll, *Larding the Lean Earth: Soil and Society in Nineteenth-Century America* (New York: Hill and Wang, 2002); Mart A. Stewart, "If John Muir Had Been an Agrarian: Environmental History West and South," *Environment and History* 11, no. 2 (2005): 139–62; Jack Temple Kirby, *Mockingbird Song: Ecological Landscapes of the South* (Chapel Hill: University of North Carolina Press, 2006); Lynn A. Nelson, *Pharsalia: An Environmental Biography of an American Plantation, 1780–1880* (Athens: University of Georgia Press, 2007); James C. Giesen, *Boll Weevil Blues: Cotton, Myth, and Power in the American South* (Chicago: University of Chicago Press, 2011); Drew Swanson, *Remaking Wormsloe Plantation: The Environmental History of a Lowcountry Landscape* (Athens: University of Georgia Press, 2012). See also Sutter, "The World with Us," 106–8.

6. Lisa Brady, *War upon the Land: Military Strategy and the Transformation of Southern Landscapes during the American Civil War* (Athens: University of Georgia Press, 2012); Megan Kate Nelson, *Ruin Nation: Destruction and the American Civil War* (Athens: University of Georgia Press, 2012).

7. Like all myths, the "discovery" of bright tobacco is greatly simplified, and may even be apocryphal. For discussion of the Slade story and accounts of early bright leaf experimentation in the region, see Drew A. Swanson, *A Golden Weed: Tobacco and Environment in the American South* (New Haven: Yale University Press, 2014), esp. chap. 2; Barbara Hahn, "Making Tobacco Bright: Institutions, Information, and Industrialization in the Creation of an Agricultural Commodity, 1617–1937" (PhD diss., University of North Carolina, 2005), 236–38; Barbara Hahn, *Making Tobacco Bright: Creating an American Commodity, 1617–1937* (Baltimore: Johns Hopkins University Press, 2011); Nannie May Tilley, *The Bright Tobacco Industry, 1860–*

1929 (Chapel Hill: University of North Carolina Press, 1949), 24–26; Frederick F. Siegel, *The Roots of Southern Distinctiveness: Tobacco and Society in Danville, Virginia, 1780–1865* (Chapel Hill: University of North Carolina Press, 1987), 100–102.

8. E. H. Mathewson, *The Culture of Flue-Cured Tobacco*, USDA Bulletin No. 16 (Washington, D.C.: Government Printing Office, 1913), 4; A. P. Brodell, *Cost of Producing Virginia Dark and Bright Tobacco and Incomes from Farming, 1922–1925*, Virginia Polytechnic Institute Agricultural Experiment Station, Bulletin No. 255 (Blacksburg: Virginia Polytechnic Institute and State University, 1927), 4; Charles E. Landon, "The Tobacco Growing Industry of North Carolina," *Economic Geography* 10, no. 3 (1934): 242; E. M. Rowalt, *Soil Defense in the Piedmont*, USDA Farmer's Bulletin No. 1767 (Washington, D.C.: Government Printing Office, 1937), 2–4; Wrightman W. Garner, *The Production of Tobacco* (New York: Blakiston Company, 1951), 88–89, 362; W. W. W. Bowie, "An Essay on the Culture and Management of Tobacco," *American Farmer* 10, no. 2 (1854): 34.

9. J. B. Killebrew and Herbert Myrick, *Tobacco Leaf: Its Culture and Cure, Marketing and Manufacturing* (New York: Orange Judd Co., 1909), 80–84; Augustus Voeleker, in John Ott, *Tobacco in Virginia and North Carolina* (Richmond, Va.: Southern Fertilizer Company, 1877), 15; Garner, *The Production of Tobacco*, 331–32; "Farmers' Meeting at the Exchange Hotel," *Southern Planter* 17, no. 4 (1857): 226; Robert L. De Coin, *History and Cultivation of Cotton and Tobacco* (London: Chapman and Hall, 1864), 258; D. Layton Davis and Mark T. Nielsen, eds., *Tobacco: Production, Chemistry and Technology* (Malden, Mass.: Blackwell Science, 1999), 128.

10. For examples of representative sales, see Williams & Carrington to William Bailey, June 17, 1859, William Bailey Papers, Records of Antebellum Southern Plantations (hereafter RASP), series E, part 1, roll 1; "To the Planters of the Tobacco Growing Sections of Virginia and North Carolina," *Milton Chronicle*, February 12, 1857, 2; "Tobacco," *Milton Chronicle*, May 21, 1858, 2; "The Dan River Valley – Its Superior Products," *Danville Republican*, July 24, 1856, 2; "Advertisement," *Virginia Echo*, August 19, 1859, 3. For an analysis of antebellum tobacco sales on the Danville market and a list of records consulted in establishing regional price differentials, see Swanson, *A Golden Weed*, appendix.

11. Diary of George Washington Jeffreys, January 10, 1845, William Bethell Williamson Papers, Southern Historical Collection, University of North Carolina Library, Chapel Hill, N.C. (hereafter SHC); W. Edward Hearn and Frank P. Drane, *Soil Survey of Caswell County, North Carolina* (Washington, D.C.: Government Printing Office, 1910), 21, 26; R. C. Jurney et al., *Soil Survey of Halifax County, Virginia* (Washington, D.C.: Government Printing Office, 1934), 17, 21, 33–34, 40–42; N. M. Kirk et al., *Soil Survey of Pittsylvania County, Virginia* (Washington, D.C.: Government Printing Office, 1922), 28, 33–34.

12. *Compendium of the Enumeration of the Inhabitants and Statistics of the United States – Sixth Census* (Washington, D.C.: Thomas Allen, 1841), 34–35, 42–43; *The Seventh Census of the United States: 1850* (Washington, D.C.: Robert Armstrong, 1853), 261, 310; *Population of the United States in 1860; Compiled from the Original Returns of the Eighth Census* (Washington, D.C.: Government Printing Office, 1864), 358–59, 516–18.

13. Swanson, *A Golden Weed*, chap. 3.

14. Joseph C. Robert, *The Tobacco Kingdom: Plantation, Market, and Factory in Virginia and North Carolina, 1800–1860* (Durham: Duke University Press, 1938), 166–68; William S. Powell, *When the Past Refused to Die: A History of Caswell County, North Carolina, 1777–1977* (Durham, N.C.: Moore Publishing Co., 1977), 116.

15. Suzanne G. Schnittman, "Slavery in Virginia's Urban Tobacco Industry, 1840–1860" (PhD diss., University of Rochester, 1987), 27.

16. Robert, *The Tobacco Kingdom*, 178.

17. List of tobacco purchased and manufactured, November 1, 1854, William Thomas Sutherlin Papers, SHC. William Thomas Sutherlin, who was the primary investor in Sutherlin & Ferrell, began manufacturing tobacco in Danville in 1844. See "Maj. William T. Sutherlin," *Southern Planter and Farmer* 10, no. 10 (1875): 596.

18. Schnittman, "Slavery in Virginia's Urban Tobacco Industry," 28; Diane Barnes, *Artisan Workers in the Upper South: Petersburg, Virginia, 1820–1865* (Baton Rouge: Louisiana State University Press, 2008), 160–61.

19. Allan M. Brandt, *The Cigarette Century: The Rise, Fall, and Deadly Persistence of the Product That Defined America* (New York: Basic Books, 2007), 25.

20. This per capita estimate is based on a national population of 31,443,008 and $21,820,535 worth of manufactured tobacco products. It assumes an average value of 30 to 40 cents per pound for tobacco products, a range drawn from wide reading. Price fluctuations outside of these estimates would vary the per capita figure, but the point that the nation consumed a great deal of tobacco would remain valid. See *Manufactures of The United States in 1860; Compiled from the Original Returns of the Eighth Census* (Washington, D.C.: Government Printing Office, 1865), 732; *Population of the United States in 1860*, vii.

21. Dickens quoted in Iain Gately, *Tobacco: A Cultural History of How an Exotic Plant Seduced Civilization* (New York: Grove Press, 2001), 174.

22. Bell Irvin Wiley, *The Life of Billy Yank: The Common Soldier of the Union* (New York: Bobbs-Merrill Company, 1952), 101.

23. Bell Irvin Wiley, *The Life of Johnny Reb: The Common Soldier of the Confederacy* (New York: Charter Books, 1962), 172; Bartlett Yancey Malone, *The Diary of Bartlett Yancey Malone*, ed. J. G. De Roulhac Hamilton, Henry M. Wagstaff, and William W. Pierson (Chapel Hill: University of North Carolina, 1919), 53–54. The letters of a Wisconsin soldier suggested that bored troops even chewed tobacco (and spit) when in local churches. See John O. Holzhueter, "William Wallace's Civil War Letters: The Virginia Campaign," *Wisconsin Magazine of History* 57, no. 1 (1973): 39.

24. Ludwell Johnson, "Contraband Trade during the Last Year of the Civil War," *Mississippi Valley Historical Review* 49, no. 4 (1963): 647.

25. Jeffrey McClurken, "After the Battle: Reconstructing the Confederate Veteran Family in Pittsylvania County and Danville, Virginia, 1860–1900" (PhD diss., Johns Hopkins University, 2002), 54–57; American Tobacco Company, *The American Tobacco Story* (Richmond, Va.: American Tobacco Company, 1964), 17; Tilley, *The Bright Tobacco Industry*, 36; Siegel, *Roots of Southern Distinctiveness*, 153.

26. Siegel, *Roots of Southern Distinctiveness*, 140–42.

27. Van Bienthussen & Crafton to William T. Sutherlin, September 7, 1861; Pemberton & Carter to William T. Sutherlin, September 9, 1861; Hill & Warren to

William T. Sutherlin, September 9, 1861, all in William Thomas Sutherlin Papers, folder 13, SHC. Quote in the latter.

28. B. F. Grasty to William T. Sutherlin, August 20, 1861, William Thomas Sutherlin Papers, folder 12, SHC.

29. Thomas Samuel to Sutherlin & Ferrell, February 19, 1863, William Thomas Sutherlin Papers, Special Collections of Duke University Library, Durham, N.C. (hereafter Duke).

30. For examples of communications between Sutherlin and his agents in the field, see Johnson H. Owen to William T. Sutherlin, September 20, 1861; Johnson H. Owen to William T. Sutherlin, William Thomas Sutherlin Papers, folder 13, SHC; W. W. Bunch to William T. Sutherlin, January 4, 1861, William Thomas Sutherlin Papers, folder 15, SHC; and S. R. Neal to William Sutherlin, November 26, 1862, William Thomas Sutherlin Papers, Duke.

31. "Advertisement," *Danville Appeal*, March 26, 1864, p. 4.

32. For this practice during the antebellum era, see Joseph C. Robert, *The Story of Tobacco in America*, 2nd ed. (Chapel Hill: University of North Carolina Press, 1967), 94.

33. Samuel Ayers to William T. Sutherlin, January 4, 1862, William Thomas Sutherlin Papers, folder 15, SHC; Elijah Torrian to Sutherlin & Ferrell, February 19, 1863, William Thomas Sutherlin Papers, Duke.

34. Johnson H. Owen to William T. Sutherlin, August 27, 1861, William Thomas Sutherlin Papers, folder 12, SHC.

35. Johnson H. Owen to William T. Sutherlin, January 18, 1862, and John Sutherlin to William T. Sutherlin, January 21, 1862, William Thomas Sutherlin Papers, folder 15, SHC; James M. Norman to William T. Sutherlin, June 1, 1862, William Thomas Sutherlin Papers, folder 19, SHC. John Sutherlin advised William that tobacco was selling two to three dollars higher per hundredweight than it had twelve months earlier.

36. E. M. Gardient to William T. Sutherlin, August 19, 1861, William Thomas Sutherlin Papers, folder 12, SHC; Middleton & Son to William T. Sutherlin, June 20, 1862, William Thomas Sutherlin Papers, folder 19, SHC.

37. James R. Millner, "To the Public," March 20, 1863, 3-5, 16, 23-24, in *Confederate Imprints*, reel 94; and John Sutherlin to William T. Sutherlin, January 19, 1863, William Thomas Sutherlin Papers, Duke.

38. William T. Sutherlin, "A Reply to the Publication of James R. Millner, Dated March 20th, 1863," July 28, 1863, 3, 20, 27, 32, in *Confederate Imprints*, reel 95.

39. Though hard figures are impossible to obtain, there is substantial anecdotal evidence of widespread wartime tobacco cultivation. For examples, see Hahn, "Making Tobacco Bright," 119-20; Probate inventory of John T. Muse, 1864, RASP, Southside Family Papers, series E, part 3, reel 3; Receipt of William A. J. Finney, September 2, 1863, RASP, Southside Family Papers, series E, part 3, reel 4; Receipt of Joel Hubbard, October 14, 1865, RASP, Southside Family Papers, series E, part 3, reel 3; Receipt of W. C. Tate, April 2, 1866, RASP, Southside Family Papers, series E, part 3, reel 6; Daniel Tatum Merritt Diary, September 12, 1863, Virginia Historical Society, Richmond, Va. After the end of the war, tobacco receipts from late 1865 and early 1866 record the sale of 1865 crops started in plant beds in the winter of 1864/1865. Most revealing was the fact that regional

manufacturers consistently bought enough local tobacco to keep their operations running at full capacity.

40. Anderson Willis to William T. Sutherlin, August 28, 1861, William Thomas Sutherlin Papers, folder 12, SHC. Willis's letter also illustrated the wartime demand for bright leaf. He offered his crop to Sutherlin, but informed the manufacturer that there was another Danville buyer waiting in the wings.

41. George Jones, in Jeffrey McClurken, *Take Care of the Living: Reconstructing Confederate Veteran Families in Virginia* (Charlottesville: University of Virginia Press, 2009), 30.

42. William R. Hatchett to Allen Hatchett, October 1, 1862, Hatchett Family Papers, Duke. Continued tobacco production could pay in other ways as well. When Caswell soldier and tobacco farmer Bartlett Yancey Malone was captured and imprisoned at Point Lookout, Maryland, his father sent him a box of bright chewing tobacco, which he parceled out and sold to his fellow prisoners for the healthy sum of $55.70 (Malone, *The Diary of Bartlett Yancey Malone*, 53–54).

43. James H. Brewer, *The Confederate Negro: Virginia's Craftsmen and Military Laborers, 1861–1865* (Durham: Duke University Press, 1969), 125.

44. Major and Quartermaster Jason G. Paxton, "To the Farmers of Campbell, Franklin, Henry, Patrick, Grayson, Carroll, Floyd, the Western Part of Pittsylvania and Halifax, and the Southern Part of Bedford Counties," *Broadside*, November 13, 1863, in *Confederate Imprints, 1861–1865*, reel 83, viewed at University of Georgia Library, Athens, GA; McClurken, "After the Battle," 64.

45. Editorial, *Milton Chronicle*, November 9, 1863, 2. See also Durwood T. Stokes, "Charles Napoleon Bonaparte Evans and the Milton Chronicle," *North Carolina Historical Review* 44, no. 3 (1969): 258.

46. Joseph C. G. Kennedy, *Agriculture of the United States in 1860, Compiled from the Original Returns of the Eighth Census* (Washington, D.C.: Government Printing Office, 1864), 104–6, 154–56, 158–60.

47. Hearn and Drane, *Soil Survey of Caswell County*, 21, 26; Jurney et al., *Soil Survey of Halifax County*, 17, 21, 33–34, 40–42; Kirk et al., *Soil Survey of Pittsylvania*, 28, 33–34; "Farmers' State Club," *Southern Planter* 11, no. 3 (1851): 76. The early twentieth-century soil surveys of Caswell, Halifax, and Pittsylvania list productivity figures for unfertilized soil series. New corn and wheat strains had slightly improved productivity, but erosion and agricultural use had also lessened soil fertility by the early 1900s, and thus the surveys should provide relatively accurate statistics for determining antebellum productivity. This claim is also supported by antebellum anecdotal evidence.

48. Colonel Larkin Smith, "Notice to Farmers and Quartermasters," June 13, 1863, Samuel Pannill Wilson Papers, Small Special Collections, University of Virginia Library (hereafter UVA).

49. Commissary Receipts of Samuel P. Wilson, 1863–1865, Samuel Pannill Wilson Papers, UVA.

50. Tax in Kind Receipt of Pleasant H. Womack, July 7, 1864, Hatchett Family Papers, Duke.

51. For an example of an impressment notice, see Impressment Notice, March 16, 186[?], in George Hairston Papers, folder 18, SHC.

52. Paxton, "To the Farmers of Campbell"; McClurken, "After the Battle," 64.

53. Commissary Receipts of Samuel P. Wilson, 1863–1865. The tax in kind continued under the new regulations as well, with quartermasters writing off 10 percent of seizures as tax, and issuing small payments of IOUs for the remainder of the seized goods.

54. For examples, see Sallie J. Sims to William Sims, n.d. (probably 1864), and James Young to Phoebe Bailey, February 29, 1864, both in Bailey Family Papers, Virginia Historical Society (hereafter VHS).

55. Benjamin Lines Farinholt to William Sims, July 31, 1864, and William Sims to Phoebe Bailey, August 17, 1864, both in Bailey Family Papers, VHS (quote in the latter). Seizures and impressment of agricultural produce appears to have been carried out in a fairly uniform manner – that is to say that in the region, privilege did not protect a well-to-do planter from impressment – as evinced by the fact that the Sims family had personal ties to General Lee, yet still faced food and slave impressments. For the family's familiarity with Lee, see Robert E. Lee to Maria C. Sims, May 16, 1862, Robert E. Lee Papers, folder 1, SHC.

56. Robert Enoch Withers, *Autobiography of an Octogenarian* (Roanoke, Va.: Stone Printing and Manufacturing, 1907), 209.

57. Brewer, *The Confederate Negro*, 8; William Alan Blair, *Virginia's Private War: Feeding Body and Soul in the Confederacy, 1861–1865* (New York: Oxford University Press, 1998), 122–24. For an example of slave rentals to the Confederate government, see Hairston Family Plantation Record Book 1, 46, Peter Wilson Hairston Papers, folder 104, SHC.

58. Blair, *Virginia's Private War*, 100–101.

59. Brewer, *The Confederate Negro*, 125.

60. Ibid., 41–42, 87–88, 141–42. This railroad spur allowed easier transportation of Caswell tobacco to Danville by the end of the war, and was the idea of a number of wealthy Southside planters and tobacco manufacturers, including William Sutherlin. See Subscribers to the Piedmont Railroad Company, February 8, 1862, William Thomas Sutherlin Papers, February 8, 1862, SHC.

61. William Sims to Phoebe Bailey, August 17, 1864, Bailey Family Papers, VHS; Commissary Receipts of Samuel P. Wilson, 1863–1865.

62. William Sims to William Bailey, March 15, 1861, Bailey Family Papers, VHS.

63. Phoebe Bailey to William Sims, March 1, 1864, Bailey Family Papers, VHS.

64. Receipt of William T. Sutherlin, August 20, 1859, and Samuel Ayers to William T. Sutherlin, January 4, 1862, both in William Thomas Sutherlin Papers, SHC; Williams and Cheatam to John Sutherlin, July 15, 1858, William Thomas Sutherlin Papers, Duke; Jordan Goodman, *Tobacco in History: The Cultures of Dependence* (New York: Routledge, 1993), 100; Hahn, *Making Tobacco Bright*, 58.

65. For an analysis of California's agricultural marketing, see Douglas Cazaux Sackman, *Orange Empire: California and the Fruits of Eden* (Berkeley: University of California Press, 2005), 84–116; Steven Stoll, *The Fruits of Natural Advantage: Making the Industrial Countryside in California* (Berkeley: University of California Press, 1998).

66. Sackman, *Orange Empire*, 87.

67. For sales to merchants in these locations, see B. H. and O. H. P. Thomas to

John Sutherlin, June 11, 1858, William Thomas Sutherlin Papers, Duke; Receipt of William T. Sutherlin, June 26, 1860, William Thomas Sutherlin Papers, SHC.

68. For the dominance of Danville-area bright leaf as plug wrappers, see S. N. Hawks Jr., *Principles of Flue-Cured Tobacco Production*, 2nd ed. (Raleigh: North Carolina State University, 1978), 5.

69. G. Melvin Herndon, *William Tatham and the Culture of Tobacco* (Coral Gables: University of Miami Press, 1969), 414; Evan Bennett, "King Bacca's Throne: Land, Life, and Labor in the Old Bright Belt since 1880" (PhD diss., College of William and Mary, 2005), 25; Schnittman, "Slavery in Virginia's Urban Tobacco Industry," 24–25; Blow and March to John Sutherlin, May 12, 1858, William Thomas Sutherlin Papers, Duke.

70. William Sours to John Sours, November 19, 1865, Sours Family Papers, folder 21, SHC.

71. Myrta Lockett Avary, *Dixie after the War: An Exposition of Social Conditions Existing in the South, During the Twelve Years Succeeding the Fall of Richmond* (New York: Doubleday, Page, 1906), 52–56; John Gilliam to William T. Sutherlin, June 14, 1865, William Thomas Sutherlin Papers, folder 23, SHC; Receipt of William T. Sutherlin, October 31, 1865, William Thomas Sutherlin Papers, folder 23, SHC.

72. For the growth and changing nature of the postwar tobacco industry, see Benjamin W. Arnold, "History of the Tobacco Industry in Virginia, 1860–1894," in *Johns Hopkins University Studies in Historical and Political Science*, ed. Herbert Adams, 9–86 (Baltimore: Johns Hopkins University Press, 1897); Richard B. Tennant, *The American Cigarette Industry: A Study in Economic Analysis and Public Policy* (New Haven: Yale University Press, 1971); Tilley, *The Bright Tobacco Industry*; Nannie May Tilley, *The R. J. Reynolds Tobacco Company* (Chapel Hill: University of North Carolina Press, 1985); Pete Daniel, *Breaking the Land: The Transformation of Cotton, Tobacco, and Rice Cultures since 1880* (Urbana: University of Illinois Press, 1985); Robert F. Durden, *Bold Entrepreneur: A Life of James B. Duke* (Durham, N.C.: Carolina Academic Press, 2003); Robert R. Korstad, *Civil Rights Unionism: Tobacco Workers and the Struggle for Democracy in the Mid-Twentieth Century South* (Chapel Hill: University of North Carolina Press, 2003); Brandt, *The Cigarette Century*.

73. Jeffrey R. Kerr-Ritchie, *Freedpeople in the Tobacco South: Virginia, 1860–1900* (Chapel Hill: University of North Carolina Press, 1999), 217, table 8.4.

74. Calculated from Historical Census Browser, University of Virginia, Geospatial and Statistical Data Center, http://mapserver.lib.virginia.edu/collections/stats/histcensus/index.html.

75. Mark Fiege, *The Republic of Nature: An Environmental History of the United States* (Seattle: University of Washington Press, 2012), 411.

76. Stanley W. Trimble, *Man-Induced Soil Erosion on the Southern Piedmont, 1700–1970* (Ankeny, Iowa: Soil Conservation Society of America, 1974), 2–3; Rowalt, *Soil Defense in the Piedmont*, 2–7; F. F. Nickels, E. F. Goldston, and E. P. Deatrick, *Reconnaissance Erosion Survey of the State of Virginia* (Washington, D.C.: USDA, Soil Conservation Service, 1934); G. L. Fuller, *Reconnaissance Erosion Survey of the State of North Carolina* (Washington, D.C.: USDA, Soil Conservation Service, 1934); P. F. Keil, "Two Centuries of Accruing Tragedy along the Dan River," *Soil Conservation* 1, no. 7 (1936): 1–5. For the SCS's demonstration work in Pittsylvania, see

surviving issues of the *Bannister River Banner* – the district's conservation organ – in the University of Virginia's Small Special Collections Library.

77. F. H. Jeter in Charles E. Landon, "The Tobacco Growing Industry of North Carolina," *Economic Geography* 10, no. 3 (1934): 253.

78. Michael Pollan, *The Botany of Desire: A Plant's-Eye View of the World* (New York: Random House, 2002), esp. chap. 3.

79. For a tobacco history that takes this cultural construction argument to its logical end, see Hahn, *Making Tobacco Bright*.

NINE

Reconstructing the Soil
Emancipation and the Roots of Chemical-Dependent Agriculture in America

TIMOTHY JOHNSON

When Gen. William T. Sherman's troops tore through eastern Georgia in late 1864 on the storied March to the Sea, there was little doubt that the Yankee war machine was a massively disruptive, if not revolutionary, force on Georgia's cotton belt. Marching from Atlanta to Savannah, sixty thousand Union troops destroyed railroads, torched cotton bales, emptied corncribs and smokehouses, and seized hogs, horses, and mules. Most significantly, the armies freed thousands and thousands of enslaved laborers along their path. Sherman was no champion of racial equality, but whether or not he was comfortable with his own role as emancipator, it was certain that a revolution in social relations was taking place in his wake. What was less apparent, however, was that an ecological revolution would soon be taking place as well.[1]

As they tramped across Georgia on the Savannah Campaign, Union troops encountered an agricultural landscape that differed from their farms back home in a number of important respects. First, much of the Deep South was parceled off into large plantations worked by enslaved laborers in large gangs, a world apart from the single-household farms common in the North. But beyond the plantation system, southerners practiced extensive agriculture – they tapped the nutrients of fresh soil to feed plants, rather than rotating crops and recycling nutrients like animal manure and home compost into the soil. Thus, their ability to feed their staple crops hinged on the native fertility of the land and the prospect of finding more fresh soil once the land's endowment had been drawn down after a few seasons of cultivation. Much of the cotton land southeast of the Mississippi Delta was composed of relatively acidic and nutrient-poor soils, which kept the pace of expansion at a fast clip. For these reasons, many historians suggest that the dual forces of slavery and cotton-fueled land hunger led southerners into the war in the first place, as extensive cotton cultivation created a westward push for new slave states that promised reservoirs of fresh soil. Importing fertilizer to maintain agricultural yields in place was not yet a major part of the equation.[2]

Yet only a few short years after the war, free laborers were cultivating the southern soil with the assistance of new blends of minerals, chemicals, and industrial byproducts marketed by the burgeoning fertilizer industry. On the heels of breakthroughs in agricultural chemistry and discoveries of nutrient-rich minerals, farmers in northern Europe and northeastern states had begun feeding their plants with commercial fertilizers in the antebellum period. Starting during the Reconstruction era, however, the cotton and tobacco belts of Georgia and the Carolinas would lead the United States in fertilizer purchases well into the twentieth century, making the path of Sherman's last great campaign the nation's proving ground for a new era of chemical-intensive agriculture that remains the standard today. Rather than turning to California or the Corn Belt to unearth this particular root of the modern fossil-fueled food system, the following pages examine a small area of the Georgia Cotton Belt centered in Hancock County. Events there can help us untangle how and why the aftermath of the Civil War created a dual revolution in social and ecological relationships.

But even during Reconstruction, farmers quickly learned that the new fertilizer regime was not without its costs. The pungent products that helped bring postwar cotton production to staggering new heights came with a debt burden that led farmers to mortgage their futures to grow staple crops. Indeed, fertilizer was a major new source of debt that emerged during Reconstruction and has been overlooked by historians of the period. By the 1880s fertilizers had become a major — if not the largest — source of farm debt among farmers in the "old" cotton states of Georgia and the Carolinas. Former slaves and poor white farmers were thus the shock troops who ushered in an ecological shift from extensive cultivation to a chemical- and debt-intensive agriculture in the United States. The proliferation of fertilizers illustrates the tight connections between exploitative politics and ecology that took root in the uncertain period after America's greatest conflict. The emergence of the new fertilizer regime reveals environmental connections between the death of bondage and the birth of a new and persistent form of debt.

A handful of scholars of the American South have noted the economic implications of the region's postwar fertilizer boom, yet environmental historians have yet to fully consider the social causes and effects of this change, nor Reconstruction more broadly. There have been longstanding debates about the environmental legacies of slavery, and the apparent "backwardness" of southern agriculture that took shape after the Civil War and continued through the first half of the twentieth century. Conversely, scholars who have examined the emergence of agricultural chemistry in the nineteenth century and the international market in fertilizers—particularly the trade in raw materials between South America and northern Europe—have largely left the American South out of their analysis. But despite these omissions, the tide of commercial fertilizers that began to remake the landscape of the South during Reconstruction signaled the nation's most decisive step into the modern era of chemical- and energy-intensive agriculture. This change would have impacts ranging in scale from microscopic alterations in soil and water chemistry to spatial realignments in crop production both in the South and worldwide.[3]

And yet it is important to note that the impact of war cannot by itself account for the South's transition from extensive agriculture into the fertilizer-fueled nutrient regime. The destruction of war and its political impacts all played a part in the process, but so too did other factors—both human and nonhuman—that were not directly connected to the national ordeal. General Sherman may have fancied his capacity to bring Georgia to its knees by "devastating the state in its whole length and breadth," but to give the federal troops all of the credit for an agricultural transformation would be misplaced. Indeed, as some keen observers of things at ground level noted, many important changes were taking place long before *any* human trod the Georgia soil.

Although the Scottish geologist Charles Lyell came to Georgia in the winter of 1845 and 1846 on a more peaceful visit than Sherman, among scientific circles at the time his purpose was also quite revolutionary. Lyell visited America while he was in the process of redefining the way scientists thought about the history of the earth. In the early nineteenth century most geologists believed that the rocks and landforms of the earth had been shaped by singular, catastrophic events. Among many so-called "catastrophists," the most notable event in the earth's history was Noah's flood, but many natural scientists also pointed to the colossal impacts of other major events like volcanic eruptions and earthquakes. Lyell was different. In contrast, he argued that most "geological changes proceeded slowly and imperceptibly." Gradual forces like erosion, and the flow of rivers and tides, in his view, had shaped the face of the earth over the millennia; the same natural phenomena of the modern era were those that had made the earth the way it was in the past. To help confirm this theory, Lyell came to North America on two separate trips to compare fossils and rocks in search of geological continuities on the other side of the Atlantic. As he visited fossil beds in Georgia and South Carolina on his second trip, he was not disappointed.[4]

With his wife, Mary Elizabeth, Lyell traversed much of the same region of Georgia that Sherman would visit nearly twenty years later. West of the state capital of Milledgeville, he encountered a yawning erosional gully of monstrous proportions. This particular gully had been formed in only twenty years, not even the blink-of-the-eye on the geologic timescale, but once farmers had cleared the native forest for cotton cultivation the process of erosion proceeded with astonishing speed. Lyell speculated that "this country has always been covered by dense forest, from the remote time when it first emerged from the sea." But once farmers felled the protective tree cover, the "excavating power" of heavy rains deepened the gully until "a chasm, measuring no less than 55 feet in depth, 300 yards in length, and varying in width from 20 to 180 feet, was the result." Rain had also worked to leach nutrients from the land, making the soil nutrient poor and acidic. In these rusty-hued soils, which modern soil scientists call "ultisols," losing just the top few inches of soil originally protected by forest cover also meant losing nearly all of the naturally occurring plant nutrients useful for growing crops. Lyell estimated that it would take decades for the land to recover, but modern studies suggest that many of the impacts will last millennia.[5]

Lyell described how the "clearing away of the woods is a source of serious inconvenience and loss" for southern farmers, but he found little evidence that they were working to stem the tide of soil degradation, because cultivating cotton remained profitable for the slaveholders of the South. Mary Elizabeth Lyell saw the connection between "soil mining" and slavery when she chatted with the first lady of Georgia in Milledgeville during their visit to the executive mansion. The governor's wife, Mary Ann Crawford, asked where ladies in London obtained their soap. When Mrs. Lyell responded that they purchased it at stores, Crawford scoffed at the idea of paying for soap when it was so easily made. To make soap, according to Crawford, one had only to fell trees, burn them and boil their ashes for potash, which, she claimed, "costs nothing but the trouble of felling the trees." The basic potash was then "mixed with the fat of sixty hogs" at slaughter time to finish the soap. The labor was all performed by the Crawford's enslaved workforce – which included nine maids for Mrs. Crawford alone. How much easier it was to avoid the "extravagance" of store-bought soap when one could command a small army of slave labor to clear trees and render the fat to make soap at home![6]

From the Lyells' encounters in the gully and in the executive mansion, it is tempting to surmise – as many visitors to the South did – that the institution of slavery by necessity encouraged a profligate attitude toward the soil that made the slaveholding class especially poor stewards of their land. After all, in the decades since the American Revolution, the regime of extensive cotton culture, largely powered by brutal slave labor, had unleashed a seemingly insatiable hunger for land that had leveled native hardwood forests, removed topsoil, and choked streams and rivers with upland sediments. Settlers drifted from South Carolina to central Texas in search of fresh soil, leaving a trail of heavily impacted "old fields" in their wake. Editors of agricultural journals rebuked planters for their misuse of land and labor alike. Most southern planters championed an agricultural system that privileged short-term gain and mobility at the expense of stewardship and permanence, and this process had a particularly deep impact on soils lacking a wealth of native fertility and that did not recover quickly from human impacts. Yet while there is no doubt that the institution of slavery was and remains objectively immoral, to assert that chattel slavery inevitably fostered what would today be called an "unsustainable" agricultural regime ignores the southern planters who used their mastery of labor toward conservationist ends.[7]

On the border of the rolling hills of the Piedmont plateau and the coastal plain, Hancock County, Georgia, was the epicenter of a drive for agricultural improvement before the Civil War in the Deep South. The region was deeply influenced by legacies of extensive agriculture fueled mostly by slave labor. Hancock's white population peaked at about ten thousand in 1800 after the State of Georgia offered up vast swaths of Indian land in a lottery. By the eve of the Civil War, the county's white population had dwindled to about one third of its initial size, while the enslaved black population had nearly doubled. In the face of these demographic shifts, and the environmental realities of badly eroded soils after decades of cotton cultivation, eighteen wealthy planters started the Hancock County Planters' Club in 1837 to try to slow the tide of westward movement by proving that agricultural improvement could restore value to the land. Specifically, they sought "the most eligible means of preparing and mode of applying manures to the exhausted fields" and the best ways to "prevent the waste of soil by heavy falls of rain." The club hosted lecturers, studied local soils, and hosted annual agricultural fairs. One of the founders of the club, William Terrell, endowed the first agricultural chair at the University of Georgia. Fawning editors from the *Southern Cultivator* gloated that the club's efforts to unlock the mysteries of the soil would encourage "fixedness and stability" to an otherwise "roving population." One member of the club harangued his peers in 1843 that "we must revolutionize our system of agriculture, we must improve our lands, or we must abandon our homes." In this light, keeping the land healthy assumed political, even moral dimensions – even as the morality of slavery remained uncontested.[8]

To be certain, members of the Planters Club were outliers in an agricultural regime that tended to be as indifferent to conservation as it was abusive to labor. These soil-obsessed planters were not motivated by impulses that would be familiar to modern environmentalists. Members of the Planters' Club wanted to preserve their wealth and position by virtue of sustained agricultural outputs – conservation was a means to a profitable and socially conservative end. But their reform efforts also tapped into a Whiggish impulse that championed permanence and economic development over time. By dint of their wealth and philosophy, they had a considerably different sense of time and place than their contemporaries whose limitations and perspective led them to search for fresh soil and better prospects beyond the horizon. Long-term thinking was a luxury that the wealthiest planters could afford.[9]

This variety of conservative conservationism among Hancock County's planters might have remained a footnote of southern history if it were not for the business acumen of a Sparta, Georgia, planter named David Dickson. Like other devotees of improved agriculture in Hancock County, Dickson read widely and studied agricultural journals to increase the productivity of his plantation. He was fastidious about directing his enslaved laborers to compost and save manure for his land, which he often bragged had been extremely poor and eroded when he bought it in 1845. He won acclaim for his "system of agriculture," which utilized special plows Dickson designed himself, along with compost and manure. But his real claim to fame was his use of Peruvian guano, a nitrogen-rich "commercial manure" shipped from South America by way of Baltimore to feed his cotton and corn. Although some northern farmers and many cultivators in northern Europe had been using guano since the 1820s and 1830s, Dickson never missed an opportunity to point out that he had been the first farmer in the Deep South to use commercial fertilizers of any kind, starting in 1846. He discovered that heavy applications of guano produced greater yields from his cotton and corn.[10]

After the success of his trials with guano, Dickson began shipping it to his farm by the ton in the decade before the Civil War. The results of his experiments with this "commercial manure" astonished his neighbors and won him attention in the southern agricultural press. What amazed visitors to his plantation the most was how Dickson was restoring old, eroded fields into green and productive ones. To those who scoffed that anyone should pay money for fertilizers and tamper with the soil, Dickson insisted that he was merely giving nature a hand. "I believe strongly in natural laws" but rather than letting fields go fallow, Dickson argued that it was "safest to add a little science, experience and art, to help old nature." And on his sprawling plantation, it looked as though fertilizers had helped unlock the secret to reversing the trend of degradation. Of course, his "secret" was not just fertilizer and manure – it also was a small army of tractable enslaved laborers who performed double duty as workers and as collateral that allowed him to take risks like experimenting with fertilizers. In 1860 Dickson held 144 slaves – the most of anyone in his county. His was an oppressive conservation, indeed.[11]

When war erupted, Dickson joined the ranks of other planters who grew cotton and food to fund and feed the Confederacy. Thus, when Sherman cut supply lines and marched through the croplands of middle Georgia, Sherman was attacking what Lisa Brady has called the "ecological foundation" of the South – slave-based plantation agriculture. When federal troops stormed David Dickson's plantation in early December of 1864, the abundance they found indicated that Dickson had built himself a firm foundation. Sherman's men burned three hundred bales of Dickson's cotton, and collected or destroyed his corn and his grain. They also walked off with at least fifty-five mules and horses – animals valued for labor as well as their manure. Most important, the army liberated about 150 men, women, and children who had lived their lives in bondage. This was a transformative moment. In a matter of minutes, the reinstatement of federal authority dissolved their status as commodities.[12]

The end of war cast uncertainty onto a southern plantation system that had been tremendously profitable to the few and oppressive to many. It was not surprising that former slaveholders wanted to recreate the conditions of slavery to restart cotton production in Georgia—which had dwindled from seven hundred thousand bales in 1860 to about fifty thousand in 1865—while freedpeople sought ways to assert their newfound freedom. To wealthy whites, a hiccup in cotton production felt especially painful considering the loss of wealth from the emancipation of slave property. To these "laborlords-turned-landlords," to paraphrase Gavin Wright, wresting value from land became an imperative once land replaced human chattel as the most valuable asset. Drought in 1866 and 1867 led to crop failures and added to the sense of disorder in the cotton market. Many white landlords tried to force freedpeople to continue to work in gangs on the same land as they had in bondage.[13]

For their part, freedpeople sought to make freedom real by moving away from the gang labor system of slavery to live and work with their own families. Many freedpeople held out hope that Sherman's Special Field Order 15, which had promised land on the Georgia Sea Coast to former slaves, would take effect across the South. The storied "40 Acres and a Mule" never materialized, but congress created the Freedmen's Bureau in 1865 to try to meet the needs of southerners as they sorted through the wreckage of war, including rations for hungry people during a postwar drought. But many observers saw the bureau as a threat to business as usual. One contributor to the *Macon Telegraph* charged that the Freedman's Bureau was "the most potent source of demoralization and the encouragement of idleness among the negroes of the South." He added, "the rations of bacon and corn that are being distributed by these selfish and unprincipled agents of the Government will lessen the crop of cotton by many thousand bales." By this logic, federal interference was slowing the restoration of cotton production and white supremacy to which many insisted the South was destined to return. But whether the South was a slave society or a free one, there was little doubt that cotton would remain king.[14]

David Dickson saw only opportunity. True, war had stripped him of his ability to intensively manage his labor and his land, and Sherman's troops had taken away the animals that had provided valuable manure. But Dickson believed he could sell fertilizer as an antidote for both the social unrest and the underproductive soils of Georgia's cotton land. In a series of letters published in the *Southern Cultivator* starting in 1867, Dickson suggested many ways that fertilizer could help speed the recovery of the southern economy. He mixed a special blend of mineral fertilizers, including guano and bone meal that he dubbed "Dickson's Compound." Then Dickson advertised his fertilizer to other former slaveholders who were frustrated by the uncertainty of a free labor market and the ongoing military occupation under Congressional Reconstruction. But he went even further, using the uncertainty of Reconstruction not just to sell fertilizers but also to sell the very *idea* of using fertilizers by creating a market of soil fertility. Transforming fertility, which had long been considered an innate quality of the land – a natural endowment – into a commodity that could be purchased on the open market took a special type of salesman.

Appealing to those frustrated by the vagaries of the postwar climate, in May 1868 Dickson bragged that unlike the freedpeople, his fertilizer was "self-sustaining; it is punctual in payments; never repudiates or asks for an extension of credit; wants no stay laws or military orders ... it makes laborers cheerful and more willing to work." Most important, he asserted, fertilizer "enables you to work freedmen when they would bring you into debt without it." This was surely a tantalizing prospect for readers who resented the new independence of black laborers, and the continued presence of federal troops once congressional Republicans wrested control of Reconstruction from President Andrew Johnson in 1867. In this sense, Dickson's rhetoric depicted commercial fertilizers as a salve for imbalances in social relations and new political realities.[15]

Dickson also made the case that fertilizers added value to the ailing postwar landscape as well. In a letter to the *Cultivator*, he limned agricultural soil as a marketplace of nutrients, in which fertilizers were an essential investment. Channeling the agricultural chemistry of Justus von Liebig in a financial metaphor, Dickson called for people to put guano "into circulation" as a "currency" by adding as much as two hundred pounds of fertilizer per acre to the soil. The land was a commodity, but he was also suggesting the nutrients flowing through it were commodities, as well. Therefore, planters had to make investments to ensure they did not run down the "principle" bestowed upon the land by nature. Dickson lived by his own advice: records show that he spent three thousand dollars on guano in 1867 alone. That same year, other farmers in Hancock spent forty thousand dollars on fertilizers, much of which, we can assume, was purchased from Dickson. By arguing that fertilizers could answer the post-emancipation "labor question" and make cotton cultivation viable through the miracles of agricultural science, Dickson pointed the direction to a new era on the Cotton Belt without upsetting the racial order of the South.[16]

It might be said, then, that David Dickson provided a spark that helped ignite the fertilizer boom in the Deep South. But a number of other trends converged to foster the shift from extensive agriculture to a fertilizer-fueled regime. One decisive factor was the movement of northern capital into new southern markets after the war. Railroad construction in Georgia and throughout the South began to gain steam during the late 1860s, quickening the transportation of goods and the cost of freight to once remote parts of the South. Sensing new opportunities, fertilizer manufacturers who had supplied truck farmers around northern seaboard cities eyed the emerging market in the staple-producing South—and particularly in the worn cotton lands of the Southeast. In an 1869 letter to a Massachusetts country merchant, Boston fertilizer wholesaler George Davenport wrote that "owing to the great demand for it South compared with the small amount wanted in New England" the Pacific Guano Company was moving its entire fertilizer business and supplies down the coast in search of better profits.[17]

Southerners also cashed in on the growing southern fertilizer market by exploiting the rich phosphate deposits around Charleston, South Carolina. Before the war, the phosphate beds had mostly drawn the attention of fossil hunters and geologists like Charles Lyell, but after the war the mineral's fertilizing value captured the attention of investors. Chief among them was the chemist Nathaniel A. Pratt, who had overseen geological surveys of the Confederate states in search of minerals for explosives and other strategic resources during the conflict. After the war, Pratt tapped his knowledge of the region's geology to help develop the Ashley River phosphate beds for fertilizer industry near Charleston. With the assistance of new rail lines and the state's proximity to the phosphate beds of South Carolina, fertilizers in Georgia in the 1880s were twelve to fifteen dollars per ton cheaper than in states to the west. As more phosphate deposits were opened in Tennessee and Florida, southeastern states became not only major fertilizer consumers, but also exporters in a growing global economy of plant nutrients. This early example of postwar industrialization in the South helped resuscitate postwar cotton production well beyond what it had been before the war began—especially in eastern states like Georgia, where the soil had been so depleted by extensive agriculture and erosion. Fertilizer played a leading role in Georgia's cotton renaissance by providing a mineral "fuel" for cotton cultivation.[18]

And yet, if the example of the fertilizer industry was a bright spot for champions of southern industrialization and for those vested in the reinstatement of King Cotton, the new fertilizer regime was less clearly a boon to rank-and-file farmers, black or white. David Dickson had touted fertilizers as a way for landowners and merchants to make sure they would still make money even as laborers claimed household autonomy, but it also took new legal instruments to make sure these claims would ring true. The legal structure of the Reconstruction-era agricultural economy virtually ensured those tilling the soil would be the least likely to profit from their toil. Lawmakers passed Georgia's first crop lien law in 1866 as a way to unfreeze the credit market of the stalled agricultural economy – especially with rural assets decimated by emancipation and Sherman's forces. The lien laws evolved over time, but in essence they allowed creditors and landlords to furnish supplies or rent land to farmers in the spring in return for a portion of the harvest in the fall. On paper this arrangement was not inherently malicious to borrowers, but in practice it allowed for landlords and merchants to dictate harsh credit terms, and to exercise a great deal of influence over a farmer's operations. The ecologically and economically insidious consequences of the crop lien system – incentivizing cotton production as a term of credit, for instance – are well documented. Less well known are the impacts of Reconstruction-era laws regulating fertilizer and its sale.[19]

Fertilizer was a major source of debt for farmers beginning in the years after the Civil War, but historians have not fully understood exactly how these products helped create a new landscape of agricultural production and debt after the war. Between 1870 and 1890, farmers purchased 75 to 85 percent of all fertilizer on credit at inflated prices, and at times, this amount peaked at 95 percent. Starting in the 1870s, farmers borrowing fertilizer for spring planting could expect to sign a "guano note." So-named after bird dung fertilizers, guano notes were financial instruments similar to crop liens – in essence they were promissory notes by which farmers offered a portion of their crop in exchange for fertilizers. Fertilizer merchants wanted to ensure that lending their products would produce returns, so they stipulated that farmers plant cotton as a condition of sale. Thus, fertilizer merchants were also in line with landlords and other furnish merchants to call in debts when the fall harvest was complete.[20]

Ostensibly, farmers purchased fertilizers because they would increase their profits by reaping a more bountiful harvest. Yet guano notes reveal how the benefits of the fertilizer were most likely divvied out to the lending merchants, rather than the farmers who applied them. Clearly, farmers recognized benefits from the application of fertilizers from the evidence they witnessed in the deep green leaves they saw in their plants. Fertilizer purchases continued in a strong upward curve for decades after the war, suggesting that people believed it was a valuable new tool in cultivation. Guano notes provide evidence that the financial risks involved with purchasing fertilizer fell on farmers more than anyone else, and these risks only became more acute over time. Beginning in 1877, the final year of federal Reconstruction, the Georgia General Assembly passed a constitutional amendment allowing debtors to waive the homestead exemption, which legally protected the homes and household goods of families from parties seeking to collect debt. After 1877, without exception, fertilizer dealers included language on their notes that required the signer to waive their homestead protection as a condition of credit. Thus, whether a farmer was advanced two dollars or two hundred dollars of fertilizer in the spring, failing to produce the cotton or cash outlined on the note in the fall could mean losing one's home, mule, or even household goods. A critic of the rapid proliferation of guano notes lamented that "farmers cannot obtain credit unless they sign a waiver note, and waive everything except their wife and baby; and dealers would require those waived if they could." These were harsh terms considering that the very best return a farmer could expect on purchasing fertilizers at the time was to break even.[21]

If farmers were to assume the risks associated with costly fertilizers and legally binding guano notes, they desired a modicum of insurance for their purchases. During the Reconstruction era, agricultural chemistry was still in its developmental phase, and although most farmers did not wade into the rarified world of experimental science they still expected to get what they paid for. Fertilizers were investments that were supposed to pay farmers back, so farmers wanted an appraisal of their value. In 1868 Georgia's state legislators created the position of state chemist to ensure that fertilizers sold in the state contained the plant nutrients that they advertised. In 1874 the Georgia General Assembly established a state-level department of agriculture to expand regulation powers and keep pace with the volume of fertilizers entering the state each year. The state inspectors attached tags to each bag of fertilizer translating the opaque language of chemistry into more legible terms. Fertilizer manufacturers paid a fee for each shipment of their products that the state chemists inspected. The profits from inspection fees funded the Department of Agriculture as the department's duties expanded to include the regulation of other commodities, agricultural research, and inventories of the state's resources. In 1875 alone, the state's inspectors tested 48,000 tons of fertilizer, encompassing 112 different brands.[22]

Inspection fees paid the bills at the Georgia Department of Agriculture, but that did not mean that its personnel approved of fertilizer's steadily growing role on the state's farms. Georgia's first Commissioner of Agriculture, Thomas P. Janes, saw the rise of farm debt across the state and pointed to an obsession with expensive fertilizers as a primary cause. "The injudicious use of high-priced fertilizers has been a fruitful source of loss and embarrassment" according to Janes, who believed that farmers were failing to use local sources of nutrients like compost and manure. A student of mixed husbandry and an educated agricultural expert, Janes regarded fertilizer as evidence that Georgia's farmers had lost their way. Why pay to feed one's plants when one could rotate crops and use composts and manures? In 1875 the department reported that Georgia farmers spent $2.5 million on commercial fertilizers, while only 15 percent of the state's farmers saved stable manure to feed their plants.[23]

In reality, however, Georgia's farmers had few options but to give themselves over to the new fertilizer-fueled cotton regime. As it had been before the war, the state and much of the region was tethered both economically and culturally to short-stapled cotton. Thus, a farmer seeking an advance on seed or land to cultivate would have to agree to grow cotton as a term of credit. On a small farm with poor soil, the manure of one or two mules proved insufficient to feed the plants. Before the war, David Dickson had forced his laborers to gather and spread manure in addition to fertilizers. By 1885, the year Dickson died, however, his account book was filled with the names of his tenants and neighbors who owed him for fertilizer and other debts. More than 120 of the debtors in the book were in "bad" or "doubtful" standing, but in spite of this he left behind a fortune valued in the hundreds of thousands of dollars. If owning slaves had been the key to wealth before Sherman came, it seemed that selling fertilizer was the best opportunity after he had passed.[24]

In 1880 the Bureau of the Census conducted a major study of cotton production across the states of the American South. A team of soil scientists and geologists fanned out across the states of the former Confederacy as well as Oklahoma and California to gauge the state of America's fiber-producing heartland in the new context of freedom. Their findings, published in 1884, provide a snapshot of a region much changed during the Reconstruction period. Cotton remained the staple crop in the Deep

South, but it was being cultivated in new ways in new places. Since the war, Mississippi was the leader in cotton production due to the "exceptional fertility" of its soil and the singular pursuit of cotton cultivation there. Quite beyond that, Mississippi was newer to cotton cultivation than states to the east, and with its combined natural advantages and somewhat shorter history of cultivation, it would remain a jewel of the cotton kingdom long thereafter.[25]

The report noted that, somewhat surprisingly, Georgia was a close second to Mississippi in cotton production in 1880, albeit for different reasons. Georgia lacked the natural advantages of the alluvial lands of Mississippi, and it had a longer history of extensive cultivation that had taxed its fragile soils. Georgia's surprising cotton resurgence came not from rich soil but from its new dependence on fertilizers. Across the state, small dealers selling phosphates, cottonseed hulls, and German potash peddled their wares on credit to farmers seeking better crops. In 1879 Georgians spent $4.3 million on fertilizers in 1879, leading the nation both in expenditures and in tonnage. And although the mineral and byproduct-based fertilizers Georgians applied lacked the concentration of modern chemical fertilizers, they were effective enough to radically change the map of cotton production within the state and to create a new consumer market for agricultural inputs that has grown steadily ever since.[26]

Whereas the extensive agricultural pattern created a westward-moving cotton frontier before the war, fertilizers provided farmers with the tools to exploit "inner peripheries" – that is, areas that had been bypassed during the initial wave of land clearing and cultivation. Because fertilizers accelerated the rate of plant growth, they allowed upcountry farmers into the cooler temperature regime and shorter growing season of southern Appalachia. Fertilizers allowed cultivation at higher elevations, thus bleeding the traditional boundary of cotton cultivation northward. The new marketplace of plant foods also moved the area of cultivation southward into the nutrient-poor soils of the coastal plain. In 1864 General Sherman had noted that on the sandy coastal plain, cotton cultivation had stopped and the land and people he encountered tended to be poor, but fertilizers helped change this. Even within the old cotton lands of the Piedmont region, fertilizers allowed farmers to look at old eroded fields with fresh eyes.[27]

"More than gold was to California, diamonds to Brazil and the Cape, or silks to France, commercial fertilizers are to the South," exclaimed a *New York Times* correspondent in 1881. In reality, farmers were conflicted about the value of fertilizers. According to farmers who submitted opinions to the 1880 cotton survey, fertilizers were at once a blessing and curse. A farmer in upcountry Hall County claimed that fertilizers "made a climate," by quickening plant growth and allowing cotton cultivation in cooler climes. In Clarke County "the best farmers use them and would not be without them." Another claimed fertilizer increased crop production by 50 percent. In contrast, others asserted that, "they increase the crops but not the net profits of farming," that they "are used for the benefit of the crops, not for any lasting addition of the soil." At worst, they "make farmers of this region poorer each year."[28]

Whether or not it stood to benefit farmers, fertilizer became the new normal first in Georgia and then across the cotton South during the region's tenuous reentry into the nation. And in spite of the end of an oppressive labor regime, under the new nutrient regime, soils continued to degrade from erosion and continuous cropping. A recent study by soil scientists estimates that the erosion from cotton cultivation in middle Georgia will take the soil as many as ten thousand years to recover. Certainly the new era carried the promise of freedom, but there was no freedom from the same tenuous soil ecology that had plagued farmers before Sherman made his famous—or infamous—March to the Sea. The Civil War did not undermine the continued agricultural and natural tolls on the soil. It merely helped to change the terms by which it was conducted by helping to usher in a new era of input-intensive agriculture. Southern agriculture was reconstructed on a new, albeit shaky social and ecological foundation.

Before the Civil War, the United States was not at the forefront of agricultural chemistry or even the largest user of mineral fertilizers. But following the war the rapidly industrializing and urbanizing nation became an agricultural powerhouse that exported not only new energy-intensive agricultural practices but also massive agricultural surpluses produced by its new fertilizer-fueled agriculture, as well. The reach of fertilizer inputs drifted far beyond its early southern staging ground to reach virtually every major agricultural region of the nation by the 1950s. This expansion was occasioned by the diminishment of native soil fertility in other agricultural regions, the replacement of manure producing draft animals with tractors, and the maturation of a fertilizer industry capable of harnessing minerals and fossil fuels to produce potent chemical products to meet rising demand for fertilizer both within the United States and beyond. But it was in the years after the Civil War that our chemical-dependent approach to feeding and clothing ourselves first took root. Reconstructing the nation, its turns out, also involved redefining how Americans related to and relied upon the land underfoot.

Notes

1. For Sherman's account of the Savannah Campaign see Michael Fellman, ed., *Memoirs of W. T. Sherman* (New York: Penguin Books, 2000); and Brooks D. Simpson and Jean V. Berlin, eds., *Sherman's Civil War: Selected Correspondence of William T. Sherman, 1860-1865* (Chapel Hill: University of North Carolina Press, 1999). For an account of Sherman's racial and political views see Michael Fellman, *Citizen Sherman: A Life of William Tecumseh Sherman* (New York: Random House, 1995).

On the environmental history of the Savannah Campaign, see Lisa M. Brady, "The Wilderness of War: Nature and Strategy in the American Civil War," in *Environmental History and the American South*, ed. Paul S. Sutter and Christopher Mangianello, 168-95 (Athens: University of Georgia Press, 2009).

2. On the relationship between slavery and land exhaustion in the Deep South see, for example, David T. Montgomery, *Dirt: The Erosion of Civilizations* (Berkley: University of California Press, 2007).

3. On the rise of agricultural chemistry in America see Margaret W. Rossiter, *The Emergence of Agricultural Science: Liebig and the Americans, 1840-1880* (New Haven: Yale University Press, 1975); Benjamin R. Cohen, *Notes from the Ground: Science, Soil, and Society in the American Countryside* (New Haven: Yale University Press, 2009); Steven Stoll, *Larding the Lean Earth: Soil and Society in Nineteenth-Century America* (New York: Hill and Wang). On fertilizers in nineteenth-century America see Richard A. Wines, *Fertilizer in America: From Waste Recycling to Resource Exploitation* (Philadelphia: Temple University Press, 1985); Jimmy M. Skaggs, *The Great Guano Rush: American Entrepreneurs and American Overseas Expansion* (New York: St. Martin's Press, 1994).

4. Leonard G. Wilson, *Lyell in America: Transatlantic Geology, 1841-1853* (Baltimore: Johns Hopkins University Press, 1998), 1-6.

5. Charles Lyell, *A Second Visit to the United States of America* (London: Spottswoodes and Shaw, 1850), 2:23-24. On southern gullies and erosion see Paul Sutter, "What Gullies Mean: Georgia's 'Little Grand Canyon' and Southern Environmental History," *Journal of Southern History* 76, no. 3 (2010): 579-616. On ultisols see Daniel D. Markewitz and Daniel Richter, *Understanding Soil Change* (Cambridge: Cambridge University Press, 2001); C. R. Jackson, J. K. Martin, D. S. Leigh, and L. T. West, "A Southeastern Piedmont Watershed Sediment Budget: Evidence for a Multi-millennial Agricultural Legacy." *Journal of Soil and Water Conservation* 60, no. 6 (2005): 298-310.

6. Lyell, *Second Visit to America*, 2:24.

7. On conservation and slavery see Lynn A. Nelson, *Pharsalia: An Environmental Biography of a Southern Plantation, 1780-1880* (Athens: University of Georgia Press, 2007).

8. Gustavus B. Maynadier and W. J. Geib, *Soil Survey of Hancock County, Georgia* (Washington, D.C.: Government Printing Office, 1909), 553. The Hancock

County Planters' Club Papers, Folder 10, Georgia Department of Archives and History (hereafter GDAH); "Address of R. P. Sasnett, esq.," *Southern Cultivator,* Jan. 1846, 4, 1. On the HCPC, see also James G. Bonner, "Profile of a Late Antebellum Community," *American Historical Review* 49, no. 4 (1944): 663–80.

9. Benjamin Cohen does an excellent job in parsing out the strains of this improvement ethic in the nineteenth century in *Notes from the Ground.*

10. One of the Party, "Hancock Farming – David Dickson, Again," *Southern Cultivator,* November 1859, 17, 11.

11. David Dickson with J. Dickson Smith, ed., *A Practical Treatise on Agriculture* (Macon: J. W. Burke and Company, 1870), 235; David Dickson, "Observations on Manures," *Southern Cultivator,* May 1867, 25, 5.

12. Lisa M. Brady, "Devouring the Land: Sherman's 1864–1865 Campaigns," in *War and the Environment: Military Destruction in the Modern Age,* ed. Charles E. Clossman (College Station: Texas A&M University Press, 2009), 62; The 1860 census shows that Dickson owned 144 slaves; other numbers about the impact of Sherman are from "David Dickson Dead," *Atlanta Journal,* February 18, 1885.

13. Gavin Wright, *Old South, New South: Revolutions in the Southern Economy Since the Civil War* (Baton Rouge: Louisiana State University Press, 1985), 17; Willard Range, *A Century of Georgia Agriculture, 1850–1950* (Athens: University of Georgia Press, 1954), 69.

14. Cotton Factors Messr. Easton & Co., New York, "Experiment Being Developed: Cotton Cultivation Diminishing, Diversification of Pursuits Essential to Restore the South," *Georgia Weekly Telegraph,* July 10, 1868, 8.

15. Dickson, *A Practical Treatise on Agriculture,* 141.

16. Ibid., 108–9; records of Dickson's purchases come from Stephen D. Heard Account Book, 1867, Stephen D. Heard Papers, SHC; Range, *A Century of Georgia Agriculture,* 121–22.

17. On the rise of early fertilizer manufacturers, see Wines, *Fertilizer in America.* Regarding railroad construction, Woodward notes that the real construction boom came after 1880: C. Vann Woodward, *Origins of the New South, 1877–1913* (Baton Rouge: Louisiana State University Press, 1951), 120. George Davenport & Co. to P. W. Dudley & Company, March 27, 1869, Warshaw Collection of Business Americana, Fertilizer Series, box 1, "Pacific Guano Co.," Smithsonian National Museum of American History.

18. N. A. Pratt, *Ashley River Phosphates: History of the Marls of South Carolina and the Discovery and Development of the Native Bone Phosphates of the Charleston Basin* (Philadelphia: Inquirer Book Job Print, 1868), 6; Shepherd W. McKinley, *Stinking Stones and Rocks of Gold: Phosphate, Fertilizer, and Industrialization in Postbellum South Carolina* (Gainesville: University Press of Florida, 2014); Harold E. Malde, *Geology of the Charleston Phosphate Area, South Carolina,* Geological Survey Bulletin vol. 1079 (1959): 1–7; See also Carville Earle, *Geographical Inquiry and American Historical Problems* (Stanford: Stanford University Press, 1992), 293. On the transition from the organic economy to the mineral-based energy economy, see E. A. Wrigley, *Continuity, Chance and Change: The Character of the Industrial Revolution in England* (Cambridge: Cambridge University Press, 1988).

19. On the crop lien start with Woodward, *Origins of the New South*; see also

Roger L. Ransom and Richard Sutch, *One Kind of Freedom: The Economic Consequences of Emancipation* (Cambridge: Cambridge University Press, 1977). On legal history see Harold D. Woodman, *New South – New Law: The Legal Foundations of Credit and Labor in the Postbellum Agricultural South* (Baton Rouge: Louisiana State University Press, 1995), 1–10.

20. Range, *A Century of Georgia Agriculture,* 101.

21. Guano notes were exceedingly common in the past but relatively rare in archival collections. The Hodgson Cotton Company Records at the Hargrett Library, University of Georgia, is an excellent place to look. On the homestead exemption, see Steven Hahn, *The Roots of Southern Populism: Yeoman Farmers and the Transformation of the Georgia Upcountry* (New York: Oxford University Press, 1983), 195. "The Brady Bill," *Atlanta Constitution,* July 19, 1887, 2. Ransom and Sutch, *One Kind of Freedom,* 188.

22. *Annual Report of the State Department of Agriculture* (Savannah: J. H. Estill, 1878), 9–10; *Acts of the General Assembly of the State of Georgia,* 1868, 1874.

23. H. C. White, *Annual Report of the State Department of Agriculture,* 1875, 37.

24. David Dickson Will, in David Dickson Papers at the Georgia Department of Archives and History, Morrow, Ga. On the fascinating story behind the contestation of Dickson's will, see Kent A. Leslie, *Woman of Color, Daughter of Privilege: Amanda America Dickson, 1849–1893* (Athens: University of Georgia Press, 1995), 79.

25. E. W. Hilgard, "Report on Cotton Cultivation in the United States: Part I" (Washington, D.C.: Government Printing Office, 1884), 7.

26. Ibid.

27. On "inner peripheries" and frontiers, see Robert B. Marks, *China: Its Environment and History* (New York: Rowman and Littlefield, 2012), 173–76. R. H Loughridge, *Report on the Cotton Production of the State of Georgia* (Washington, D.C.: Government Printing Office, 1884), 56.

28. C. R. M., "The Soil of the South," *New York Times,* October 16, 1881. Loughridge, *Report on the Cotton Production,* 165.

TEN

Walking, Running, and Marching into an Environmental History of the Civil War

MART A. STEWART

Environmental historians often start with the obvious: How do people create livelihoods for themselves? Where do they live, and what do they eat? How do they get from one place to another, and what do they do along the way (and how do movements of organisms from one place to another change those places)? As a field, it has also had deep roots in the last question – and especially in the history of walking – as a way to travel, as a means of experiencing nature, as a mediating activity between us and the environment. Accounts and analyses of walking, like the analysis of how we are what we eat, produce an understanding of something fundamental in our experience with the world around us, first of all. For millennia, humans walked all of the time, to move ahead of the weather; to stalk deer, monkeys, and crabs; to gather roots, grubs, and leaves. Then about a half-minute ago, we stooped to sow some seeds, and now here we are with air travel, Hummers, the Internet, and couch potatoes. More specifically, the discourse on walking and the environment was partly developed out of a preoccupation with the perambulating considerations of nature generated by naturalist-philosophers – by Gilbert White, William Bartram, Henry David Thoreau, John Muir, Gary Snyder, and a host of others who explored nature on foot. Thoreau's essay on walking, or more accurately, on the value of *saun-terre-ing*, is a pivotal text in the history of environmental thought; its compelling conclusion, after Thoreau had proclaimed the value of plunging deep into a figurative swamp of wildness, "In Wildness is the salvation of the world," is a walker's manifesto as well.[1] After it had been metabolized by John Muir, who changed the word "wild" to "wilderness," it became the call to battle for the first important environmental activist organization in the United States cofounded by Muir, the Sierra Club.

What does this have to do with an environmental history of the Civil War? If the Civil War was the first modern war, it was also the last one where participants, both combatants and noncombatants, for the most part moved to and around the landscape of war mainly on foot. Enlistees were mustered in with a single stride, traveled from one engagement to another on foot, sometimes straggled off in the same way, and then returned home the way they went – by walking. When noncombatants fled armies or rushed to join in their trail, roamed through southern fields and forests looking for sustenance, or traveled to visit relatives who were soldiers or to check on kin on other plantations, they usually did this on foot. Historians are finally beginning to engage the environmental history of the Civil War, and the first entries into what has the potential to be a rich future scholarship have been published. As this scholarship develops, and if one of the fundamental experiences with the environment of war for both combatants and noncombatants was astride – whether walking, running, or marching – then we can learn a lot from some good footwork on this experience.[2]

Walking

The literature of walking out of which an environmental ethos developed was, first of all, a literature and a genre that explained how a solitary (almost always) stroll through nature could be both instructive and virtuous. The early literature in this genre, inspired by English writer William Hazlitt's influential 1821 essay, "On Going for a Journey," was meant to provide instruction on a ritual for middle class walkers who had both the leisure and the education to worship at the altar of nature. Hazlitt's essay and the genre it inspired were always conventional, explains Rebecca Solnit in her history of walking, *Wanderlust*: "Both walk and essay are meant to be pleasant, even charming, and so no one ever gets lost and lives on grubs and rainwater in a trackless forest, has sex in a graveyard with a stranger, stumbles into a battle, or sees visions of another world." It was an occasion for thinking about nature, with both the scenery of the walk and the education of the walker on view – Hazlitt managed to quote, in a short essay, works by Virgil, Shakespeare, Milton, Dryden, Gray, Cowper, Sterne, Coleridge, Wordsworth, and of course Rousseau.[3] The walking essay also put natural history on view. Both Bartram's and Muir's accounts of their perambulating journeys were notable for the botanical knowledge they displayed, and include sensitive and astute accounts of flora and fauna – and for Muir, ecological processes – encountered on the trail. So it is a stretch to talk about Civil War walkers as part of this tradition. Their purpose was not to parade knowledge of the classics, to reflect on nature, to generate bourgeois virtue, or even to describe the surrounding landscape – but to stumble into battle.

We do have, however, a compendium from the Civil War, which even if not used very often was nonetheless intended to be used as a source of botanical knowledge – and that gathered together information of the kind that was important to and sometimes generated by Bartram, Thoreau, and Muir. It also took for granted a kind of perambulation, to gather and use what was described and explained in this collection. This was Francis Peyre Porcher's *Resources of Southern Fields and Forests*, published in Charleston, South Carolina, in 1863. Porcher was the Surgeon General of the Confederate States, and *Resources* was designed to provide information about the flora of the region and its uses, for everything from coffee to cooking oil, but with an emphasis on medical botany: the subtitle of the book was *Medical, Economical, and Agricultural. Being also a Medical Botany of the Confederate States; with Practical Information on the Useful Properties of the Trees, Plants, and Shrubs*. This massive compendium of information about southern flora was also a catalogue of both vernacular and scientific knowledge about southern botany. It drew from published works on botany and medical botany, both classical and recent, Porcher's own research as a botanist and doctor, and from information he gathered from oral accounts of plants and plant uses by southerners both white and black. It was meant to helve to the ground; the introduction included brief instructions on the gathering and drying of useful plants, as well as a short list of plants that could be useful for medicinal purposes by soldiers, "while in service in any part of the Confederate States," and a similar list of southern trees "adapted to the purposes of the Manufacturer and Wood Engraver." Just how often it was used is not known, but it had embedded within it assumptions about walking through the landscape and paying attention to nature that connect it to the larger literature of walking.[4]

Resources of Southern Fields and Forests was a collection informed by exploratory walking that was also meant to be used by soldiers who were covering the ground by foot. While it did not espouse or express the improvement of character when it advised readers about the many uses of the plants they could find by searching southern fields and forests, it was infused with the same traditions of natural history that were active in accounts of walking by White, Bartram, and Thoreau. It also had a larger philosophical and political goal in mind: the encouragement of innovation and self-sufficiency for soldiers of the newly formed Confederate States of America. It argued for larger political virtue, rather than the bourgeois individualism of Hazlitt's and Thoreau's accounts of walking; it espoused botanizing for national self-sufficiency and independence.

For example, the bark of the members of the "dogwood tribe," especially the *Cornus florida*, a common understory tree throughout the South, was an adequate substitute for the quinine extracted from the Peruvian cinchona, which was not available during the war. Porcher explains how to prepare it, and lists accounts of its success in treating intermittent fever and malaria from medical practitioners who were his colleagues, as well as anecdotal information he had gathered – that dogwood bark "has been used from time immemorial among the Huguenot families of the Santee" for treating malaria, for example. A scarlet color had been extracted from the fibrous roots of the plant by "Indians," he explained by the way, and the "common people of South Carolina" had long whitened their teeth by rubbing them with the young branches of the tree.[5]

Another significant plant discussion that is representative of the larger goals of the volume, and of a plant that was on Porcher's short list of useful plants for both medical and manufacturing purposes, is the one of sesame, or bené. Bené was an exotic introduction from Africa, and a cultivated rather than wild plant, but it had acquired importance in the domestic economy of the southern lowcountry, mainly because of its use for both oil and food by African American slaves. Sesame seed, Porcher explained, easily yielded a high quantity of high-quality oil, which could be used for all kinds of purposes: a mucilaginous tea made from sesame seed was almost as useful as sassafras in treating dysenteries and pulmonary diseases; sesame oil was just as accomplished as castor oil as a purgative, and "free from the nauseous taste peculiar to castor oil"; the oil was as versatile as Mediterranean olive oil in cooking, and could also be used in the manufacture of soap or as a foundation for varnish or paint; the seeds could be parched (the common method of the "Africans of South Carolina") and preserved for several years, or cooked in stews or mixed with sugar to make candy; and the leaves of the plant could be steeped into a tea that had several medical benefits. One of the most versatile plants in this compendium of more than eight hundred was significantly also not a wild plant. The absence of clear distinctions in *Southern Fields and Forests* between wild and domestic, as well as between native and exotic plants, except in terms of where they could be found, how they could be produced or collected, and the natural history of each, reflected the absence of these distinctions in southern natural history and environmental thinking in general. The products of both southern fields and forests were useful to both Confederate soldiers and civilians as they moved through the wartime environment of the South.[6]

One more useful southern plant, saltwort, that appeared on Porcher's short list was hardly known to most southerners, unless they lived on the southeast Atlantic coast or were knowledgeable in botany. *Salsola kali*, or saltwort, which could be processed to yield the soda that was required in the manufacture of soap, grew along the Atlantic coast from Georgia north. Porcher explained that the Spanish once cultivated it, and it could be planted in places where it could be flooded periodically with salt water – as well as gathered from the salt marshes of South Carolina. He explained how it could be processed to yield soda – of a better quality than that extracted from seaweed or corncobs – and also included several soap recipes. He also here explained, by way of a quotation from an article in the *Richmond Dispatch*, just why botanizing and its products were necessary:

> In these times of war and blockade, when our people are thrown almost entirely upon their own resources, every item looking to domestic economy and home production should be carefully observed. Our people are passing through a trying ordeal, but they are learning lessons which will be of practical utility in after times. Habits of economy, and elements of self-reliance, which have been pushed aside by the pressure of an extravagant sentiment, by an increasing love for easy and luxurious living, and by the versatility of Yankee genius in supplying our almost every want, are now, from the influences of necessity, being resumed, while they are found to embody all of practical utility which they possessed in days of yore.

By searching through the fields and forests and marshes and swamps of the South, the self-sufficiency and self-reliance of the region could be enhanced, and independence from "Yankee genius in supplying ... almost every want" could be achieved. Traveling through the floral South was in Porcher's compendium deepened by connections to classical botanical sources and propelled by its value in supporting sustenance and saving lives. But it was also a means to political virtue and southern success in the war for Confederate independence.[7]

At the very least, *Southern Fields and Forests* acknowledged formally practices that became increasingly common among southerners as the Civil War ground up usual supplies of food and medicine – practices that became common among soldiers both blue and gray, too, of moving through southern fields and forests to gather and glean and beg and sometimes steal, for sustenance and fuel. Experience of the environment here began with the belly and was exercised on foot; it read landscape, sometimes with considerable nuance, to find what was needed to feed the participants in the war. Soldiers both blue and gray gathered chestnuts and muscadines; picked blackberries, persimmons, huckleberries, walnuts, hickory nuts, and pecans; cut oak for all kinds of purposes, some of them medicinal; caught fish, eels, and crustaceans; barbecued opossum and made soup or pie out of rabbits, and occasionally boiled an alligator. They hardly lived off the land, and when they did it was off the production of the cultivated rather than uncultivated landscapes of the South, and especially during the harvest season. But at the end of the day while they were making camp or were out on the flanks of the march or in an advance guard, they used the opportunities provided by less distraction and a route off the road to add to their trail larder.[8] Walking through nature was not an occasion for reflecting on it, but more often an effort to eat it. But this dimension of the Civil War was a fundamental one and needs to be recovered in full to understand the environmental history of the war.

Running

African Americans during the Civil War were more likely to run than walk – if not actually, then figuratively. At the same time, the act of running to Union lines also erased decisively the antebellum meaning of the term "running." The decision of tens of thousands of slaves to expedite emancipation by fleeing to Union lines – a Confederate officer in North Carolina in August 1862 estimated a million dollars worth a week – had deep roots in antebellum practices of running away. If not in the relatively rare but often imagined northward trek toward freedom, fleeing to Union lines came out of the far more common act of laying out or circulating surreptitiously through the plantation neighborhood. It also had deep roots in the environmental practices of slaves, who because of nocturnal hunting, visiting of relatives on neighboring plantations, growing patches of vegetables in the woods and swamps, or gathering resources from fields and forests, often knew the surrounding natural landscapes better than their masters.

Slaves who ran during the Civil War usually left the plantations at night, concealed themselves in woods or swamps during the day, and then sprinted for the nearest Union camp as soon as they came close. A few examples will suffice here. In lowcountry South Carolina, Jack Flowers hid in the rice swamps during the day and slowly made for the woods and a nearby river, where he patched together a boat of reeds, caulked with cotton from nearby fields and sealed with pitch, and paddled his way to freedom. A couple of Louisiana families spent two days and nights in waist-deep mud and water in the swamps, with children clinging to their backs, before making a break for Union lines. Sometimes slaves hid out for extended periods in swamps and forests near the plantations – in the neighborhoods of the known – where they depended on their ability to wrest something to eat from local environments, and also from food supplied by kin in the neighborhood, to survive until Union troops drew near. In some places runaways formed small colonies; a slave patrol in South Carolina found such a settlement in a nearby swamp that was well supplied with everything they needed to keep a permanent camp, including "twelve guns and an ax." In Surrey County, Virginia, another patrol tracked down a similar colony but was not able to report on it, because the fugitives killed them.[9] In all cases, the environmental knowledge of slaves was crucial: "They know every road and swamp and creek and plantation in the country," shrieked the usually reserved Reverend Charles Colcock Jones of Georgia, noting that slaves not only ran away easily, but then sometimes came back as guides to the troops they ran to – "They are traitors who may pilot a enemy into your *bedchamber*!" he added.[10]

What historians have somewhat austerely called "terrains of struggle" and the "geography of resistance" here needs to be examined in a way that recovers the environmental dimension of running away – just how important environmental knowledge was to this act – or in fact, just what kind of geographers slaves were.

The best one-stop source to do this comes not from the Civil War, but from a slave narrative published in 1836, Charles Ball's *Slavery in the United States: A Narrative of the Life and Adventures of Charles Ball*, which includes an extended account of a yearlong trek Ball took from Georgia to reunite with his wife in Maryland. Ball's was a walking narrative that in detail and dramatic verve and environmental meaning rivals those by the founding *peregrinati* of environmental history. From beginning to end, the narrative was shaped by Ball's understanding of fugitive environments, and how these worked themselves out by way of natural ones. He kept in his sights always the path of the North Star, first of all, and usually traveled in the deep night not only to avoid slave patrols but to keep his direction – and when the sky was cloudy, he laid out in thickets of oak, whortleberry, or cedar or in uninviting tangle of swamps until he could see the stars and plot his way again. He also lived off the land – both cultivated and uncultivated. He headed off in the first place in August, because this was when corn could begin to be harvested; he savored the large naturalized Indian peaches he found growing in Georgia and South Carolina, and was grateful for the strength he gained at crucial times in the trek by opossums and a wild pig he killed – though he lamented not having a dripping pan that would catch the fat when he cooked them. He had to manage all kinds of weather – his trek ended in spring of the next year – and a stone, steel, and tinderbox, along with a knack for finding dry fuel, gave him fire when he could risk having one.[11]

What was most striking about this account as an explanation of slave environments was how Ball gathered and analyzed geographic information. He had traveled south by foot when he was first brought to South Carolina and then Georgia from the upper South, so he had some previous experience with the topography of the Carolinas and Georgia on a regional scale. When he set out at first from middle Georgia he reckoned he would go a little east of north to intersect the systems of roads that he recalled from this previous trip. But after several days of walking and not crossing major rivers, he estimated that he was traveling more east than north, and at just thirty miles from Charleston, turned west and north again – to regain country with more relief and the hills that gave him cover during the day (he understood that slave patrols traveled on horseback on roads that were mainly in the low places) and to find roads that at night might also take him north. He knew he had strayed by reading the land he was crossing – he knew that he should be crossing rivers, not traveling parallel to them – and then analyzing it within the context of his understanding of the topography of the region. He then confirmed what he suspected by hiding out near a road and listening in on the conversations of passersby (one of the ways he gathered information in general while on this trek). His ability to read landscape to locate himself within the larger region, with the general guidance of the North Star, indicates an ability not only to remember and use environmental knowledge but to analyze and imagine from what he experienced in the context of what he already knew to what he expected to find.

Ball had what geographer Carl Sauer in a classic essay, "The Education of a Geographer," calls a "morphologic eye," the ability to intuitively understand form and pattern in geography as well as in vegetation, and put the two together to understand how landforms and vegetation communities are related. This is more than description and memory. The range of possible forms is enormous, Sauer explains, so it is necessary to note relevance and understand how each form is related to others in a kind of grammar of geography that requires analysis and explanation rather than mere description. He notes that the native guides who helped him years before in Mexico always had this "eye"; some of the students who were training with him at the University of Chicago to be geographers, alas, did not.[12]

Ball's understanding of landform and vegetation was, moreover, conditioned by the need to hide, to move undetected through a landscape shaped by slavery. *His awareness of form was a double one*; he had to understand the movements and behaviors of slave patrols and indeed of anyone, once he moved beyond the locale where he knew his way around and was known. He also used well-practiced skills in listening in to confirm what he had already reckoned, to identify where he was by learning the names of the places he was near. He may have had a keen sense of how landforms connect and are arranged, but as a geographer he was also shaped by the conditions of running in a strange place in the slave South.

Slaves who ran to Union lines did not usually—though not always—need to know as much or reckon as much as Ball did. Freedom was much closer. "See how much better off we are now that we was four years ago," one successful runaway in Kentucky exclaimed, "it used to be five hundred miles to get to Canada from Lexington, but now it's only eighteen miles! *Camp Nelson* is now *our* Canada."[13] But environmental knowledge of the neighborhood as well as the terrains of forests and swamps they might have to cross gave slaves the skill and confidence they needed to make this trek. Environmental knowledge—and a morphologic eye—was the most important component of the geography of resistance. Without it, the systems of cooperation where slaves supported one another or the fierce determination to acquire freedom from slavery might have become merely the handmaidens of dumb luck. We need to put running away—and *to*—by African Americans during the Civil War down on the ground and begin to recover some of the rich texture of this understanding and what it meant to slaves who were emancipating themselves.

Marching

If some ran and a few walked, most participants in the Civil War marched. They moved through the landscape in large organized groups, more or less in unison if not in step, and under orders and with a clear destination in mind. Just how well they did this is apparently a matter of debate, but the war itself would have been impossible without soldiers who had an aptitude or who acquired a habit for marching. That soldiers marched, and marched well, is not only supported by hundreds of personal accounts that describe the often extraordinary treks that they took from one battlefield to another but also by the very fact of Civil War battles themselves. Soldiers were trained to move in unison up to and on the battlefield, and military action would have been impossible without it. The ferocity of these battles and discipline with which soldiers on both sides often maneuvered, at least as the war proceeded – and were slaughtered – underlines the importance of marching and the constant drill that educated soldiers to do it well. The Civil War soldier was a good fighter because he was a good soldier, mechanized and educated to war through drill and training. Several interpretations explain the willingness of Civil War soldiers to walk into slaughter in battle after battle during the war – a proclivity to violence, community and kin allegiances, the stamina and endurance engendered by rural hardships, Celtic heritage, citizenship in the Republic of Death, and so on – but soldiers both North and South were also drilled hard and taught the habits of regimental movement.[14]

This kind of movement had little in common with walking or running – soldiers rarely marched in small groups and were never alone (unless they were deserting, and then they ran and hid out rather than marched in the open). Marching, even if while on the road from one battlefield to another and more a kind of ambling than marching, was always done in a group, was always pushed along by orders from commanders, and nearly always had a clear destination in mind – there was never a trace of the saunter in Civil War marching. It was just what Whitman said it was, "A March in the Ranks Hard-Presst" – its primary benchmark was not river or forest, but a dim light in a hospital and the face of a dying soldier, and then back on the road and marching on again, and the road unknown. Soldiers noticed the landscape through which they marched – especially Union soldiers, as they traveled into a region largely unknown to them. When Sherman's troops were ordered to cut down on their baggage and live off the land in Georgia, they also learned firsthand about the resources of southern fields and forests – and especially the fields, as they traveled from Atlanta to the sea right at the end of harvest season, with corn in the crib and slips banked on most farms, and the hog butchering almost done. They also had to rustle up firewood, and moss or pine needles for bedding, and they acquired an intimate experience with weather and terrain.

And mud. By the time Sherman's troops left Savannah on the five-hundred-mile trek from Savannah to Goldsboro, North Carolina, it was winter, the difficult and often swampy terrain was made swampier (and colder) by heavy winter rains, and many of the soldiers by this time were shoeless or nearly shoeless—by the time they reached Goldsboro, nearly four thousand men in the 17th Corps alone were barefoot. The trek was notable for its mud and for five large rivers the troops had to cross, as well as several swamps they had to wade. Thousands of men tramping across a landscape already muddy turned it into a slurry of red mud and feet—and sometimes, bloody feet. If the boot, according to anthropologist Tim Ingold, has been one of the most important technological innovations separating humans on foot from nature, one that gave them leverage at the same time against topography and variation, then thousands in Sherman's troops were more in touch with swamps and mud and wildness than Thoreau himself. But still they marched on, in the ranks, hard-pressed, and the road unknown; the sixty thousand troops that Sherman led north in the winter and early spring of 1865 averaged twelve miles a day.[15]

In general, marching taught soldiers to move differently in the landscape, and to think differently about it at the same time. Civil War marching, along with the mobility provided to some troops by railroad transport, may have by itself contributed to the transformation of American society from a premodern to a modern one. Historian Willam G. Thomas explains: "Those who controlled their own bodies, their movements, and their geographic surroundings experienced what they thought was modern. Those who did not or who had their movements curtailed and restricted were placed outside the modern world." Moving across and experiencing unfamiliar landscapes was a rehearsal for the movements of modern society. Railroads, what Thomas in this context calls an "extension of the body," and which allowed soldiers to race across high bridges and through deep tunnels, were the ultimate experience of this kind of modernity. But marching from one place to another and ultimately to diverse parts of the nation and then back again, and in spite of the challenges thrown up by the environment, also erased some of the obstacles to unrestricted movement and enhanced the experience of modernity. Marching in the ranks hard-pressed for hundreds of miles by itself contributed to the emergence of modern America and also a set of sensibilities that took for granted the control of nature.[16]

As Drew Gilpin Faust has contended, becoming a soldier was also not unlike becoming an industrial worker in nineteenth-century America. Soldiering and working in factories required self-control, personal discipline, and steady work habits, as well as habituation to the regulations and monitoring that encouraged these. Civil War soldiers were like many of the first industrial workers. From pre-industrial backgrounds, they had to learn new values and internalize a new set of expectations that required more steadiness and attention to the regulation of others than had been their practice back on the farm. The extent to which many soldiers, backcountry southerners, especially, shed their individuality and internalized this discipline remains controversial and was at least very uneven.[17] But one way or another, soldiers had to march, to move in groups across the countryside, with regimented and disciplined action on battlefields as their goal and destination. Though the Civil War was the last war in which most troops moved mostly by foot rather than by rail or other means, it was the first modern war, and soldiers learned how to move through the environment in a way that was consonant with the larger economic and social changes that were occurring around them – changes that also did not tread lightly as they traveled. Marching armies were giant streams of organisms, moving in a way that changed the environment as well as those who marched through it.[18]

Marching and its consequences linked many soldiers to the postwar order in another way. Around forty-five thousand soldiers lost arms or legs (or both) during the Civil War – a loss that, when it was a leg, made someone less than a man at first because he could no longer move around as he once did. Once these soldiers were fitted, with support from the U.S. government, with some of the new prosthetic devices, however, these technological wonders restored some traditional mobility while at the same time linking them to the new Union and the post–Civil War technological present. Marching along a road unknown, when it ended, rather than was marked by, an amputation in a hospital, was for many soldiers a path to a postwar future.

What does this mean for an environmental history of the Civil War? It is important for us to put participants, noncombatants as well as combatants, back into the environment if we are to begin writing an environmental history of the Civil War – not just about battlefields or occasional events that might be resonant in what they tell us about participants and environments but the substrate of interaction with the environment: how soldiers and civilians, white and black, moved through the environment differently and tellingly. An environmental history of the Civil War should even begin and end with this – which will also tell us something about the environmental history of postwar America. Even if they did not leave us a literature of walking, these interactions told stories about the war that often began and ended with putting one foot in front of the other. Even if walking was not an occasion for reflecting on nature, it was the mode by which nature was experienced, and by looking more closely at it we can put legs on how soldiers and civilians sensed the environment, and start where they did, from the ground up, and by hitting the ground, one foot after the other.

Notes

1. Henry David Thoreau, "Walking," *The Atlantic,* June 1862, http://www.the atlantic.com/magazine/archive/1862/06/walking/304674/. This influential essay was published after Thoreau's death from tuberculosis and in the second year of the Civil War, when his kind of walking was overwhelmed by the other kinds discussed in this essay. My thanks to Rand Jimerson for assistance at the beginning of this project, and for his recommendations of relevant scholarship.

2. Several recent works have demonstrated just how much can be learned that is new about the Civil War, by applying to the study of it the methods and perspectives of environmental history. At the same time these entries into the field demonstrate just how much yet needs to be done: Lisa M. Brady, *War upon the Land: Military Strategy and the Transformation of Southern Landscapes during the American Civil War* (Athens: University of Georgia Press, 2012); Megan Kate Nelson, *Ruin Nation: Destruction and the American Civil War* (Athens: University of Georgia Press, 2012); Mark Fiege, "The Nature of Gettysburg: Environmental History and the Civil War," in *The Republic of Nature: An Environmental History of the United States* (Seattle: University of Washington Press, 2012): 199–227. Fiege briefly discusses the fact of walking as a window into the environmental experience of Civil War soldiers (223).

3. Rebecca Solnit, *Wanderlust: A History of Walking* (New York: Penguin, 2000), 119–20. Environmental historians have acknowledged the importance of walking to environmental history, and informal considerations of this importance abound within environmental history scholarship and in presentations at professional conferences in the field. Aside from Joseph Amato, *On Foot: A History of Walking* (New York: New York University Press, 2004) and Solnit's *Wanderlust,* this potentially rich area of inquiry has not however yet received the formal attention it deserves.

4. Francis Peyre Porcher, *Resources of the Southern Fields and Forests, Medical, Economical, and Agricultural. Being also a Medical Botany of the Confederate States; with Practical Information on the Useful Properties of the Trees, Plants, and Shrubs* (Charleston, S.C.: Evans and Cogswell, 1863); Electronic Edition, Documenting the American South, University of North Carolina–Chapel Hill, http://docsouth.unc.edu/imls/porcher/porcher.html. For a discussion of the published sources Porcher mined for information, see vi–v, 1–4, and the numerous citations throughout the collection.

5. Porcher, *Resources of the Southern Fields and Forests,* 59–63.

6. Ibid., 450–59. For a discussion of the relative absence of ideas about wilderness in the U.S. South, and the dominance of agrarian and pastoral traditions as

mediating ones for ideas about nature in this region, see Mart A. Stewart, "If John Muir Had Been an Agrarian: American Environmental History West and South," *Environment and History* 11, no. 2 (2005): 139–62.

7. Porcher, *Resources of the Southern Fields and Forests*, 133–35.

8. See Kelby Ouchley, *Flora and Fauna of the Civil War: An Environmental Reference Guide* (Baton Rouge: Louisiana State University Press, 2010), for examples. For an explanation of how Union soldiers perceived the southern landscape in general, and the exotic fauna, people, and institutions in it—as they marched—see Reid Mitchell, "The Landscape of War: The Union Soldier Views the South," in *Civil War Soldiers: Their Expectations and Their Experiences* (New York: Simon and Schuster, 1988), 90–147.

9. Leon F. Litwack, *Been in the Storm So Long: The Aftermath of Slavery* (New York: Vintage, 1979), 51–59. For a relevant discussion of the distinction slaves made between the relatively well-known terrain of the plantations and local environments in proximity to the ones on which they were slaves, and the environments and plantations in other neighborhoods beyond these, see Anthony E. Kaye, "Terrains of Struggle," in *Joining Places: Slave Neighborhoods in the Old South* (Chapel Hill: University of North Carolina Press, 2007), 119–52. See also Mart A. Stewart, *"What Nature Suffers to Groe": Life, Labor, and Landscape on the Georgia Coast, 1680–1920* (Athens: University of Georgia Press, 1996), esp. 126–46, 174–86. Walter Johnson has devised an apt term, "carcerol landscape," for the landscapes both off and on the plantation as they were experienced by slaves: Walter Johnson, *River of Dark Dreams: Slavery and Empire in the Cotton Kingdom* (Cambridge, Mass.: Harvard University Press, 2013), 209–43. Though his account of this landscape includes an appreciation of the use of environmental knowledge as a weapon of resistance by slaves, it is strangely abstract and detached from the particular environments that yielded that knowledge. The reader has to go elsewhere to find an understanding of the richness and meaning of this knowledge, especially as it was attached to particular places. A partial corrective can be found in Christopher Morris, *The Big Muddy: An Environmental History of the Mississippi and Its Peoples* (New York: Oxford University Press, 2012), 108–39. For a discussion of gender and networks of support for runaway slaves, see Stephanie Camp, "The Pleasures of Resistance: Enslaved Women and Body Politics in the Plantation South, 1830–1861," *Journal of Southern History* 68, no. 3 (2002): 533–72.

10. Rev. C. C. Jones to Lt. Charles C. Jones Jr., July 16, 1862, quoted in *The Children of Pride*, ed. Robert Mansom Myers (New York: Popular Library, 1972), 929.

11. *Slavery in the United States* was republished several times—material in this paper is from the 1859 edition, published under the title *Fifty Years a Slave: Charles Ball, Fifty Years a Slave or, the Life of an American Slave* (New York: H. Dayton, 1859), 310–93 (electronic edition, Documenting the American South, University of North Carolina/Chapel Hill, 1997, http://docsouth.unc.edu/fpn/ball/ball.html). Like most slave narratives, Ball's had an interlocutor, Isaac Fisher, to whom Ball recalled his story and who then wrote it down and gave it a literary style that would appeal to readers at the time. The extent to which Fisher controlled the production of Ball's narrative is debated. Some scholars consider the published account to be a mere "voiceover," with Ball a mere puppet to Fisher's purposes. Such a

view overlooks the complexity of its authorship, and has the effect of denying it a legitimate place in the historical record. Others view the genre of slave narrative as a contest for voice between the ex-slave and the white editors and supporters: ex-slaves agreed to tell their stories only if the potential white editor respected blacks, for example, and thus asserted some control over the narrative. See John W. Blassingame, "Using the Testimony of Ex-Slaves: Approaches and Problems," in *The Slaves' Narrative*, ed. Charles T. Davis and Henry Louis Gates Jr. (New York: Oxford University Press, 1985), 81. James Olney cites the formulaic framework of the genre of slave narratives as evidence that white domination over the ex-slave's voice circumscribed the content. The dynamics between fugitive and white editor with regard to narrative authorship were analogous to the master–slave relationship (he calls the formulaic framework characteristic of the genre the "Master Plan," with intentional irony). Narratives were a kind of hybrid, in his view, of a narrative by the ex-slave of his life, and the editorial intervention of the "witness," the editor who shaped the narrative into publishable form: Olney, "I Was Born," 156. Ball's description of the material conditions of his trek, which are the subject of this investigation, are much more likely to have survived intact the shaping of the larger narrative by Ball's editor and his supporters.

12. Carl Sauer, "The Education of a Geographer," Presidential address given by the Honorary President of the Association of American Geographers at its 52nd annual meeting, Montreal, April 4, 1956. Sauer, of course, was an important pioneer in the development of environmental history.

13. Quoted in Litwack, *Been in the Storm So Long*, 51.

14. Mark A. Weitz, "Drill, Training, and the Combat Performance of the Civil War Soldier: Dispelling the Myth of the Poor Soldier, Great Fighter," *The Journal of Military History* 62, no. 2 (1998): 266–67. The manuals that were used to drill soldiers in different formations and kinds of marching are useful sources here. For Confederate troops, the standard manual that had been used before the war continued to be used when its author became an officer in the Confederate Army: William J. Hardee, *Rifle and Light Infantry Tactics for the Exercise and Manoeuvres of Troops When Acting as Light Infantry or Riflemen* (Philadelphia, Lippincott, Grambo, and Co., 1855). The Union Army used an adaptation of this text by Silas Casey, *Infantry Tactics for the Instruction, Exercise, and Manoeuvres of the Soldier, a Company, Line of Skirmishers, Battalion, Brigade or Corps d'Armée* (New York: D. Van Norstrand, 1862).

15. Joseph T. Glatthaar, *The March to the Sea and Beyond: Sherman's Troops in the Savannah and Carolinas Campaign* (Baton Rouge: Louisiana State University Press, 1985), 115; Tim Ingold, "Culture on the Ground: The World Perceived through Feet," *Journal of Material Culture* 9 (2004): 319–21; Clemont Eaton, ed., "Diary of an Officer in Sherman's Army Marching Through the Carolinas," *Journal of Southern History* 9 (May 1942): 239–40. Soldiers left a wealth of diaries and journals about their experiences in the war that often include accounts of their movements – these may constitute the main "walking literature" for the Civil War.

16. William G. Thomas, *The Iron Way: Railroads, the Civil War, and the Making of Modern America* (New Haven: Yale University Press, 2011), 9–10.

17. Even the Rebel yell was a discordant matter – and especially compared to

what Gen. "Jube" Early called the "studied hurrahs of the Yankees" (Bell Irvine Wiley, *The Life of Johnny Reb: The Common Soldier of the Confederacy* [New York: Bobbs-Merrill Company, 1943], 71). At the least, the ranks of both Confederate and Union armies contained extraordinary diversity, quite beyond any effort to homogenize all of them. See the chapter on the Confederate soldier, "What Manner of Men," in Wiley, *The Life of Johnny Reb*, 322–47.

18. Drew Gilpin Faust, "Christian Soldiers: The Meaning of Revivalism in the Confederate Army," *Journal of Southern History* 53 (February 1987): 63–90, esp. 73–75; Charles E. Brooks, "The Social and Cultural Dynamics of Soldiering in Hood's Texas Brigade" *Journal of Southern History* 67 (August 2001): 557–59. An assessment of military drill and marching that identifies a deeper consequence of it, dating back at least, if not to ancient Greek and Roman infantry training, to the drill devised (and written about) by Maurice of Orange, Captain General of Holland from 1585–1625, is William H. McNeill's *Keeping Together in Time: Dance and Drill in Human History* (Cambridge, Mass.: Harvard University Press, 1995), esp. chap. 5, "Politics and War." McNeill argues that close-formation military drill forged a "muscular bonding" among soldiers from diverse backgrounds into a singular community and effective fighting machine. This argument reinforces and deepens Faust's. One of the most compelling chapters in Megan Kate Nelson's *Ruin Nation* is devoted to a discussion of the ruining of soldier's bodies by amputations of legs; see Nelson, *Ruin Nation*, 160–227.

EPILOGUE

"Waving the Muddy Shirt"

PAUL S. SUTTER

It is usually the job of a concluding chapter in an essay collection such as this one to sing the praises of the volume's achievements. So I should say up front that I judge *The Blue, the Gray, and the Green* to be one of the most important explorations of the environmental history of the American Civil War to date, and one undertaken by an adept expeditionary party. While this volume is not a systematic or thorough survey of the full possibilities of Civil War environmental history, reliant as it is on the specific research interests of a diverse group of authors, it nonetheless succeeds at sketching many of the landscape's major features. It has done commendable work, and I will hit on some of the highlights. Having led with praise, however, I also want to play the skeptic and ask what is missing from this volume and where it might fall short in its proselytizing mission. This is not to suggest that I am skeptical of bringing environmental approaches to the study of Civil War history; to the contrary, I am an enthusiast. Rather, it is to recognize that skepticism about such approaches—sometimes mixed with apathy or wariness—remains among the broader historical community, and that overcoming said skepticism requires that we seriously plumb its causes.

This is not the first effort to wed Civil War history and environmental history, and the impetus for such efforts has usually come from environmental historians. That may be one cause of skepticism. To flog the wedding metaphor to near-death, it is the father of environmental history that is holding the shotgun at this wedding, and most of the guests are sitting on environmental history's side of the church. Even the task of writing an epilogue to this volume has fallen to an environmental historian. Thus, I have tried to imagine what a Civil War historian unfamiliar with or suspicious of environmental approaches might conclude from this volume. Would the evidence contained herein be sufficient to give her a clear and thorough sense of the larger environmental history project? Would the analytical attractions of this volume be sufficient to woo her into a sustained relationship with environmental approaches to the Civil War? Why, this historian might ask, have environmental historians been so enthusiastic about the consummation of these two fields? What is it that environmental historians see in the Civil War, and why have Civil War historians been colder to the union?

One reason for skepticism might be the features of the Civil War that seem to most attract environmental historians. Surprisingly, environmental approaches to the war often have focused on traditional military history topics. This volume is no exception. If, as Brian Drake rightly suggests in his excellent introduction, Civil War historians have spent the last several decades "marching away from a narrow focus on battlefield events and sectional crises to explore the lives of individual soldiers, freed slaves, women, the home front, motivation, memory, and a host of other topics," many environmental historians of the Civil War seem intent on returning to, or at least beginning with, that older narrow focus and reviewing it through an environmental lens. It is a slightly odd way to begin what is supposed to be a cutting-edge historiographical maneuver, but there are a couple of good reasons for doing so. The first – as Drake intimates – is that environmental historians came to the Civil War as part of a larger effort to make sense of the environmental dimensions of war and militarization, a foray meant to push American environmental history beyond its early preoccupations with the transformative powers of capitalism and the rise of state conservation. Environmental historians thus arrived at the field of battle just as many Civil War historians were retreating from it. Second, to the extent that environmental historians have been on a mission to prove that "nature matters" to explanations of historical causation, the battlefield has seemed like fruitful ground, for environmental forces were at play there in many obvious ways. For these reasons, a focus on traditional military topics has appealed to environmental historians interested in the Civil War. Nonetheless, I wonder how well such a focus has worked to sell environmental history as a novel approach to the Civil War.

Despite this concern, I do think environmental history brings important new questions to this traditional focus on battlefield events. The essays in this volume pay careful attention to the environmental spaces within which the war played out, and they argue that environmental conditions and forces shaped the course of war in consequential – rather than random or ephemeral – ways. Now, truth be told, most Civil War historians would not find it news that, as Kenneth Noe wryly notes, the "American Civil War was largely fought outdoors." If making that point in more elaborate ways is all that environmental history is going to bring to our understanding of the Civil War, then Civil War historians are right to be skeptical. But something more sophisticated is going on in these essays. Environmental historians often maintain that historians have not paid sufficient attention to the environmental *specifics* – that they have treated the environment not only as a backdrop but also as a black box, and that they need to open the category up and explore its inner workings. Many of the essays in this volume do just that – they show, for instance, that the behavior of Maj. Isaac Lynde makes new sense when we understand peculiar aspects of the desert environment, and human physiology in interaction with it; or that "straggling," a frequent behavior of the common soldier usually chalked up to indiscipline, makes much more sense when we consider "self-care" as an environmental strategy; or even that battlefield tactics and outcomes are not merely the products of military minds and soldierly actions but also of the dynamics of weather, terrain, soil type, disease, and other nonhuman entities and forces. By adding depth to the traditional two-dimensionality of historians' treatment of the environment, many of the essays in this volume have convinced me that the environment mattered to Civil War military conflict in more than ambient ways.

Yet, despite these virtues, I fear that the insistent "nature matters" logic that we environmental historians sometimes engage in – what I call "waving the muddy shirt" – may, in its apparent partisanship, get in the way of reaching across the aisle to Civil War historians. More than that, it may stop us short of a more radical claim that these essays might lead us toward: that environmental history is not merely a subdiscipline that seeks to give "agency to nature," but one that, by pointing out how entangled human actions have been with nonhuman entities and forces, actually offers a fundamental challenge to still-dominant notions of *human* agency. Until environmental historians can make that case with greater sophistication, we will be all too easy to marginalize. Part of the problem is the application of agency to nature, for many historians would still argue that agency is, by definition, a human quality. But "nature" may also be part of the problem, for by cramming all that is outside the realm of the human (and sometimes even the material human body) into that single category, we tend to obscure important causal and moral distinctions that we need to make about our world. "Nature," then, may be tenuously holding together what we need to tease apart, while the personifying logic of its "agency" risks caricaturing environmental history's causal claims.[1]

Lisa Brady's reconceptualization of friction is telling here. Brady, arguably the leading theorist of Civil War environmental history, astutely suggests that friction is more than the stochasticity that intercedes between plan and execution, and she rightly insists that we see much of what Clausewitz called friction as fundamentally environmental.[2] Her skillful repurposing of Clausewitz ought to get Civil War military historians to stand at attention. But here's the rub: Brady then uses friction as a way of suggesting that "nature" has "agency," while, to me, friction is better conceptualized as agency's opposite, as a concept that embodies a set of countervailing forces that limit, divert, ensnare, and reshape our best-laid plans. Indeed, friction strikes me as a tremendously promising concept for rethinking human agency from an environmental standpoint.[3] My point is more than a semantic one. For many non–environmental historians, agency, defined by the capacity to convert individual free will into action, is the very quality that separates humanist history from a nature that is external to it. If we are to make claims for the causal importance of environmental entities and forces, then we must first confront the ways in which the concept of agency has itself defined a nature that exists outside of history. It is a logic that continues to thwart our efforts to convince others to bring the "outdoors" into history.

While many of the essays in this volume engage the causal claims of environmental history, others take a more conceptual approach. Perhaps the most ambitious is Tim Silver's effort to see the war – and particularly the movement of the Black Mountain Boys during the Peninsula Campaign – as a biotic event. Silver shows how the removal of human labor from the fields of Yancey County undermined the constant ecological negotiation that is agricultural production; he details the ways in which troop concentration, in interaction with other environmental forces like mosquitoes and microbiota, produced disease; and he demonstrates that troop movement was part of a larger mammalian migration that had its own implications for both human and animal health and military success. Silver boldly suggests that this larger biotic story was "*the* story" of the Civil War. In doing so, he makes causal claims akin to those made by other essays in this volume, but he also expands our frame and reimagines what constitutes the proper subject of Civil War history. He asks us not just to recognize that nonhuman forces shaped human history but also to see that the Civil War was a significant event in the history of the environment. In doing so, he hints at another radical aspect of the environmental history project: a conceptualization of the nonhuman environment not only as a shaper of human history (or a victim of it), but as itself a product of change over time. Understanding that natural systems, even absent human actors and impacts, are products of history requires us to stretch beyond the humanist boundaries that have traditionally defined the discipline. In other words, environmental history is a project that asks historians to expand their circle of concerns. That demand, which is a quiet part of many of this volume's essays, will be a challenging one for many historians to stomach, but it is one that we must put on the table with more relish.

Non–environmental historians encountering this volume might also come away confused about environmental history's moral agenda, for the essays herein tend to treat environment more as an analytical category than a normative one. Why, they might ask, do we so fervently wave the muddy shirt? What's our cause? The essays in this volume are not altogether clear on that point, and that lack of clarity might also be a source of skepticism. Environmental historians need not have a singular or simple moral position; in fact, the field's maturation over the last several decades has meant that we have often moved away from simple *environmentalist* lessons. But most of our work does stem from a desire to use history to explain how we came to live in the world as we do, and to bring historical perspectives to our current environmental predicaments. We probably need to be more forthright about that, and what that means for Civil War environmental history, if we are to win more converts.

When we insist on environmental causation, for instance, we are offering a critique, often an implicit one, of a modernist hubris premised on the notion that humans can completely master the environment around them – a hubris to which metaphors of war were critical, as Ed Russell has shown. To argue for the importance of environmental causation, then, is often to advocate for a less controlling and more negotiated way of being in the world.[4] This critique is one of the things at stake when we wave the muddy shirt.

When environmental historians argue for attention to the ways in which different groups have historically experienced and known the natural world – as Mart Stewart's essay on the Civil War foot travel does – we are often arguing for the importance of environmental intimacy to proper conceptualizations of and resolutions to our contemporary environmental problems. Stewart's discussion of African American environmental knowledge – what he calls the "environmental dimension of running away" – is particularly important here, for it counters a different narrative of environmental mastery that long was central to justifications of slavery: that white planters were the agroecological masters of the lands that they "worked," and that black slaves were nothing but brute labor. While the racial tenets of that master narrative have long ago been discredited, historians have only recently tackled its environmental assumptions.[5] Focusing on environmental knowledge not only gives us a richer picture of how African Americans took their freedom during the Civil War – and as John Inscoe's essay so nicely suggests, freedom was an environmental imaginary – but it also makes the wartime experience of African Americans critical to genealogies of environmental justice. More than that, it brings slavery, the Civil War, and African Americans' experiences more broadly into the critical history of environmental politics.

Another part of our moral agenda is to chart the environmental destruction produced by the Civil War, and to examine the war's place in a larger nineteenth-century history of human-environmental interactions. A few of the volume's essays do this well. But by repositioning Civil War historiography so that we might better view the war's environmental impacts and legacies, we need to be sensitive to how such a diversion might appear to slight the human causes and human suffering that have defined the war. I am *not* suggesting that environmental historians have been cold to these human concerns; most of us, if we do not explicitly address them, take them as a given. But doing so has created absences in this volume that might lead some to misunderstand environmental history's moral center. In noting the parallel cultural fascinations between arboreal and human stumps, we need to be careful not to give the impression that we consider them equivalents, or that we are ultimately more concerned about the former (even as we take it as our duty to explicate the former where others have not). Rather, our analyses of environmental impacts are meant to suggest – as Aaron Sachs's essay in fact does – that this republic of human suffering cannot be teased apart from larger landscapes of destruction, and that some of the trauma of war – visible in dead animals, splintered forests, and wasted agricultural fields – was centered in human-environmental interaction. The war's environmental destruction and its human suffering were inextricable.

This volume gestures at another crucial argument, one that ought to be more overt in our courtship of Civil War historians: that the American

Civil War was an environmental watershed for the nation. Aaron Sachs's essay – as well as recent books by Sachs, Megan Nelson, and Lisa Brady – provides us with a promising start by pointing to the cultural meanings to be found in the war's environmental impacts and traumas.[6] The Civil War, they argue, functioned as a powerful example of modern environmental destruction, one that would lead in direct ways – as Sachs suggests – to the conservation movement and away from other environmental ideals. It was no mistake that the war years saw the setting aside of the Yosemite Valley as a public park; or that George Perkins Marsh's *Man and Nature*, which Lewis Mumford famously called the "fountainhead of the conservation movement," appeared in 1864; or even that the nation's biggest trees, the mighty sequoias of the Sierra Nevada Mountains, would come to be named for Civil War generals (mostly Union generals though Lee too would get a tree). These examples suggest some of the ways in which the destruction of the war – to environments as well as to human bodies and psyches – reshaped concern for the natural world as a source of finite resources and as a therapeutic retreat. Moreover, as Civil War historiography has been transformed in part by a focus on memory, surely there is important work to be done by environmental historians in that arena as well. As the environmental historian Brian Black has shown, ideas of nature have been central to how we have managed, and argued about how to manage, our Civil War battlefields as preserved memorials, and to an understanding of why Americans – and, more specifically, the National Park Service – have so assiduously protected these naturalized landscapes of this war.[7] The Civil War, in other words, was a critical moment in the history of American environmental thought and politics.

While most former Civil War battlefields, like those who died upon them, now lie in pastoral repose, we ought not to forget that questions about how best to *work* the land were also central to the Civil War. It is, of course, an old saw that the divergent economies of North and South, and particularly the peculiar nature of the South's agricultural economy, led inexorably to the sectional conflict that produced the Civil War. Union and Confederate soldiers not only fought in the dirt and mud, but they fought over how it would be used, and by whom, to produce food, fiber, and the other commodities of the soil. Two general conclusions might thus be made about this intersection: that we cannot understand the Civil War without paying detailed attention to the history of farming in nineteenth-century America, and that we cannot understand the trajectory of agriculture in U.S. history without attending to the legacies of the Civil War.

The essays in this volume that most directly address the intersection of agriculture and the Civil War, those by Drew Swanson and Tim Johnson, are interested in the relationship between sectional conflict and southern agriculture's destructive reputation. This is a venerable inquiry. Behind Tim Johnson's history of the rise of fertilizer use in the post–Civil War South, as he intimates, is a bigger story about the relationship between soil fertility and sectional conflict, a story that reminds me of William Chandler Bagley's obscure but important study, *Soil Exhaustion and the Civil War* (1942). Bagley argued that the southern plantation strategy of exhausting soils and then moving to fresh lands – what we today call shifting cultivation – is "the key to an understanding of the economic significance of the territorial limitation of slavery." To territorially limit slavery was, given this ever-expanding agricultural pattern, to threaten it with extinction.[8] For Bagley, how southerners farmed, and the relation between their farming practices and their commitment to slave labor, led in a direct way to the Civil War. One can find Bagley's influence in Eugene Genovese's later argument that slave labor necessarily exhausted the soil, leading to agricultural expansion and irrepressible sectional conflict.[9] More recently, environmental historians such as Steven Stoll and Jack Temple Kirby have portrayed a southern antebellum agricultural reform tradition that urged soil stewardship and agricultural permanence as tactics for dealing with this apparently ruinous expansiveness (there is actually a healthy debate about whether shifting cultivation was, in fact, an ecologically destructive practice or whether it was a sensible adaptation to southern environmental conditions) and for strengthening the Southern cause.[10] Indeed, in a provocative recent book, John Majewski has argued that the "constraints of the southern environment," from soil quality to livestock diseases, led most southerners to rely on shifting cultivation to manage southern soil fertility, which in turn meant low population densities and lots of economic "dead space" that, in combination with slavery, inhibited the development of markets and cities. He also insists that many of the region's most ardent secessionists understood these economic weaknesses, and that the cornerstone of their imagined independent Confederacy would have been a reformed agriculture that replaced the rule of shifting cultivation with a new regime of sedentary soil stewardship. Only then, they believed, could the South's economy truly urbanize, industrialize, and exist within a bounded region.[11] In other words, it was no mistake that Edmund Ruffin, a pioneering agricultural reformer and arguably the South's most important antebellum environmental thinker, fired one of the first shots of the Civil War from Charleston Harbor in 1861 – or that he fired his last shot, four years later when the war's outcome became clear, in taking his own life. Such were the tight connections between shifting cultivation, agricultural reform, and the Civil War.

While a modernized Confederate regime premised on a reformed agriculture never came to be, we can see Tim Johnson's essay as an exercise in placing soil fertility and its management at the center of the Civil War, Reconstruction, and New South stories. While the meat of Johnson's story of the rise of a southern fertilizer industry is in the postwar years, the fertility crisis that that industry addressed had its origins well before the Civil War, and the war was a product of it. Drew Swanson's essay takes a different tack, giving us the story of bright leaf tobacco's rise as a counterintuitive case study in agroecological complexity and specificity. One of the most remarkable things about bright leaf tobacco, the quality that made it seem like a providential crop, was precisely that it thrived in the *absence* of soil fertility, and was thus immune to the soil fertility crisis that shaped the war. Where the traditional dark tobacco that had dominated the northern Piedmont for two centuries prior to the Civil War had been demanding of soil nutrients, bright leaf tobacco enjoyed acidic, sandy, and nutrient-poor soils – sometimes the very soils that other crops had exhausted. As a result, Swanson gives us a story in which the war, far from destroying or demanding the reconstitution of a particular crop culture, actually left it relatively unscathed. Indeed, the wartime demand for bright leaf advanced its cause, even as the Confederacy desperately needed food crops to feed its army. We cannot fully appreciate this story, or the ways in which it bucks larger narratives about agriculture and the Civil War, Swanson insists, unless we attend to the agroecological specifics of this crop and its place in the region. That's a vital message, one that's central to some of the very best work now being produced in agroecological history more broadly.

There is another important point to be made about agricultural history and the Civil War's importance as an environmental watershed. Perhaps the single most important piece of legislation in shaping the modern history of American conservation was a product of a Civil War Congress largely devoid of southerners and animated by a free labor vision of what the nation's agricultural future would be. I refer, of course, to the Homestead Act of 1862, a democratic vision for how to settle the American West that largely ignored the region's environmental realities and led, in turn, to a series of legislative revisions that eventually ended in conservation. From the establishment of the nation's first forest reserves in 1891 –

which came as a part of the General Revision Act of that year, a comprehensive overhaul of homesteading law – through the Taylor Grazing Act of 1934, which withdrew from the public domain most of the remaining lands open to homesteading and put them under permanent federal management, eventually under the auspices of the Bureau of Land Management – conservation largely arose as a series of federal responses to homesteading's failures. The Civil War also saw the creation of the U.S. Department of Agriculture and the passage of the Morrill Act, which created the nation's system of land grant colleges. For reasons too numerous to explicate here, both were also monumental developments in the environmental history of the nation's farmlands and deserve to sit at the center of our assessments of the Civil War's larger environmental legacies. Indeed, as these examples suggest, the Civil War gave birth to the environmental management state.

The point of this volume, then, is not merely that "nature mattered" to the Civil War, though in every imaginable sense of that phrase it clearly did. It is, rather, that environmental history can be a powerful way of rethinking the very *matter* of the war, its lived material realities, and their formative relation to that roiling ideological formation that we call nature.

Notes

1. I have written more extensively about this in "The World With Us: The State of American Environmental History," *Journal of American History* 100 (June 2013): 94–120; I have been heavily influenced by Linda Nash's wonderful short essay, "The Agency of Nature or the Nature of Agency?," *Environmental History* 10 (January 2005), 67–69.

2. Lisa M. Brady, *War upon the Land: Military Strategy and the Transformation of Southern Landscapes during the American Civil War* (Athens: University of Georgia Press, 2012); Brady, "From Battlefield to Fertile Ground: The Development of Civil War Environmental History," *Civil War History* 58, no. 3 (2012): 305–21; Brady, "The Future of Civil War Era Studies: Environmental Histories," *Journal of the Civil War Era* 2, no. 1 (2012): http://journalofthecivilwarera.com/forum-the-future-of-civil-war-era-studies/the-future-of-civil-war-era-studies-environmental-histories/.

3. Here we might consider putting Brady's environmental reading of Clausewitz in conversation with Anna Tsing's use of friction in her ethnography of globalization in the rainforests of Indonesia. See Tsing, *Friction: An Ethnography of Global Connection* (Princeton: Princeton University Press, 2004).

4. Edmund Russell, *War and Nature: Fighting Humans and Insects with Chemicals from World War I to Silent Spring* (Cambridge: Cambridge University Press, 2001).

5. Judith Carney's work particularly influenced this point. See Carney, *Black Rice: The African Origins of Rice Cultivation in the Americas* (Cambridge, Mass.: Harvard University Press, 2001).

6. Aaron Sachs, *Arcadian America: The Death and Life of an Environmental Tradition* (New Haven: Yale University Press, 2012); Brady, *War upon the Land;* Megan Kate Nelson, *Ruin Nation: Destruction and the American Civil War* (Athens: University of Georgia Press, 2012).

7. Brian Black, "The Nature of Preservation: The Rise of Authenticity at Gettysburg," *Civil War History* 58, no. 3 (2012): 348–73.

8. William Chandler Bagley, *Soil Exhaustion and the Civil War* (Washington, D.C.: American Council on Public Affairs, 1942), 8. Bagley was of course influenced by the work of earlier southern agricultural historians, particularly Avery O. Craven, Lewis C. Gray, A. R. Hall, and U. B. Phillips.

9. Eugene Genovese, "Cotton, Slavery, and Soil Exhaustion in the Old South," *Cotton History Review* 2, no. 1 (1961): 3–17.

10. Steven Stoll, *Larding the Lean Earth: Soil and Society in Nineteenth Century America* (New York: Hill and Wang, 2002); Jack Temple Kirby, *Poquosin: A Study of Rural Landscape and Society* (Chapel Hill: University of North Carolina Press, 1995).

11. John Majewski, *Modernizing a Slave Economy: The Economic Vision of the Confederate Nation* (Chapel Hill: University of North Carolina Press, 2009), esp. 22–52.

CONTRIBUTORS

Lisa M. Brady is a professor of history at Boise State University and editor of *Environmental History*. Her most recent publications include *War upon the Land: Military Strategy and the Transformation of Southern Landscapes during the American Civil War* (University of Georgia Press, 2012); "From Battlefield to Fertile Ground: The Development of Civil War Environmental History," in *Civil War History* (2012); and "The Future of Civil War Era Studies: Environmental Histories," in *Journal of the Civil War Era* (2012).

Brian Allen Drake is a lecturer in the University of Georgia's history department, where he teaches environmental and United States history. He is the author of *Loving Nature, Fearing the State: Environmentalism and Antigovernment Politics before Reagan* (2013); and "The Skeptical Environmentalist: Senator Barry Goldwater and the Environmental Management State," in *Environmental History*.

John C. Inscoe is the Albert B. Saye Professor of History and a University Professor at the University of Georgia. He has written widely on nineteenth-century Appalachia, and is currently at work on a book, tentatively titled "Appalachia on Film: History, Hollywood, and the Highland South."

Timothy Johnson is a PhD candidate in the history department at the University of Georgia whose research explores the origins of fertilizer-fueled agriculture in the United States and the expansion of America's agricultural-industrial complex in the era of the World War.

Kathryn Shively Meier is an assistant professor of history at Virginia Commonwealth University and author of *Nature's Civil War: Common Soldiers and the Environment in 1862 Virginia* (2013).

Megan Kate Nelson is a freelance writer and a cultural and environmental historian of nineteenth-century America and the American Civil War. After earning her PhD in American studies from the University of Iowa in 2002, she taught at Texas Tech University, California State University at Fullerton, Harvard University, and Brown University. She is the author of *Trembling Earth: A Cultural History of the Okefenokee Swamp* (University of Georgia Press, 2005) and *Ruin Nation: Destruction and the American Civil War* (University of Georgia Press, 2012), in addition to numerous articles, film and television reviews, and columns for the *New York Times* Disunion blog. Her current book project is a narrative history of the Civil War in the desert Southwest.

Kenneth W. Noe is Alumni Professor and Draughon Professor of Southern History at Auburn University. He is most recently the author of *Reluctant Rebels: The Confederates Who Joined the Army after 1861* (2010) and the editor of *The Yellowhammer War: The Civil War and Reconstruction in Alabama* (2013). His current research involves the role of weather in the Civil War.

Aaron Sachs is an associate professor of history and American studies at Cornell University and a 2013–14 Fellow at the Charles Warren Center for Studies in American History, Harvard University. He is the author of *The Humboldt Current: Nineteenth-Century Exploration and the Roots of American Environmentalism* (2006) and *Arcadian America: The Death and Life of an Environmental Tradition* (2013).

Timothy Silver is a professor of history at Appalachian State University. He is the author of *Mount Mitchell and the Black Mountains: An Environmental History of the Highest Peaks in Eastern America* (2003).

Mart A. Stewart is a professor of history at Western Washington University and an affiliate professor in their Huxley College of the Environment. He is the coeditor of *Environmental Change and Agricultural Sustainability in the Mekong Delta* (2011) and the author of "Plantations, Agroecology, Environmental Thought, and the American South," in *The Environmental History of the Plantation*, edited by Frank Uekotter (2014).

Paul S. Sutter is an associate professor of history at the University of Colorado at Boulder. He is the author of *Driven Wild: How the Fight against Automobiles Launched the Modern Wilderness Movement* (2002), coauthor of *The Art of Managing Longleaf: A Personal History of the Stoddard-Neel Approach* (University of Georgia Press, 2010) and coeditor of *Environmental History and the American South: A Reader* (University of Georgia Press, 2009). Sutter's next book, *Let Us Now Praise Famous Gullies: Georgia's "Little Grand Canyon" and the Soils of the South*, is forthcoming in 2015.

Drew A. Swanson is an assistant professor of history at Wright State University. He is author of *A Golden Weed: Tobacco and Environment in the Piedmont South* (2014) and *Remaking Wormsloe Plantation: The Environmental History of a Lowcountry Landscape* (University of Georgia Press, 2012).

INDEX

acoustic shadows phenomenon: overview, 10, 147, 149–51; Fort Donelson battle, 151–53; Iuka battle, 153–56; Perryville battle, 156–59
Adventuring in the Andes (Frazier), 130
African Americans. See *Cudjo's Cave* (Trowbridge); fertilizer regime, postwar; slaves
agency, concept of, 227–28. *See also specific concepts*
agriculture: Civil War connections summarized, 231–34; emancipation's impact, 191, 197–98; northerner critiques, 163–64; as scholarly opportunity, 164–65; Sherman's destruction, 5, 191, 197; shifting cultivation strategy, 53, 191–92, 232–33; slavery's role, 176–77, 194–95, 232; soil fertility attitudes, 195–97; taxation/confiscations, 175–76, 188n55; twentieth-century soil survey, 187n47. *See also* fertilizer regime, postwar; tobacco, bright leaf
Agriculture and the Civil War (Gates), 4
air temperature factors. *See* acoustic shadows phenomenon
Alcott, Louisa May, 81
American Forests (Starr), 103, 110n16
American Space (Jackson), 112n25
amputees, 96, 98, 108n2, 220
Appalachia, as refuge
—freedom associations, 114–15
—for fugitive soldiers, 121–24, 127
—guerrilla activity correlation, 120–21
—literary portrayals: overview, 9; *Cold Mountain* (Frazier), 130–37; "Crowder's Cove: A Story of the War" (Woolson), 125, 128–29; *Cudjo's Cave* (Trowbridge), 115–20, 139n17; "A Strange Land and Peculiar People" (Harney), 124–25, 141n27; "The Yares of Black Mountain" (Davis), 125, 126–28, 141n39
—wilderness image development, 113–14

Appalachia on Our Mind (Shapiro), 141n37
Appleton's Journal, 128
Arizona, in Southern Manifest Destiny, 36–37
"Armies of the Wilderness, The" (Melville), 96
Arndt, Hartmut, 149
artillery damage, 100, 109n7
Ashby, Turner, 70
Ashley, David, 86, 87

Bachman, Aaron E., 79
Bagley, William Chandler, 232
Bailey, Phoebe, 178
Balicki, Joseph, 26
Ball, Charles, 215–17, 222n11
Ballard, Michael, 154
Banks, Nathaniel P., 72
Bartlett, Napier, 22–23
Bartlett, W. H., 104
bathing opportunities for soldiers, 68, 71, 86
Batteau, Allen, 113–14, 124
Battling the Elements (Winters), 17
Baylor, John, 35, 39, 41, 43, 45
Becks, Lutz, 149
bené plant, 212
Benjamin, Judah, 78
Bennett, Judith, 5
Berry, Stephen, 5–6, 8
Beyerchen, Alan, 148, 160n14
Bierstadt, Albert, 102
biotic event, Civil War as, 228–29. *See also* agriculture; disease
Bird, W. H., 80
bison herds, drought impact, 19–20
Black, Benjamin, 231
Blackington, Jacob, 82, 87
Black Mountain Boys: battle casualties, 57, 60–61; disease vulnerability, 8, 57–58, 60; enlistment rates, 52, 54, 55. *See also* Yancey County, North Carolina

Black Mountains, location, 141n41
blacks. See *Cudjo's Cave* (Trowbridge); fertilizer regime, postwar; slaves
blockade impact, tobacco market, 169–71
botanical knowledge from walking, 211–14
Botany of Desire, The (Pollan), 182
Boulware, James Richard, 88
Brady, Lisa M.: chapter by, 144–62; comments on, 5, 9–10, 18, 47, 90n10, 115, 165, 197, 228
Bragg, Braxton, 22, 153, 156, 158–59
Briggs, David, 5
Brown, Joe, 121
Brown, John, 113, 116, 118
Buckner, Simon Bolivar, 152
Buell, Don Carlos, 151, 156–59
Burnette, Dorian, 20
Burnside, Ambrose, 144–45, 146, 153
Burnsville, population statistics, 53
Burson, William, 122–24

Caldwell County, North Carolina, in fugitive's memoir, 122
camels, military use, 49n11
camp conditions: bathing opportunities, 68, 71, 86; morale problem, 77–78, 81–82; officers vs. troops, 76–77, 84–85; and rainy weather, 57–59, 67, 71, 72–73, 74; sanitation problems, 58, 59, 72; as scholarly opportunity, 26. *See also* disease; marching conditions; straggling
Camp Misery, 72–73
Canby, Edward R. S., 34–35, 46
Cape Fear River, in *Cold Mountain*, 132
Carpenter, Kinchen Jahu, 72, 82
Carter, Robert G., 74, 86
Cashin, Joan, 12
Casler, John, 85
Castleman, Alfred, 81
Caswell County, North Carolina, agriculture. *See* tobacco, bright leaf
catastrophism, geological, 193–94
cattle fever, 60
caves. See *Cudjo's Cave* (Trowbridge)
cemeteries, 103–4, 111n19
Cemetery of Mount Auburn (Bartlett), 104

Century, The, 122
Chancellorsville battle, 60
chaos theory and Clausewitz's friction concept, 148–49
Chaplin River, Perryville battle, 157
Chapman, William, 34
chemical fertilizers. *See* fertilizer regime, postwar
Chickahominy River, camp conditions, 58–59
Chickamauga, Battle of, 22, 23
Chinese poetry, 130–31, 142n52, 142n59
Chivington, John, 46
Church, Frederic, 102
Civil War studies, environmental history perspectives: overview, 7–12; cautions and skepticisms, 225–35; scholarly contribution potential, 1–7, 63–64. *See also specific topics of study*
Civil War Weather in Virginia (Krick), 16–17
Clarke County, Georgia, fertilizer use, 205
class bias, health problems, 77
Clausewitz, Carl von. *See* friction concept, Clausewitz's
"Clausewitz, Nonlinearity, and the Unpredictability of War" (Beyerchen), 148, 160n14
climate and weather patterns: definitions, 17–18; farming impact, 7, 19–22, 55, 198; as friction element, 146–47; human response themes, 25–27; and military campaigns, 23–25, 27–29, 63, 70, 152–53; scholarship inadequacies, 16–17, 18–19, 21, 31n25. *See also specific weather-related topics*
Clingman, Thomas, 54
Closmann, Charles, 5
Cold Mountain (Frazier), 130–37
cold weather. *See* frost/freeze events; rains and mud
Cole, Thomas, 96, 97, 102, 111n23
colonies, runaway slaves, 215
Comanche people, 19–20
compost applications, 196–97, 203
conscription, 70–71, 178
Conscription Act, 55

conservation/preservation movements, 9, 102–3, 105, 107–8, 112n25, 231, 233
Cooper, Samuel, 75
Corinth, Mississippi, 153–54
corn crops, 20, 31n25, 55, 166, 174, 175
Cornus florida, 212
cotton production. *See* agriculture
Cozzens, Peter, 155–56
Crawford, Mary Ann, 194–95
creosote bushes, 42
Crilly, F. J., 39–40, 42, 43, 44, 45
Crittenden, Thomas, 157
Crook, George, 120
crop lien laws, 201
Crosby, Alfred, 52
"Crowder's Cove" (Woolson), 128–29, 137, 142n47
Cudjo's Cave (Trowbridge), 115–20, 135–36, 139n17
Cullum, G. W., 151
Curtis, Samuel, 23

Danville, Virginia, area. *See* tobacco, bright leaf
Darwin, Charles, 136
Davenport, George, 200
Davis, Jefferson, 37–38, 49n11
Davis, Mike, 19
Davis, Rebecca Harding, 125–26, 141n39
Dayton National Cemetery, 105
debt, farm. *See* fertilizer regime, postwar
dehydration, 42–43, 44, 46
DeLay, Brian, 37
Denby, characters in "The Yares of Black Mountain," 126–28
desert ecosystem characteristics, 40–42, 47
desertion, 8, 61, 68–69, 70–71, 75–76, 122. *See also* straggling
diarrhea, 58, 85
Dickens, Charles, 168
Dickinson, Emily, 108n2
Dickson, David, 10, 196–97, 198–99, 203
diet, 59. *See also* food supplies
disease: botanical remedies, 87, 211–14; as the Civil War story, 62–63; livestock, 8, 22, 59–60, 63; medical care complaints, 79–81; soldier vulnerabilities, 8, 57–59, 71–72, 85–86; as straggling justification, 8, 69, 74, 82–84, 88
Doctor's Creek, Perryville battle, 157
dogwood bark, 212
Donahower, Jeremiah, 25–26
Douglass, Frederick, 113
Downing, Andrew Jackson, 101
Down to Earth (Steinberg), 4
Drake, Brian Allen: chapter by, 1–15; comments on, 25, 226
Drake, J. Madison, 122
Dred (Stowe), 139n13
drought, 19–21, 55, 198
Dyer, Jonah Franklin, 86–87
dysentery, 58, 74

"Education of a Geographer, The" (Sauer), 216–17
Elinor, character in "Crowder's Cove," 128–29
Ellis, Thomas, 74
El Niño–Southern Oscillation (ENSO), 19–20
Elson, Henry, 100
Environmental Histories of the Cold War (McNeill and Unger), 5
environmental history, emergence, 3–4. *See also* Civil War studies, environmental history perspectives
environment as enemy, 90n12
erosion, 181, 194, 205
Evans, Charles N. B., 174

Fair Oaks battle, 57, 59
famine, 19–20, 61. *See also* food supplies
Fannin County, Georgia, 121
Fast and Loose in Dixie (Drake), 122
Faust, Drew Gilpin, 219–20
fertilizer regime, postwar: beginnings of, 192–93, 205–6; cost problem, 10–11, 192–93, 201–3, 204; Dickson's impact, 196–97, 198–99; emancipation's role, 197–98, 199; as market opportunity, 200; production impact, 203–5; regulatory approaches, 202–3; tobacco requirements, 181

244 Index

Fiege, Mark, 4–5, 181
field rotation system, 53
Final Harvest: Emily Dickinson's Poems (Johnson), 108n2
Fisher, Isaac, 222n11
Fletcher, Private, 87
Flowers, Jack, 215
Floyd, John, 152
fog metaphor, Clausewitz's, 145–48, 160n14
food supplies: foraging for, 4–5, 68, 86–87, 214, 216, 218; guerrilla raids, 61; military appropriation, 56; shortage-related riots, 7, 31n25, 61; tobacco production conflicts, 173–76; weather-related problems, 19–20, 55–56
Foote, Andrew, 151, 152
foot travel: overview, 11; running away, 214–17, 222n11; walking, 209–14. *See also* marching conditions
foraging, 4–5, 68, 86–87, 214, 216, 218
Forrest, Nathan Bedford, 152
Fort Craig, 34–35, 45–46
Fort Donelson battle, 150–53
Fort Fillmore, 34, 38–40, 46, 47
Fort Henry, 151
Fort Stanton, 35, 46
Fort Stanton Road, 41–45
Frank Leslie's Illustrated Newspaper, 72, 73
Frazier, Charles, 130–37, 142n52, 142n59
Fredericksburg battle, 60
Freedman's Bureau, 198
Frémont, John C., 72, 73, 77, 81, 92n47
friction concept, Clausewitz's: overview, 145–48, 159–60; Beyerchen's argument, 148, 160n14; nature arguments, 149–50, 228; Watts's argument, 148–49. *See also* acoustic shadows phenomenon
frost/freeze events: farming impact, 20–22, 55; and military campaigns, 23–25, 70, 152–53. *See also* rains and mud
Ft. Sanders, Knoxville, Tenn., 99
fugitives, 214–17, 222n11. *See also* Appalachia as refuge; straggling
Fulkerson, Samuel V., 78–79
furlough debate, 75, 78–79, 84

Gains Mill battle, 57, 59
Gates, Paul W., 4, 20–21
Genovese, Eugene, 232
geography of flight phenomenon, 140n29. *See also* Appalachia as refuge; running away
geological history, Georgia, 193–94
Georgia, cotton production. *See* agriculture
"Gettysburg and the Organic Nature of the American Civil War" (Fiege), 4–5
Gettysburg battle, 60
Gibbs, Alfred, 42, 45
Gifford, Sanford Robinson, 106
glanders, 22, 60
Glatthaar, Joseph, 79
goat woman character, in *Cold Mountain*, 132–34, 137
Goodrich, William, 114
gradualism, geological, 193–94
Grant, Ulysses S., 97, 100, 151–54
Greeley, Horace, 40
guano, agricultural uses, 10, 196–97, 199
guano notes, 10–11, 201–2
guerrilla activity: civilian impact, 56, 61–62; literary portrayals, 130, 134–35, 137; wilderness area correlation, 119–21, 136–37
Gunn's Domestic Medicine, 87

Haines, Alanson, 163, 180
Halifax County, Virginia, agriculture. *See* tobacco, bright leaf
Hall County, Georgia, fertilizer use, 205
Halleck, Henry Wager, 151, 152
Hämäläinen, Pekka, 19
Hamblin, Jacob Darwin, 5
Hancock County, Georgia, prewar soil conservation activity, 195–97. *See also* fertilizer regime, postwar
Hancock County (Georgia) Planters' Club, 195–96
Handerson, Henry E., 67–68, 69–70, 88–89
Han-shan, 130–31, 142n52, 142n59
Hapgood character, in *Cudjo's Cave*, 116–18, 119, 137
Harney, Will Wallace, 124–25, 137

Harper's Weekly, 122, 123
Harsh, Joseph, 72, 89n8
Hatchett, William, 173
Haydon, Charles, 84
Hayes, Rutherford B., 120
Hazlitt, William, 210
heat stroke, 42–43, 46
hog cholera, 60
Holt, J., 157–58
Home Guard, 56, 61–62, 127, 130
Homestead Act, 233–34
homestead protection, in credit conditions, 202
horses: and diseases, 22, 59–60; during Lynde's retreat, 43; military confiscation, 56, 176; and weather extremes, 22–23
hospitals, 80–81, 177
Howard, O. O., 140n22
Hunter Mountain, Twilight (Gifford), 105, 106, 107–8
Huntington, Ellsworth, 138n3
hurricanes, 20

illness. *See* disease
impressment policy, Confederate, 56, 176–78, 188n55. *See also* conscription
Indian conflicts, 37, 49n11
industrial workers, soldiers compared, 220, 223n17
Inge, M. Thomas, 142n52
Ingold, Tim, 219
Inman, character in *Cold Mountain*, 130–37
Inman, W. P., 130
Inness, George, 105, 106, 107, 111n23
Inscoe, John C.: chapter by, 113–43; comments on, 6, 9
insect pests, 58, 74, 86
inspection fees, fertilizers, 202–3
Invention of Appalachia, The (Batteau), 113–14
Iuka battle, 151, 153–56

Jackson, John Brinckerhoff, 112n25
Jackson, Thomas "Stonewall," 70–71, 75
James, Henry, 128
Janes, Thomas P., 203

Jenks, Andrew, 5
Johnson, Bushrod, 152
Johnson, Thomas H., 108n2
Johnson, Timothy: chapter by, 191–208; comments on, 10–11, 232, 233
Johnston, Joseph E., 60, 71–72, 78
Jones, Charles Colcock, 215
Jones, Frank B., 71, 84
Jones, George, 173
Jones, John B., 25

Keeping Together in Time (McNeill), 224n18
Keiser, Henry, 79–80, 84
Kelman, Ari, 36
Kendall, E., 82
Kiesling, Eugenia, 160n14
Kirby, Jack Temple, 1–2, 4, 12, 18, 232
Krick, Robert K., 16–17

labor shortages, agricultural, 54–55, 62, 178, 199. *See also* slaves
Lackawanna Valley, The (Inness), 105, 106, 107
landscape. *See specific geographical topics*
Las Cruces, New Mexico, 34, 35, 45–46
Late Victorian Holocausts (Davis), 19
Lee, Robert E., 72
lice, 74, 86
Lincoln, Abraham, 74–76, 97, 116
Lincoln, Albert C., 70
Lincoln Memorial College, 140n22
Lippincott's, 124, 126
Lively, Robert A., 139n9
livestock: and diseases, 8, 22, 59–60, 63; during Lynde's retreat, 43; military confiscations, 56, 175–76, 176, 197; mountain farms, 53, 56; and weather extremes, 21, 22–23
Lonn, Ella, 4
Lowrey, John Robert, 121
Ludlum, David, 22, 23
Lumpkin County, Georgia, 121
Lyell, Charles, 193–94
Lyell, Mary Elizabeth, 194–95
Lynde, Isaac: overview, 7–8; accusations against, 35, 40, 47; arrival at Fort Craig,

Lynde, Isaac (*continued*)
34–35; command at Fort Fillmore, 34, 38–39; heat afflictions, 44–45; retreat orders, 35, 39–40; retreat problems, 41–44, 46–48

Macon Telegraph, 198
Madison County, North Carolina, guerrilla activity, 120
Majewski, John, 232
malaria, 58, 59, 74, 77, 79, 212
Malone, Bartlett Yancey, 187n42
Man and Nature (Marsh), 110n16, 139n11, 231
Manassas battles, 60
Manifest Destiny, Southern, 36–38
manufacturing, tobacco's contribution, 167, 169–70
manure applications, 196–97, 203
marching conditions: overview, 217–21; bonding argument, 224n18; mud and darkness, 18, 25–26, 83, 144–45, 154, 219; officers vs. troops, 76–77; as straggling incentive, 70–71. *See also* camp conditions; Sherman's March
"March in the Ranks Hard-Presst, A" (Whitman), 218
Marsh, George Perkins, 110n16, 139n11, 231
Marx, Leo, 105
maximum effect category, weather-military campaign database, 23–24, 29
McClellan, George, 8, 35, 57, 58–59, 63, 74–75
McClellan, William C., 83–84
McClernand, John A., 152
McDonald, Bob, 86
McEvoy, Arthur, 6
McGee, W. J., 44
McKee, J. Cooper, 45
McKim, Randolph, 82
McNeill, John, 5, 7
McNeill, William H., 224n18
McPherson, James, 144, 151, 155, 158
Meade, George, 180
measles, 57

Mechanicsville battle, Black Mountain Boys, 57
medical botany, 68, 87, 211–14
medical care, quality of, 62, 72, 76–77, 79–81, 177. *See also* disease
Meier, Kathryn Shively: chapter by, 67–95; comments on, 8, 17, 25, 47
Melville, Herman, 96
Menendez, Albert, 139n9
Merritt, Bill, 85
Mesilla skirmish, 35
Miller, James T., 74
Millner, James, 172–73
Mill Springs Campaign, 26
Milton Chronicle, 174
minimal effect category, weather-military campaign database, 27–28
mining, the Wilderness area, 100–101
Mississippi, cotton production, 203
Mitchell, Elisha, 54
Mitchell County, North Carolina, 54, 55
Mock, Cary, 20
Moore, Samuel P., 76
moral agenda, environmental history tradition, 229–30
moral landscape theme. *See* Appalachia as refuge
Morgan, William H., 71
morphologic eye, 216–17
Morse, Charles Fessenden, 72–73
mosquitoes, 58, 74
mountains as refuge theme. *See* Appalachia as refuge
Mount Mitchell, location, 141n41
Muir, John, 209–11
mules, 22–23, 43, 56, 59–60, 176
Mumford, Lewis, 231
Murfree, Mary Noialles, 124, 141n39
Murphy, Robert, 153

Nash, Roderick Frazier, 109n4
national cemeteries, 104–5, 111n19
National Park Service, 231
Native American conflicts, 37, 49n11
Natural Enemy, Natural Ally (Russell and Tucker), 4, 5, 90n12

Neal, T. D., 171
Nelson, Megan Kate: chapter by, 35–51; comments on, 7–8, 165, 224n18
New Mexico. *See* Lynde, Isaac; Southwest region
New York Times, 204–5
Noe, Kenneth W.: chapter by, 16–33; comments on, 7, 47, 48, 55, 120, 157
no effect category, weather-military campaign database, 27
nonlinear dynamics and Clausewitz's friction concept, 148–49

oat crops, 174, 175
O'Donnell, Kevin, 141n39
Olmsted, Frederick Law, 101, 102–3, 110n15
Olney, James, 222n11
"On Going for a Journey" (Hazlitt), 210
On War (Clausewitz), 145–48
Ord, Edward O. C., 154, 155, 156
Organ Mountains, 35, 40–41
Owen, Johnson, 171

Pacific Guano Company, 200
Paludan, Phillip, 120–21
Pangle, character in *Cold Mountain*, 134–35
Parker, Theodore, 116
Patterson, Private, 83
Paxton, Elisha F., 84
Paxton, Jason, 175
Pearson, Chris, 5
Pender, William Dorsey, 57
Peninsula Campaign, illness rates, 8, 69, 90n11. *See also* Black Mountain Boys; straggling
Penland, Milton, 53, 61–62
Penn Hapgood, character in *Cudjo's Cave*, 116–18, 119, 137
People's History of the United States, A (Williams), 31n25
Perkins, George, 82
Perryville battle, 151, 156–59
phosphate deposits, South Carolina, 200
Pickett's Charge, 60
Piedmont farming. *See* tobacco, bright leaf

Pillow, Gideon, 152
Pinchot, Gifford, 105, 107–8
Pinchot, James, 105, 107
Pittsylvania County, Virginia, agriculture. *See* tobacco, bright leaf
plantation system. *See* agriculture
Plummer, Augustus H., 46
Polk, Leonidas, 156–57
Pollan, Michael, 182
Pomp, character in *Cudjo's Cave*, 117–18, 137
population statistics, 53, 167, 181, 195
Porcher, Francis Peyre, 11, 211–14
portmanteau biota, 52
Pratt, Lorenzo N., 87
Pratt, Nathaniel A., 200
preservation/conservation movements, 9, 102–3, 105, 107–8, 112n25, 231, 233
Price, Sterling, 153–55, 156
publishing statistics, Civil War, 139n9
punishment approach, straggling, 68–69, 72, 75–76, 85

Quagmire (Briggs), 5
quinine, 212

Race for Liberty, A (Burson), 122–24
railroads: in painting by Inness, 105, 106, 107; postwar construction, 200; slave impressments for, 177; in southerners' expansionist plans, 36–37; for tobacco transport, 188n60; troop/supply transports, 153, 156, 219
rains and mud: as acoustic shadow element, 154; camp conditions, 57, 58–59, 71, 72–73, 74; in database of military campaigns, 24; marching challenges, 18, 25–26, 144–45, 154, 219; as straggling justification, 83–84. *See also* climate and weather patterns; disease
Rappahannock River, 144–45
Ray, Montreville, 61–62
Rebel yell, 223n17
Reed, George M., 108n2
Resources of Southern Fields and Forests (Porcher), 11, 211–14

Richmond Dispatch, 213
Rio Grande, fort locations, 37
Roberts, Benjamin S., 40
Robinson, Armistead, 21, 31n25
Rodman's Keeper (Woolson), 142n47
Romney campaign, 70
Ropes, Hannah, 81
Rosecrans, William, 22, 154–55, 156
Ross, Charles, 150, 152, 155, 158–59
Ross, L. F., 155
Routes of War (Sternhell), 114
Ruby, character in *Cold Mountain*, 135
Ruffin, Edmund, 232
running away, 140n29, 214–17, 222n11.
 See also Appalachia as refuge
rural cemetery movement, 103–4
Russell, Edmund, 5, 90n12, 229
Ryan, George, 43
rye crops, 174

Sachs, Aaron: chapter by, 96–112; comments on, 9, 230–31
Sackman, Douglas, 179
Sally, character in "Crowder's Cove," 129
Salsola kali, 213
Salt as a Factor in the Confederacy (Lonn), 4
salt supplies, 4, 56, 175
saltwort, 213
San Augustin Springs, 35, 41, 42, 43, 44–45, 46
Sanitary Commission, U.S., 77, 81, 110n15
Sarris, Jonathan, 121
Sauer, Carl, 216–17
scurvy, 59, 76, 86–87
sesame plant, 212
Seven Days campaign, Black Mountain Boys, 57
Seven Pines battle, 57, 59
Shapiro, Henry D., 141n37
Sharrer, G. Terry, 63
shelter for soldiers, 26, 69
Shelton Laurel massacre, 120
Shenandoah Valley Campaign, 69, 70–71, 90n44
Shepard, Lewis, 80
Shepard, Norton C., 101

Sheridan, Philip, 157
Sherman's March: agricultural destruction, 5, 191, 197; slave liberations, 197, 198; weather conditions, 23, 24, 26, 218–19
Shields, James, 72
shrub-steppe ecosystem, 40–41
Sibley, Henry H., 37–38
significant effect category, weather-military campaign database, 23, 24, 28–29
Silver, J. Wilburn, 60
Silver, Timothy: chapter by, 52–66; comments on, 8, 228–29
Sims, William, 176, 178, 188n55
Slade, Abisha, 165
Slavery in the United States (Ball), 215–17, 222n11
slaves: and food shortages, 62; and fugitive prisoners of war, 121–22; military impressments, 176–78, 188n55; in prewar agricultural practices, 191–92, 194–95, 197; running actions, 214–17; Sherman's liberations, 191, 197, 198; in southerners' expansionist plans, 36–37; and tobacco cultivation, 165, 166–67, 176–77; Yancey County, North Carolina, 53–54. See also *Cudjo's Cave* (Trowbridge); fertilizer regime, postwar
Sloan, David Charles, 111n19
smallpox, 80
smelters, the Wilderness area, 100–101
Smith, Edmund Kirby, 156
Snake Creek Gap, Georgia, 24
snow, 70, 71, 152
Snyder, Gary, 130–31
soap, 194–95, 212, 213
soil conditions. *See* fertilizer regime, postwar; rains and mud; tobacco, bright leaf
Soil Exhaustion and the Civil War (Bagley), 232
Solnit, Rebecca, 210
song sheets, veteran uses, 108n2
sound absorption factors. *See* acoustic shadows phenomenon
Sours, William, 180
South, The (Trowbridge), 139n15
Southern Cultivator, 196, 198–99
Southwest region: Confederate goals, 37–

38, 45–46; Rio Grande fort locations, 37, 39, 40, 47; in Southern Manifest Destiny, 36–37. *See also* Lynde, Isaac
Spotswood, Alexander, 100–101
Starr, Frederick Jr., 103, 110n16
Staunton River Bridge, 176
Steinberg, Ted, 4, 18, 21, 30n15, 31n25
Stephen (slave), 165
Sternhell, Yael, 114, 140n29
Stewart, A. M., 80
Stewart, Mart A.: chapter by, 209–24; comments on, 11, 229–30
Stilwell, William, 86
Stobrod, character in *Cold Mountain*, 135
Stoll, Steven, 232
Stowe, Harriet Beecher, 115, 139n13
straggling: absenteeism problem, 68–69, 70, 72, 73–75; for clean water, 85–86; conflation with desertion, 68–69, 89n8; for forage, 86–87; as friction example, 90n10; furlough debate, 78–79; Handerson's experience, 67–68, 88–89; illness-caused, 69, 85; leadership assumptions about, 8, 72, 76–78, 84–85; and medical care, 79–81; for morale boost, 81–82, 87–88; punishments for, 68–69, 72, 75–76, 85; for relief from marching conditions, 70–71; research challenge, 69–70, 91n14; as self-care technique, 8, 68, 69; for shelter seeking, 82–84. *See also* camp conditions; disease; marching conditions
"Strange Land and Peculiar People, A" (Harney), 124–25, 137, 141n37
Strother, David, 73, 82
stumps. *See* Wilderness landscape
Sutherlin, William, 170–73, 180
Sutherlin & Ferrell, 167, 170–71
Sutter, Paul S.: chapter by, 225–35; comments on, 7, 11
swamplands, 74, 77, 215, 219
Swanson, Drew A.: chapter by, 163–90; comments on, 10, 233

Taken at the Flood (Harsh), 89n8
Talcott, T. J., 171

taxes, agricultural commodities, 175, 176
Taylor, Amy Murrell, 12
Taylor, Thomas I., 80
Taylor, William, 79
Taylor Grazing Act, 234
temperatures, desert, 40–43. *See also* climate and weather patterns; frost/freeze events; straggling
Terrell, William, 196
thirst, death from, 44
Thomas, Emory M., 31n25
Thomas, James, Jr., 170
Thomas, William G., 219
Thoreau, Henry David, 209, 221n1
ticks, 74
Tilghman, Lloyd, 151
timber cutting, 100–101, 194
tobacco, bright leaf: agency arguments, 182; blockade impact, 169–71; demand for, 168–69, 171, 185n20, 185n23, 186n39, 187n40, 187n42, 233; during federal occupation, 179–80; food production conflicts, 10, 173–76; and freedpeople land conflicts, 181; marketing strategies, 171–73, 178–79; origins, 165–66; postwar production, 180–81; profitability, 166–68; railway transportation, 188n60; slavery's role, 165, 166–67, 176–77; Sutherlin's success, 170–73, 180
tourism, 54, 61, 139n14
Tripler, Charles S., 73, 76
Trowbridge, John Townsend, 115–20, 135–36, 139n11, 139n13–15, 139n17
Trueheart, Charles W., 70
Tucker, Richard, 90n12
Tullahoma Campaign, 26
typhoid, 57, 58, 68, 85

ultisols, defined, 194. *See also* rains and mud
Unger, Corinna, 5
Unidentified Soldier with Amputated Arm . . . Cannonballs, 98
Union India Rubber Company, 26
Union Refugees in East Tennessee, 122, 123

Valley of the Yosemite (Bierstadt), 102
Vance, Zebulon, 55, 56
Van Dorn, Earl, 153, 154
Victim (Paludan), 120–21
View of the Mountain Pass . . . , A (Cole), 96, 97
Vinovskis, Maris, 2
volunteers and discipline, 68, 89n6

Wade, Horace M., 83
Walker, character in *Cold Mountain*, 135
walking, 209–14. *See also* running away
Wallace, Lew, 152
Wanderlust (Solnit), 210
War and Nature (Russell), 5
War and the Environment (Closmann), 5
Warfield, Edgar, 71
water supplies: camp sanitation, 58, 72; and Perryville battle, 157; Rio Grande forts, 37, 39, 40, 47; at San Augustin Springs, 43, 45; and straggling, 68, 85–86
Watts, Barry D., 148–49
Waud, Alfred, 99
Way, Albert, 131
weather, defined, 17. *See also* climate and weather patterns
Webster County, Virginia, guerrilla activity, 120
Weigley, Russell, 155, 156–57, 158
Weirding the War (Berry), 12
West, William, 85
wheat crops, 20–21, 166, 174, 175–76
whiskey, 40, 43, 74
Whitman, Walt, 104, 218
wilderness: before Civil War, 100–101; and cemeteries, 103–4, 111n19; conservation/preservation movements, 102–3, 105, 107–8, 112n25; meanings of, 9, 96–97, 101–2; war's destruction, 99, 100, 103, 109n7. *See also* Appalachia as refuge
Wilderness, Battle of the, 60, 97, 99
Wilderness and the American Mind (Nash), 109n4
"Wilderness of War, The" (Brady), 5
wildlife, Yancey County, North Carolina, 61
Wiley, Bell Irvin, 16, 169
Williams, David, 31n25
Willis, Anderson, 173, 187n40
Wilson, Mark, 26
Wilson, Samuel, 175–76
Winder, Charles S., 75
wind factors. *See* acoustic shadows phenomenon
Winters, Harold, 17, 144, 145
Withers, Robert, 176
Womack, Pleasant, 175
Wood, Ephraim A., 86, 87
Woolson, Constance Fenimore, 125, 128–29, 142n47
World War II, 5
Wormeley, Katherine, 77
Worster, Donald, 6–7, 194
Wounded Escaping from the Burning Woods (Waud), 99
Wright, Gavin, 198

Yancey County, North Carolina: agricultural challenges, 8, 53–55; enlistment patterns, 52, 54, 55; guerrilla activity, 61–62. *See also* Black Mountain Boys
Yankee hurrah, 223n17
"Yares of Black Mountain, The" (Davis), 126–28, 137, 141nn39–41
Yosemite Valley, 102–3, 110n15
Young, Kevin, 53

UnCivil Wars

Weirding the War: Tales from the Civil War's Ragged Edges
    edited by Stephen Berry

Ruin Nation: Destruction and the American Civil War
    by Megan Kate Nelson

America's Corporal: James Tanner in War and Peace
    by James Marten

The Blue, the Gray, and the Green: Toward an Environmental History of the Civil War
    edited by Brian Allen Drake

www.ingramcontent.com/pod-product-compliance
Lightning Source LLC
Chambersburg PA
CBHW032213230426
43672CB00011B/2535